Winning
Model
United
Nations
Teams

Related Titles from Potomac Books

Pick Up Your Own Brass: Leadership the FBI Way
—Kathleen McChesney and William Gavin

Inside a U.S. Embassy: Diplomacy at Work—All-New Third Edition of the Essential Guide to the Foreign Service
—Edited by Shawn Dorman

Coaching Winning Model United Nations Teams

A TEACHER'S GUIDE

Ed Mickolus and J. Thomas Brannan

Potomac Books
Washington, D.C.

ISBN 978-1-61234-603-8 (pbk. : alk. paper)
ISBN 978-1-61234-604-5 (electronic)

Printed in the United States of America on acid-free paper that meets the American National Standards Institute Z39-48 Standard.

Potomac Books
22841 Quicksilver Drive
Dulles, Virginia 20166

First Edition

10 9 8 7 6 5 4 3 2 1

To our families, both at home and at school

CONTENTS

PREFACE

Since the early years of the twenty-first century, Model United Nations (MUN) has become the single most popular extracurricular academic activity among high school students. Its popularity has extended into many middle schools (grades 6–8) as well. More than two million high schoolers and college students have had occasion to call "point of order, Mr. Chairman!" at some point since the founding of the United Nations in 1945. MUN alumni include actor Samuel L. Jackson, Chelsea Clinton, U.S. Supreme Court Justice Stephen Breyer, and World Court (International Court of Justice) Justice Stephen Schwebel. MUN has even been mentioned at the movies, with Jennifer Aniston and Ben Stiller playing MUN alumni in the film *Along Came Polly*. MUN clubs or classes can be found in schools in all regions of the United States, and in dozens of countries around the world.

At MUN conferences, students have the opportunity to step out of their high school roles for a day or more, and step into the role of the ambassador of a country they may never visit. They learn geography; their adoptive country's history, politics, economics, society, culture, and language; issues facing that country and its place in its region and the world; international politics; and a myriad of issues that have challenged their predecessors and that they will likely confront as adults. They can and will make friendships within their school and with members of other teams that can last a lifetime.

We resurrected our high school's MUN team (at George C. Marshall High School in Falls Church, Virginia) in September 2002, when Ed's daughter was an entering freshman and Ed volunteered to help Tom reactivate the team. We soon found, however, that although there are numerous sources on what the UN is all about, there was no one source of practical information on the care and feeding of an MUN team. This volume is our attempt to help other sponsors and coaches learn from our mistakes and jump-start or revitalize your own team.

1
Introduction

Model United Nations (also Model UN or MUN) is commonly defined as an academic simulation of the United Nations that aims to educate participants about current events, topics in international relations, diplomacy, and the United Nations agenda.

Whether at a formal MUN conference, in classroom setting, or at an informal club practice, students take on the roles of diplomats representing a nation or nongovernmental organization (NGO) in a simulated session of a United Nations committee, such as the Security Council or other committees of the General Assembly (GA). Conferences often present a tier of committee assignments, aligned by skill levels, with GA committees open to novice MUNers, and the more specialized committees (e.g., UN Security Council) open to more experienced delegates. Crisis simulations are usually reserved for the most experienced delegates, with national organizations such as the United States Security Council and similar agencies of other UN member states interacting in real time situations controlled by the conference organizers. In these crisis committees, rather than representing a country, students role play specific people (e.g., secretary of state, secretary of defense, or secretary of the treasury).

Participating in an MUN conference typically requires a skill set that includes researching a country, taking on roles as diplomats, investigating international issues, debating, deliberating, negotiating, and drafting working papers and resolutions that propose solutions to world problems.

Each MUN conference has a set of rules for the operation of the conference and awards criteria; the conference rules are published in advance, but the awards criteria are often stated in quite general terms. Those participants that the conference organizers or Secretariat consider to be most contributing are given awards, such as "Best Delegate." Conferences will also often recognize "Best School" (with separate awards for large and small delegations). During a conference, participants must employ a variety of communication and critical thinking skills in order to represent

1

the policies of their respective countries. These skills include public speaking, group communication, research, policy analysis, active listening, negotiating, conflict resolution, parliamentary procedure, note-taking, writing, and editing.

The several approaches to teaching/coaching MUN can be boiled down to two: academic/noncompetitive and competitive. The approach you pick will be determined largely by the philosophy you bring to the table and by what you are trying to accomplish with MUNing.

We teach MUNing as a **competitive sport** with academic overtones, much the way similar intellectual endeavors (e.g., *High School Bowl, It's Academic,* debate, forensics, DECA) are regarded in public, private, and parochial schools in the United States and overseas. We believe that a focus on winning can generate all the benefits of the noncompetitive approach but has the added value of

- **motivating** the students;
- helping to **generate funds** from boosters, corporations, and other monetary sources;
- generating **publicity** for your program; and
- boosting **recruiting** (via the added funding and publicity, and the word of mouth created in the hallways from your winning students).

The competitive approach gives your students focus on a shared goal, and leads them to do all of the other things they should be doing anyway, including

- developing **critical thinking** skills;
- supporting **ethical practices**, **academic integrity**, and **rule of law**;
- **researching**;
- **writing** argument-based, evidence-driven papers, resolutions, amendments, and press releases;
- practicing several forms of **public speaking**;
- honing **interpersonal/persuasive skills** (what we call "schmoozing");
- learning about **parliamentary procedure** and how to use it; and
- developing **creative problem-solving** abilities.

While you have the opportunity to teach them a host of **substantive content issues**—the history and political science of terrorism, weapons proliferation, child soldiers, women's rights, AIDS, the status of international treaties, etc.—you may soon be overwhelmed with the sheer breadth of issues that any given conference's committees will cover. Although high schoolers can only exert limited influence in solving the world's most complex problems, lessons learned through MUN—the skills of diplomacy, the value of empathy, and looking at international issues from multiple points of view—can advance international understanding and global perspective.

For teachers, MUN coaches, and club sponsors, you have the opportunity to give your students life lessons that will stay with them far beyond a conference or a season of conferences. You can bring out in them such qualities as

- empathy;
- self-confidence;
- social skills;
- persuasiveness;
- leadership skills;
- organizational skills;
- knowing how to get to the heart of the matter;
- active listening;
- grace under pressure;
- thinking on one's feet;
- acting skills; and
- the ability to prioritize.

MUN skills include **acting**—students are portraying the ambassador of another country. But rather than playing a role during a one- or two-hour performance on stage, MUN delegates portray that character for days at a time. The students are no longer mere high schoolers—they put on the costume (either Western business attire or local formal business garb) of the country they represent, and *are* ambassadors (for their adoptive country and for your school) from the moment they arrive at an MUN conference until the time the conference adjourns.

MUN skills include those found in other **team sports**—knowing and abiding by the rules, learning to play a specific role on the team, cooperating with other members of the team, and sometimes sacrificing personal goals for the good of the team.

MUN skills include the same type of representational skills that one needs to practice **law**. The successful attorney does not reveal his/her own opinions about the case at hand, but rather represents his/her client in the best light possible. So, too, should the student represent his/her country. At an MUN conference, the views that matter are those of the government which the student represents.

This brings us to a fundamental difference between the competitive and non-competitive philosophy of MUNing. Noncompetitive sponsors will argue that the purpose of the United Nations is to resolve differences among nations by discussing these differences and coming to compromises peacefully. Gentle give-and-take will thus prevent military conflicts and resolve major international and regional crises. You will often see variants of these sentiments in the welcoming documents issued by the Secretariats (organizing committees) of the conferences you attend.

The competitive viewpoint argues that one should focus on **representing your adoptive country** well, and that may mean taking on a hardline role, eschewing compromise, or trying to divide blocs of nations, etc. While the articulated purpose of the United Nations may well be as previously described, this may or may not be the view of what the Foreign Ministry of your adoptive country wants its delegations to do. Rather, delegations are there to get the best deal for their country through diplomacy. Under this view, it does not matter if you lose a vote in the 193-nation General Assembly by 192–1 if you correctly represented the principles articulated by your government's leadership. Delegates are *not* at a conference to unilaterally rewrite their adoptive nation's policies, and are *not* being evaluated by how many resolutions they passed, sponsored, or supported. If a real-world diplomat does not correctly represent his or her government's policy positions, he or she is soon out of a job (and perhaps before a firing squad), or may choose to resign in protest.

We come down strongly on the side of competitive MUNing, although we suspect that you'll also be able to pick up a useful hint or two from this guidebook if you're of the noncompetitive spirit. So let's get started.

2
Getting Started

Recruiting

So now you're enthused, have the support of the school's administration, and need just one more thing: the students. Unless you're inheriting an already formed team, you've got to go out and find your team members and keep them motivated and interested once you've found them. Often the most receptive audience is students who have lived in foreign countries and are fluent in foreign languages.

There are several techniques you can use in putting your team together.

Initial Call for Volunteers: Most high schools have several ways to get the word out, including morning announcements (over public-address systems, closed-circuit television, or PowerPoint presentations), posters (hand-drawn or more professionally designed), ads/articles in the school newspaper, PTSA and Boosters newsletters, and word of mouth via staff announcements cascaded through home-room announcements.

E-mails: If your school or parent-teacher-student organization has a School_All e-mailing option, you can send broadcast e-mails to all faculty members, and sometimes all parents and students. You can also post a call for students on various computer bulletin boards/discussion groups. Some will be specific to your school; others will be specific to an interest group. Yahoo, for example, sponsors a discussion board for Model Arab League students. The website http://modelun.livejournal.com/ offers students the opportunity to chat about their school's programs, schedules, etc.

Scouting: While you should be prepared to welcome all interested students—and you can mold absolutely anyone into a first-class MUNer with patience and the techniques we'll talk about elsewhere in this guidebook—you'll have an easier time of things if you scout out and recruit students who already have some of the interests and skills you'd like your team members to have. Students who have writing, research, and especially presentation experience—including acting—will do well in MUN.

Referrals: Talk to teachers in the Social Studies Department, foreign language teachers, even sponsors of science clubs (MUN teams offer the more technically proficient student an opportunity to discuss scientific issues) to see if they'd recommend specific students, or if they'll simply spread the word for you.

Activities Fairs: Schools often will have fairs at the beginning of the year to showcase the variety of extracurricular or cocurricular activities offered to students. Make sure you get a table/booth and have plenty of handouts (include one with information on when/where the team meets, and also include any colorful ones available from the UN or other countries). In some cases, even if you cannot attend the fair because of schedule commitments, you can still recruit via flyers. Here's what we used one year:

Welcome to the Marshall High School Model United Nations Team

Sorry we couldn't be here in person to chat with you about how much fun this is, but tonight we're competing at the North American Invitational Model United Nations (NAIMUN) championships in Washington, D.C., which brings together more than 2,500 students from across the U.S., Canada, Mexico, the Caribbean, and Europe. Each of the 200+ plus schools at the conference represents an individual country at the United Nations, and each member of the team is an ambassador to one of the UN's committees. Our MUN team members will be debating resolutions (legislation) on key issues of the day, including the India-Pakistan conflict, international terrorism, peaceful uses of outer space, nuclear weapons proliferation, the Korean conflict, and dozens of others. We learn such things as public speaking techniques, how to use parliamentary procedure to get things done (and prevent things that our country is against), how to form coalitions with other nations, and how to write international law (UN resolutions).

In addition to the NAIMUN conference, this season includes competing in several other local conventions held at local high schools, including: George Mason, Thomas Jefferson, Hylton, Bishop Ireton, and Georgetown Visitation. We've represented such countries as Canada, Lebanon, Tunisia, Ukraine, Fiji, the U.S., Malaysia, and Mexico, winning awards at every convention we've attended. We'd be delighted for you to continue our winning tradition.

Want to learn more? You can visit with our faculty sponsor, Mr. Brannan, who teaches in the Social Studies Department. Or you can call our coach, Dr. Edward Mickolus (who was national college MUN champion for four years, coached the Yale University team, and cofounded the National High School championships).

Rising Freshmen Orientation Sessions: 8th graders are your future. You can meet them at orientation sessions held for them and their parents. Usually the parents will be more excited about the opportunities than the students, who will be overwhelmed with all of the opportunities offered at this new level of education, but talk to both students and parents. These sessions are usually held between May and June. You can also contact the activities directors of your middle school/junior high school feeder schools to determine whether they have MUN clubs or other clubs that would attract the type of students you seek. If so, visit them and invite students to one of your end-of-year practices.

It's your call as to whether you want to have **tryouts/auditions** to make your team. Some schools require auditions (with the possibility of *not* making the team early on) as a prerequisite for a program being eligible to give an academic letter in MUNing. Others, us included, take a come-one, come-all approach. As a teacher and coach, you'll find MUNing much more rewarding when you develop a heretofore inarticulate wallflower (who might not survive a first cut) into a self-confident, outgoing speaker ready to take on the world.

Once the students arrive at your first meeting, keep in constant contact with them. Here's what we tell our new team members:

> Welcome to the team. We're delighted to have you with us. Spend as much or as little time with the team as you can. Don't worry about making the team, tryouts, auditions, etc. Your expressing interest in joining the club got you on the team. We fully understand that you've got other school things in your lives, homework, sports, etc. In case of a conflict for your time, first do your homework; we'd prefer that everyone had all A's rather than was able to attend one-a-day practices (don't worry, we won't have one-a-days.) Attend as many practices and conferences as you can. This is a year-round sport, and if you have to take a couple of months off, you're always welcome back later in the year. We'll keep a spot open for you.
>
> Don't worry about the size of the team, or how many people come to a particular practice session. Small teams will permit us greater one-on-one coaching opportunities. Larger numbers will give us more people to comment on performances during practice sessions at our meetings.
>
> Our first meeting will be in Mr. Brannan's room on Tuesday, at 2:30 p.m. It's particularly important that our new team members attend this one—I'll give you an overview of what being on the team means, and what the sport is all about. Our veterans are also welcome; it'll be good seeing you again. Our

first scrimmage will be on Thursday at 6 p.m. in Michael Hall. Our first car wash fund-raiser will be on Saturday from 10 a.m. to 2 p.m. in front of Marshall High School. (Let us know what hours you can attend. We'll figure out who brings brushes, towels, etc. You may well see pizza involved with this event.)

At George C. Marshall High School, we come from a recent history that is marked by a lot of MUN competition, and we approach it much the way a sports coach would (think of the styles of coaches like Joe Gibbs or Phil Jackson).

We propose to show you the techniques we used to win at the high school and college levels. You'll do the same types of research that other teams do, but you'll do it more efficiently, within an overall system that actually has plays similar to sports plays. You'll learn a lot about the UN, public speaking, parliamentary procedure, coalition building, politics, and politicking—all skills that will help you in class and in life. It's our goal for other teams to expect that GCMHS teams come prepared to compete for the major awards. As students and prospective MUNers, you bring to the table skills upon which we can build another first-class team. In our first year, we started from Square One, and by the end of the year, eighteen of our team members had won individual speaker awards.

In our practices, you'll learn about the following:

- using parliamentary procedure as a tool, how to chart the order of precedence of the rules, how to stall, how to efficiently move a resolution through to adoption
- public speaking tactics appropriate to this type of forum (Dr. Ed also coached debate teams, does a lot of public speaking in his job, and was a stand-up comic at one point in life)—this will include when you should directly address the other side's arguments and when to ignore them and focus on the bigger (your view) picture, the importance of being first speaker to frame the debate, extemporaneous speaking (you will not be writing/reading speeches), etc.
- organizing and running a regional caucus, forming coalitions, horse trading on nonsalient or side issues, what's in it for their country (not yours)
- researching one's UN committee topic (including contacting the local embassy and visiting it for a briefing)
- writing position papers, resolutions, and amendments

- acting as a team during sessions
- a little background information on the UN Charter, the UN as an institution, etc.
- committee/plenary organization—what the Chair, director, secretary, parliamentarian, and pages do, and how they can help you

During the year, we'll also look a bit at our country's (or countries', if we represent more than one nation at a conference) people, customs, etc.

The drama background many of you have will put you in good stead for Model UN competitions. MUN organizers often grade you on staying "in character," meaning that you remain faithful to your country's interests and positions. Essentially, you're adopting a role—that of a UN diplomat, a delegate from a specific country—which you'll portray 24 hours a day for the duration of that conference. (You'll almost certainly have different countries to portray in different MUN competitions. It's rare that you'll get to specialize in only one country or one region throughout the year.) To that end, if you can, please consider our practices as dress rehearsals. For those of you who think in drama terms, this is your costume. If you're sports-oriented, consider these to be practices in full uniform. We'd like men to wear jacket-and-tie, business outfits for women, or national dress if we know our country (and if the sponsoring organization approves). Part of your character is the "look" of a diplomat. We will not complain if you don't dress up for practice, but it sure helps you get used to the "look and feel" of being your character and will subtly change your public speaking style along the lines you'll need on conference day. Part of being a leader is looking the part.

We look forward to working with you this year. Again, welcome to the team!

In recent years, as funding for many public schools has come under constraints, after-school buses, which in the past have been available to bring students home after extracurricular activities, have now been reduced to running once a week or in some cases have been eliminated entirely. Therefore, MUN Clubs like the one at Marshall have been forced to improvise. Beginning in 2009, Marshall's MUN Club began relying heavily on its fall training conference as the main training venue for new MUN recruits and using the BlackBoard service to post conference notices, fill delegation slots at conferences, and otherwise stay in touch with its membership. After-school sessions on late-bus days were reserved for one-on-one help sessions for new MUNers writing their position papers.

At some point, MUN club sponsors will be involved in fund-raising to offset conference, travel, and other costs. (There's usually a nominal conference registration fee charged by the hosts.) Travel costs should be minimal if we find enough local conferences and parents are willing to drive, and students can access the club's and conferences' websites to download essential materials (UN Charter, which is on the Internet, etc.).

There are other local practice sessions that area schools have to prepare for the large college-hosted conferences such as NAIMUN. They are often open to sharing their sessions with neighboring schools. You can develop those contacts through word-of-mouth, etc.

During Marshall High School's first year of its rejuvenated MUN, we averaged about one conference a month. We try to maintain that schedule, knowing that all MUN club members will not be able to attend all of the conferences (we set the magic number at three conferences per year for students who wish to consider themselves active members). You don't have to attend that many, but the more conference experiences your students get, the more confident they will become. You'll also develop contacts with other schools that you'll meet again at other conferences. Consider the amount of time you'll have to devote to preparation— remember, the kids' schoolwork comes first—and the cost. For example, local high-school-run conferences usually cost $20 to $25 per student; college-run conferences usually have registration fees for both your school ($50 to $60) and each delegate you bring ($40 to $60). Some college-hosted conferences also charge a fee for each sponsor ($50 to $60), a dubious practice since many sponsors are not paid for being a club sponsor or faculty advisor.

Do not worry about which countries you will be representing. While you can request countries of your students' national heritage, the actual country you represent does not make that much difference. Although you would think that more prominent countries would give us a better chance of getting called upon because of their heavy involvement in key issues up for debate, Chairs generally attempt to be fair and give everyone a chance to speak. The specific country has no bearing upon your likelihood of winning—that depends on your delegates' initiative and skills, not your assignment.

For example, here are the countries we represented in one year:

Algeria	Australia
Austria	Cameroon
Canada	Central African Republic

Chile	China
Djibouti	Dominican Republic
Egypt	Finland
France	Germany
Ghana	Greece
Haiti	Honduras
India	Italy
Jordan	Kazakhstan
Kenya	Latvia
Mexico	Moldova
Nepal	New Zealand
Nigeria	Oman
Pakistan	Paraguay
Portugal	Philippines
Qatar	Romania
Russia	Saudi Arabia
Spain	Syria
Tunisia	Turkey
UK	Uruguay
USA	

Where to Meet

While you're recruiting, you'll also need to think about where to host your practices. Among the places you might consider are the following:

- **Your classroom**. If you can hold your meetings here, you will have the advantage of being in control of the room's scheduling and look. However, the space might not be adequate if you have a large influx of students.
- **The school library**. Depending upon the layout of the library, you might be able to host more students than in your classroom. However, you might be competing with other individuals/groups for available time slots.
- **External locations**. Local public libraries often will have conference rooms that they make available to patrons. Depending upon your group's needs, the public library might be a suitable spot, with the added advantage of giving you access to materials that might not be housed in your school's library.

3
Fund-Raising

In addition to the time demands on you and your team members—who may routinely be involved in numerous other activities in school and possibly several others outside of school *and* who will have heavy academic workloads—the other key limitation on the extent of your program will be funding. You can respond to this by lowering costs and generating revenue.

Costs can quickly add up for a team. The lowest-cost conferences we attend are friendly evening scrimmages with local schools at an average cost of $8 to $10 per delegate (this usually pays for pizza and paper). A one-and-a-half-day conference sponsored by a local high school generally runs $20 per delegate, plus another $20 school fee. Moving a step up, college-sponsored conferences can run $40 to $60 per student, with an additional $40 to $60 school fee. Some colleges also charge a sponsor fee. The larger conferences, with thousands of participants, can charge even more—and that's just the registration fees.

Travel and hotel costs can soon become a problem. Staying local means keeping costs down, but limits the exposure of your team to better—or at least different—styles of competition and to different students. We discourage students from driving themselves to conferences. You can usually keep transportation costs down by relying upon parents to pitch in with driving to local conferences. However, every now and then you may need to rent a school bus. Some districts do not absorb the costs of the bus, which means a few hundred dollars coming out of your team's budget. Renting a commercial bus for an out-of-area conference can get well into four figures. Transportation is a major opportunity to involve parents. Delegate the responsibility for lining up parent drivers to a parent or committee of parents. They are often looking for an opportunity to get to know the students with whom their children are spending time. This is their chance.

Going to college-run conferences, even if they are local, will also greatly increase your budget due to hotel costs. Being within thirty to forty minutes of the campus or conference site makes it possible for you to be a commuter school; however, a disadvantage to this is that your students will probably miss some of the late-night/early-morning socialization with students from out-of-town schools that stay at hotels. Moreover, college students hosting MUN conferences find declaring midnight crises (generally running three to four hours) to be attractive draws. If you're a commuter school, it probably means that you'll need to get hotel rooms for the students who will be involved in these "surprise" sessions. (So make sure, when you are signing up for a college-run conference, that you know precisely which committees will have these midnight sessions, so that you can get better rates for the hotel rooms, rather than be truly surprised and have to scramble to get hotel rooms for your students. We do *not* recommend commuting in the wee hours.) Depending upon the area in which you're staying, hotel rooms can go as high as $300 for a quad per night. When making hotel reservations, public schools should be sure to ask for the government rate as often it is less than the usual discount rate.

One way you can shave a few dollars from transportation and hotel costs is to develop **alliances with other schools**. You can often save money by sharing the costs of a school bus/commercial bus with a nearby school's MUN team. (One caution—and this has happened to us—get a cash commitment from the other school, so that if they pull out at the last minute, your school is not stuck with the additional cost.) Trains and hotels often offer group rates to twenty or more customers, a breakpoint you might be able to reach if you join forces with another school. (Alliances with other schools also allow you the opportunity to conduct joint practices, jointly host a conference [a great profit source], create joint delegations [if permitted by a host Secretariat], and e-caucus with your contacts among students and teachers.) Again, from experience, we recommend against adding students from other schools to your school's conference delegation unless a teacher or other school official from that student's school is a chaperone.

Fund-Raising Ideas

There are only so many ways that you can cut costs, however, and ultimately you'll find yourself looking for ways to generate revenues, including funds to help those students whose participation would otherwise be limited by their families' incomes. Most how-to books will suggest the time-honored bake and pizza sales, gift wrap, designer tea and coffee sales, car washes, etc. But every other club in your school will be elbowing you for the same types of fund-raising activities and same spots on the school calendar (e.g., getting the concessions for the football/basketball games), and chasing the same sources of revenue (parents). Here are a few other things you might try:

Partner with a nearby college, neighboring high school, or your MUN alumni to host your own Saturday training conference. You have to train your own new MUN club members, so why not invite students from other schools and charge them a reasonable fee to learn the essential skills of being an effective MUN delegate?

Your students will gain the experience of putting on a conference. This includes recruiting experienced adults including ex-MUNers with special skills (often found among schoolteachers, school librarians, parents, and business leaders from your school's corporate partners) to teach the fundamental skills, such as Internet research, writing policy papers, and public speaking. It also includes enlisting college students (perhaps alumni from your high school) who are experienced at chairing MUN sessions at the collegiate level, and MUN writing. Your students will also get the experience of writing the major conference documents, e.g., the conference program and the all-important background guide.

Schedule your training conference for the early fall so that those attending will be energized for the coming year's schedule of MUN conferences. This requires some advance planning be done over the summer, but students (who are running the conference, with adult advisors) generally have more free time at the start of rather than during the school year. Limit enrollment to twenty-five times the number of college chairs you can get. Small afternoon sessions led by a college chair will allow the novice MUNers to practice what they learned in the morning instructional sessions. Limit the number of students attending from visiting schools to a reasonable number—say, fifteen; that way you will not be left with a major unreimbursed expense if the school does not show up on conference day. And remember to save enough slots for students from your own high school. They are, after all, the main purpose of your training conference. You may argue that by doing this you are training your future competition. Just remember that the strength of your own MUNers depends in part on how strong their competition is. By boosting the overall level of MUN competition, you are elevating your own MUN students' abilities.

The **Parent Teacher Student Association** and the **Boosters Club** in your school will find your activity an interesting addition to their portfolios. Even a few hundred dollars will give you a running start in being able to assist students with registration/hotel/transportation fees. As you develop a winning record, you'll find that these groups like backing a winner, and will be delighted to sponsor your attendance at big-time conferences such as those hosted by major universities.

Corporate sponsorships offer ways for your team to quickly get a lot of money in a short amount of time. While the time-honored car washes, will get you some money and help build team cohesion and help with recruiting, they are enormously demanding of your time and your students' time. As a cost-effective method, car washes, bake sales and the like often generate less revenue than if you simply worked at a fast-food restaurant for minimum wages. Asking companies for money, however, can easily get you hundreds of dollars. There are several options for you and for them:

- You can run a simple ad for their company on your website, such as a straightforward "Thanks to our sponsors, including Vinyard Software, Inc." and include a link to their website(s). (Check with your school's legal department regarding specifically prohibited language.)
- You can run an ad or congratulatory note from the corporation in the program of the conference you host. Fees can vary depending upon the size and complexity of the ad.
- Some firms offer matching grants. Sound out your students' parents on whether their company offers these deals.
- Consider getting approved as a charity for the United Way or the Combined Federal Campaign. In addition to getting the money specifically designated to your organization, you also get a portion of the undesignated funds, based upon the percentage of total revenues that your charity attracts.

Here's a note we used to get our foot in the door. We then follow up on any expressions of interest with visits to the companies.

George C. Marshall High School
7731 Leesburg Pike
Falls Church, VA 22043
DATE

Dear XXXX,

Your firm has the opportunity to assist the Model United Nations Club at Marshall High School, which, since its reconstitution in September 2002, has become one of the country's leading programs.

The MUN club, a cocurricular activity at Marshall, attends high school– and college-sponsored conferences where, over the course of a weekend, students act as ambassadors and simulate the discussions, debate, decorum, and crisis sessions that take place at the UN in New York. In advance of MUN conferences, we are assigned countries (there are 193 member states in the UN) and topics of current interest. We research our country's positions on key issues and write position papers that spell out our position on topics of interest to UN member states. During the conference, our student delegates use parliamentary procedure and skills of persuasion to build support for resolutions that we help draft. Conferences typically recognize outstanding performances by individual schools, delegates, or delegations by awarding the coveted MUN "gavel."

During one school year, Marshall's MUN club won the outstanding school award at the National Model Arab League championships hosted by the National Council on US-Arab Relations, the Outstanding Small School Award at the University of Virginia MUN Conference, and the Secretary General's Award for Outstanding School at the Thomas Jefferson High School for Science and Technology's TechMUN Conference. While attending fourteen conferences that year, the Marshall MUN Club won eighty-six individual speaking and writing awards. Two dozen students won Best Speaker "gavels," some of them winning several. Forty-one students won a speaking or writing award; most won several.

While winning gavels and other individual or team awards is certainly exciting, even more gratifying is the growth in poise and self-confidence that our students develop as the year progresses. The MUN experience offers our students the opportunity to practice thinking on their feet, speaking extemporaneously, and writing persuasive resolutions and position papers under rather tight time constraints. They have learned to research issues of international importance and to construct international policies and laws that take into account the differing perspectives and priorities of both developed and developing nations. In short, our students are preparing to become not only informed American citizens but also good citizens of the world.

This past year has certainly proven to be a breakout one for the Marshall MUN team. We would very much like to build on this record of success by offering our best students the opportunity to compete at the national MUN conference at the UN in New York next year. To do that, we have stepped up our fund-raising activities and have made appeals to businesses and community service groups in our area. We estimate the cost of sending one delegate to the three-day New York MUN Conference at $1,000 (including $200 for transportation, $500 for accommodations, and $300 for school and delegate registration fees). We are aware of the many ways in which your organization supports many worthwhile activities in our community, but we would like to ask you to consider any amount that you can afford to assist us in our efforts to attend Nationals and other conferences this year and in future years. We believe it would be a most worthwhile investment in the future of our country. Sponsors will also be listed on the front page of the Marshall MUN Club's website.

Checks can be made out to the Marshall MUN Club and be sent to George C. Marshall High School, 7731 Leesburg Pike, Falls Church, VA 22043.

Thank you again for this opportunity to share with you the good news about Marshall's resurgent MUN Club. If you would like further information about the club, please contact Tom Brannan, our faculty advisor, or our parent volunteer, Dr. Edward Mickolus, who serves as our coach.

Sincerely,

Chambers of Commerce and local philanthropic organizations (Optimists, Rotary, Elks, similar groups) sometimes will help fund your group or take on all costs of a single conference. You might also be able to get corporate sponsorships from some of the individual members of the Chamber of Commerce/group. Marshall's team sends a few of our students to conduct a truncated MUN session during lunch or dinnertime meetings of one of these groups—we like to think of it as a variation of singing for your supper. Each student sits at a different table, thereby creating a rooting interest among the organization's participants at the table in how well "their" student does. In only twenty minutes, the students give shortened General Debate speeches, debate resolutions, offer amendments, ask questions, and vote. Be sure to bring handouts similar to the letter above with you to the meeting.

Parents of your students will often fund most of their children's participation needs (hotel, transportation, food, registration fees, uniforms, research supplies, computers, cell phones). They can also provide very useful corporate contacts. In some cases, firms will provide in-kind expertise in writing, speaking, and research skills. Members of the international departments of firms welcome opportunities to address your practice sessions.

Awards from philanthropic, educational, or UN-affiliated groups sometimes have monetary prizes attached to them. Be sure to check out what is available in your area.

The Embassy and UN Mission of your adoptive country will have a political and/or cultural counselor who will be glad to provide your students with materials from their country. It can't hurt to ask if they would also be willing to fund the delegation.

Hosting a competitive (not training) MUN conference. Staging a competitive conference with awards and multiple committee sessions, each requiring its own background guide and an adult, college student, or experienced high school MUNer to act as Chair, is labor intensive and requires months of preparation. It is, however, a great way for the students to get leadership experience. And if you are cost-efficient, you can generate hundreds of dollars to support your own conference schedule. This is also a major commitment of time by students who must prepare the background guide covering all of the committee sessions and topics set for discussion.

4
Scheduling

Where to Go

After you have introduced yourselves to each other and you have laid down a few goals for the team, you should also include in your first meeting a discussion of where the team will go for its first conference(s). You can pick any month during the school year—you'll probably find an organization within driving distance that will be hosting a conference (the United Nations Association of the United States [UNA-USA] hosts an online calendar of MUN conferences). Pick conferences that will provide a learning experience for your students. This means you're looking for conferences that promise college chairs and have a solid record for producing excellent background guides. Those conferences will draw the MUN clubs that are serious about MUNing, and those are the conferences that will reinforce what you've been teaching and allow your kids to see firsthand the best delegates in action. Nothing will improve your team more than competing against the best MUN clubs.

While September is a bit early to start on the conference circuit—schools are just starting, and teams have not have much time to get organized—you can take this opportunity to run **scrimmages** within the team to give your students practice in a conference setting. You might even invite local schools with a few veterans to stop by to give your students an idea of the level of competition they will face. At this stage, you do not need to burden your students with researching two to five topics (which you will normally find at conferences), writing position papers, etc. Let them pick whatever country they would like (for scrimmages, it is okay for students to choose the same country), and give them all the same topic and same committee for this practice. You should draft a short background guide on the topic, offering a statement of the issue(s), some previous UN attempts to solve the problem(s), suggestions for further research, and some questions that will guide their deliberations. Here's a background guide we have used in our early scrimmages:

Welcome to our first practice. At most conferences, you'll have on average about two weeks to research your country, the topic(s), and your country's positions on the topics. In this case, we'd like you to not worry about such time pressure, and come in confident of your knowledge.

For our first scrimmage, which we'll hold on Thursday, September 21, from 6 p.m. to 8 p.m., we'll discuss global terrorism. It's a topic on which virtually every country has something reasonably substantive to say—after all, every diplomat is potentially in the terrorists' sights. You can explore pretty much whatever aspect of terrorism you want. Here are a few things you might want to consider:

- Should the UN get involved in specific terrorist campaigns? Does, say, the Sri Lankan conflict merit UN mediation? Palestine? Kashmir? Colombia? You name it, virtually every region has some terrorist group, however small, that you might wish to discuss.
- What more can the UN do regarding al Qaeda?
- Should the UN create its own independent antiterrorist force to track down terrorists and bring them before the International Criminal Court?
- What constitutes state support to terrorists? Are some types of support more worrisome than others? What should the UN do, if anything, to outlaw such activities?
- Can the UN do anything to remedy the causes of terrorism? What are those causes?
- There are numerous anti-terrorist conventions (international agreements), be they global, regional, bilateral, etc. Do we need any more? Should the UN consider setting up a review conference to examine the effectiveness of one or more of these conventions? Below is a list of the global conventions (this does not include UN Security Council or General Assembly resolutions). Make sure you know which ones your country has joined, which ones you're not in, and why.
  - Convention on Offenses and Certain Other Acts Committed on Board Aircraft (often referred to as the Tokyo Convention, 1963)
  - Convention for the Suppression of Unlawful Seizure of Aircraft (Hague Convention, 1970)
  - Convention for the Suppression of Unlawful Acts Against the Safety of Civil Aviation (Montreal Convention, 1971)
  - Convention on the Prevention and Punishment of Crimes Against Internationally Protected Persons (1973)

- Convention on the Prohibition of the Development, Production, and Stockpiling of Bacteriological (Biological) and Toxin Weapons and on Their Destruction (BTWC, 1975)
- International Convention Against the Taking of Hostages (Hostages Convention, 1979)
- Convention on the Physical Protection of Nuclear Material (Nuclear Materials Convention, 1980)
- Protocol for the Suppression of Unlawful Acts of Violence at Airports Serving International Civil Aviation, Supplementary to the Convention for the Suppression of Unlawful Acts Against the Safety of Civil Aviation (1988)
- Convention for the Suppression of Unlawful Acts Against the Safety of Maritime Navigation (1988)
- Protocol for the Suppression of Unlawful Acts Against the Safety of Fixed Platforms Located on the Continental Shelf (1988)
- Convention on the Marking of Plastic Explosives for the Purpose of Identification (Montreal Convention, 1991)
- International Convention for the Suppression of Terrorist Bombings (1997)
- International Convention for the Suppression of the Financing of Terrorism (1999)

• Should the UN keep a list of international terrorists who can be extradited to requesting countries even in the absence of a bilateral extradition treaty?

Here's your next step: Let us know what country in the UN General Assembly (pretty much any country you can think of) you would like to represent. We'd like to give preference to students from that country, or who have that ethnic heritage, but if you'd really like that country and no one else has picked it, by all means, ask. We will try to give everyone their first choice.

Once you have your country assignment, be sure to contact your respective UN mission and local embassy for information on your positions. Below are a few other sources you might find helpful (all of which you can get from me [the MUN faculty advisor] if you can't find them in local public or university libraries—and don't forget the Library of Congress:

• *Patterns of Global Terrorism 2004* (and 2003, and 2002, etc.) available from the U.S. Department of State; more recent versions are available from the National Counterterrorism Center. *Patterns* and its successor publications have discussions of the positions of virtually every country, and useful chronologies of domestic and international attacks, legislation, regional agreements, etc.

- *Encyclopedia of World Terrorism* documents the latest on the texts of the conventions named above, plus a bunch of regional conventions, UN resolutions and documents, etc.
- **Dr. Mickolus's series of terrorism chronologies**, reaching from 1968 to 2012; available from Greenwood Press, Iowa State University Press, and McFarland Publishers, and from Vinyard Software.

Once you've done that research, figure out what you'd like to say in your opening speech. Then contact the rest of our team members who are representing countries that might have positions similar to yours. See if you can draft resolutions ahead of time (some conferences outlaw "canned" resolutions, and for good reason: they stifle negotiations and discourage consensus building). After we've listened to everyone's opening speeches, we'll see if you can get these resolutions passed. Via separate attachment, we have sent you the "Rules of Procedure" for the University of Virginia MUN, which will be our first college-hosted conference of the season; you might as well get used to their rules now so that you'll be better prepared.

As ever, e-mail or phone Dr. Mickolus or Mr. Brannan if you have questions.

The summer months and the early part of the school year are also an excellent opportunity to attend a **novice-only conference**, some of which are competitive, but many of which are designed solely as learning experiences. You can find them on both coasts—University of Maryland, Baltimore Campus, George C. Marshall High School, and the University of California system host noncompetitive sessions for rookies (both students and coaches). Attending these early-season conferences will give you an opportunity to talk to other teams, and find out what conferences are on their schedule for the year. You might find a few that will be of interest to your team.

Once you have conducted such internal and external practices, it's time to hit the road and attend conferences, both competitive and noncompetitive. You can **research** what's available as follows:

- Run a **web search** on "Model United Nations," "MUN," and "Model UN." You can further refine your search by searching within those categories, and asking for "high school" conferences, or conferences in your area, e.g., "Virginia," "Maryland," or "Washington, D.C." Note that many conferences are not indexed, and many do not have a website.

- Check the United Nations Association of the United States of America's **Calendar of Model UN Conferences** at http://www.unausa.org/global -classrooms-model-un/model-un-conferences/model-un-city-conferences. You can search by month, country in which the conference is held, and school level (middle school, high school, college, or mixed). The site offers such useful information as the conference's website, contact names, addresses, and phone numbers, the dates and size of the conference, and the committees that are offered.

- Join a Model UN **e-mail group** on the Internet. MUN-e-news@yahoogroups .com is an international list-serv that gives you access to thousands of individuals interested in MUNing (and related activities). Just send a note asking "anyone know of anything at our level in this region" and you'll get several responses. You can also expect to receive ads from conferences that are looking for participants from around the world. Don't be at all surprised to hear from conferences in Cuba, Russia, Hong Kong, Mexico, Turkey, Egypt, you name it!

- Join a **Model UN discussion group** on the Internet. There are several available through livejournal.com. You can set one up for your students, or visit the more general one at http://modelun.livejournal.com/ where you'll find comments by students on the value of conferences they have attended, requests by students for contacts at upcoming conferences, suggestions on research, etc. UNA-USA offers a similar service for students only on their website http://www.unausa.org/global-classrooms -model-un/model-un-conferences. Coaches should take the role of "lurker" rather than participant; students are freer with their peers in how forthright they are in their comments on conferences. Conferences sometimes set up conference-specific discussion groups, such as the Model Arab League (there are more than a dozen of them throughout the U.S. for college and high school students) at http://groups.yahoo.com/group /modelarableague/.

- Check the **websites of Model UN teams**, both at the college and high school level, paying particular attention to their calendars of upcoming conferences.

- Contact **teachers** at schools in your area and ask them for leads to conferences.

- Contact your local **UNA-USA chapter**.

For example, here is a sample of what we considered for our schedule one year, focusing mainly on MUN conferences on the Atlantic seaboard. We did not attend all of these; we limited our schedule to fourteen conferences.

High School MUN Calendar

This calendar is not intended to be comprehensive, but rather a representation of the many MUN high school conferences offered in all regions of the United States. For a comprehensive list that includes current-year conference dates, consult the following website: bestdelegate.com/model-un-conferences-database/. A roster of middle school MUN conference can be found at bestdelegate.com/model-un-conferences-database/#middle-school-global.

September
"My First MUN" Training Conference, George C. Marshall High School, Falls Church, Virginia, http://www.fcps.edu/marshallhs

Intergenerational Model United Nations Conference, Alameda, California, https://sites.google.com/site/astimodelunitednations/useful-links

South Orange County Model United Nations (SOCOMUN), Santa Margarita Catholic High School, Rancho Santa Margarita, California, http://www.smhs.org/apps/pages/index.jsp?uREC_ID=161629&type=d&termREC_ID=&pREC_ID=330695

October
George Mason High School MUN Conference, Falls Church, Virginia

University of Connecticut MUN Conference, Storrs, Connecticut, http://www.uconnmodelunitednations.com

Diplomat for a Day MUN Workshop, University of Maryland–Baltimore Campus, Baltimore, Maryland, http://www.umbc.edu/politicalsci/stuorgs/modelun.php

Horace Mann High School MUN, Riverdale, New York, http://mun.horacemann.org

Baylor Model United Nations, Waco, Texas, http://www.baylor.edu/modelun/index.php?id=49251

Cerritos High School Model United Nations (CHSMUN), Cerritos, California, http://cerritosmun.weebly.com/

Georgia Tech Model United Nations (GTMUN), Atlanta, Georgia,
http://www.gtmun.org/

UC Santa Cruz Model United Nations (UCSCMUN), Santa Cruz, California,
http://mun.soe.ucsc.edu/

Washington University Model United Nations Symposium (WUMUNS),
St. Louis, Missouri, http://wumuns.com/WUMUNS/Home.html

November

Brown University Simulation of the UN (BUSUN), Providence, Rhode Island,
http://www.busun.net

Appalachian State University Fall HS MUN Conference, Boone, North
Carolina, http://www.ira.appstate.edu

University of Pittsburgh MUN, Pittsburgh, Pennsylvania, http://www.pitt.edu
/~modelun/

Juniata College MUN Conference, Huntingdon, Pennsylvania, http://www.juniata
.edu/departments/pacs/modelun.html

Duke University International Security Conference, Durham, North Carolina,
http://discon.org/information

University of Virginia VAMUN, Charlottesville, Virginia, http://virginia-iro.org
/vamun/index.html

William and Mary MUN (WMHSMUN), Williamsburg, Virginia,
http://www.wmhsmun.org

Princeton University PMUNC, Princeton, New Jersey, http://irc.princeton.edu
/pmunc/

Rutgers University, New Brunswick, New Jersey (RUMUN), http://www.idia.net
/rumun.aspx

East Carolina High School MUN Conference, Greenville, North Carolina,
http://www.ecu.edu/polsci/mun/index.html

Brigham Young University Model United Nations (BYUMUN), Provo, Utah,
http://kennedy.byu.edu/student/modelun/

Contra Costa County Model United Nations (CCCMUN), Pleasant Hill,
California, http://www.cccoe.k12.ca.us/supe/events/modelun.htm

St. Ignatius Model United Nations (SIMUN), Chicago, Illinois, http://simun.org/

Verona Area High School Model United Nations Conference (VAHSMUN),
Verona, Wisconsin, https://sites.google.com/site/vahsmun/

Philips Academy Interscholastic Model United Nations (PAIMUN), Andover,
Massachusetts

Phillips Exeter Academy Model United Nations (PEAMUN), Exeter, New
   Hampshire
Triton Model United Nations (TritonMUN), University of California–San
   Diego, San Diego, California, http://modelun.ucsd.edu/index.html
University of Colorado Model United Nations, Boulder, Colorado, http://www
   .coloradomun.org/
Georgia State University Model United Nations (GSUMUN), Atlanta, Georgia
University of Connecticut Model United Nations (UCMUN), Storrs, Connecticut
McGill Secondary Schools United Nations Symposium (SSUNS), Montreal,
   Quebec, Canada, http://www.ssuns.org/

December
Concord Academy MUN (CAMUN) Concord, Massachusetts, http://www
   .concordacademy.org/camun
Cleveland Council on World Affairs MUN Conference, Cleveland, Ohio,
   http://www.ccwa.org/model_un.aspx
Prince William MUN, C.D. Hylton Senior High School, Woodbridge, Virginia,
   http://www.cdhylton.com
Model OAS, Organization of American States, Washington, D.C.
Delaware MUN, Salesianum High School, Wilmington, Delaware
Eagle MUNC, Boston College, Boston, Massachusetts, http://www.eaglemunc.org/
Chicago International Model United Nations (CIMUN), Chicago, Illinois,
   http://www.cimun.org/
North County Regional Conference for Model United Nations (NCRCMUN),
   High Tech High and Pacific Ridge School, San Marcos, California,
   http://www.ncrcmun.org/
Regis High School Model United Nations, Aurora, Colorado, http://www
   .coloradomun.org/
CASC Summits, Lansing, Michigan, http://www.mamunonline.com/summits
   /index.html
Colorado Springs Model United Nations, Colorado Springs, Colorado,
   http://www.coloradomun.org/

January
Harvard MUN, Boston, Massachusetts, http://hcs.harvard.edu/~hmun
Central New York MUN Conference (CNYMUN), Syracuse, New York,
   http://www.fmschools.org/webpages/cnymun/

Chantilly High School Model UN Conference (CHMUN), Chantilly, Virginia, http://chantillymun.org/

Columbia MUN Conference & Exposition (CMUNCE), New York, New York, http://www.cmunce.org

Yale MUN, New Haven, Connecticut, http://ymun.yira.org/

Ivy League MUN (ILMUNC), University of Pennsylvania, Philadelphia, Pennsylvania, http://www.ilmunc.com

Model United Nations of San Antonio (MUNSA), San Antonio, Texas

Central New York Model UN (CNYMUN), Syracuse University, Syracuse, New York, http://www.fmschools.org/webpages/cnymun/

University of Michigan Model United Nations (UMMUN), Ann Arbor, Michigan, http://munum.org/

Dallas Area Model United Nations (DAMUN), Irving, Texas

Houston Area Model United Nations (HAMUN), Houston, Texas

February

Penn State, Middletown, Pennsylvania

Bergen County Academies MUN Conference, Hackensack, New Jersey, http://www.academymodelun.org

North American Invitational Model UN (NAIMUN), Georgetown University, Washington, D.C., http://www.modelun.org/naimun

Yeshiva University MUN Conference, New York, New York, http://yu.edu /admissions/events/yunmun/

Old Dominion University, ODUMUNC, Norfolk, Virginia, http://al.odu.edu /mun/conference/index_2013.shtml

Catholic University MUN (CUMUNC), Washington, D.C., https://nest.cua.edu /organization/cumunc/about

Gar-Field High School MUN, Woodbridge, Virginia

Miami University of Ohio Model Arab League, Oxford, Ohio (college level, but willing to take a high school team), http://ncusar.org/modelarableague /uregionals/uohio.html

Johns Hopkins MUN, Baltimore, Maryland, http://www.jhumunc.org

Carnegie Mellon University, Pittsburgh, Pennsylvania, http://www.contrib .andrew.cmu.edu/~iro/?page_id=23

Philadelphia MUN Conference (PhilMUN), Philadelphia, Pennsylvania

GatorMUN, University of Florida, Gainesville, Florida, http://www.gatormun.org/

Santa Clara Valley Model United Nations (SCVMUN), Santa Teresa High

School, San Jose, California, http://cygnusmgi.wix.com/scvmun

Massachusetts Institute of Technology Model United Nations Conference (MITMUNC), Boston, Massachusetts

Model United Nations at the University of Chicago (MUNUC), Chicago, Illinois, http://www.munuc.org/

Mid-South Model United Nations (MSMUN), Memphis, Tennessee

Alaska Model United Nations, Anchorage, Alaska, http://www.uaa.alaska.edu /modelun/

Boston University Model United Nations (BosMUN), Boston, Massachusetts, http://bosmun.org/

Laguna Hills High School Model United Nations (LHHSMUN), Laguna Hills, California, http://www.lhhsmun.org/joomla/

Surf City Model United Nations, Huntington Beach High School, Huntington Beach, California

University of Georgia Model United Nations Conference (UGAMUNC), Athens, Georgia, http://modelun.uga.edu/Home.html

UNA-USA Global Classrooms New York City (GC NYC), New York, New York, http://www.unausa.org/global-classrooms-model-un/model-un -conferences/model-un-city-conferences/new-york-city

Yeshiva University National Model United Nations (YUNMUN), Stamford, Connecticut, http://yu.edu/admissions/events/yunmun/

Alabama Model United Nations (ALMUN), Tuscaloosa, Alabama, http://bama.ua.edu/~almun/index.html

March

Fox Chapel High School, Pittsburgh, Pennsylvania

George Mason University MUN spring conference, GMUMUN, Fairfax, Virginia, http://mun.gmu.edu/masun/

National High School Model United Nations, NHSMUN, New York, New York, http://imuna.org/nhsmun/conference

Senior Hi-Y MUN, Parkersburg, West Virginia, http://www.yla-youthleadership .org/MUN.html

VISIMUN Georgetown Visitation Academy, Washington, D.C.

Cornell University, Ithaca, New York, http://www.cmunc.net/

Berkeley Model United Nations (BMUN), Berkeley, California, http://bmun.org/

Indianapolis Model United Nations (IMUN), IUPUI, Indianapolis, Indiana, http://liberalarts.iupui.edu/modelun/

Wisconsin High School Model United Nations (WHSMUN), Milwaukee,
  Wisconsin, http://www4.uwm.edu/cie/educators/1081
Bentley University Model UN High School Conference (BMUN), Waltham,
  Massachusetts, http://student-organizations.bentley.edu/modelun/hs
  /index.html
Arizona Model United Nations (AzMUN), Tucson, Arizona, http://arizonamun
  .org/wp/?lang=en
Boston College High School Model United Nations (BCHSMUN), Boston,
  Massachusetts, http://bchighmodelun.org/
Canadian High Schools Model UN (CAHSMUN), Richmond, British
  Columbia, Canada, http://www.cahsmun.org/

April

Thomas Jefferson High School for Science and Technology, TechMUN,
  Alexandria, Virginia, http://activities.tjhsst.edu/mun/techmun
Appalachian State Model Security Council, Boone, North Carolina,
  http://ira.appstate.edu/high-school-model-un
George Washington University MUN, Washington, D.C., http://www.wamunc.com/
Lock Haven University, Lock Haven, Pennsylvania, http://www.lhup.edu/lfarley
  /munhome.htm
Model Arab League High School Nationals, Georgetown University,
  Washington, D.C., and other locations in the United States and overseas,
  http://ncusar.org/modelarableague/
Osbourne Park High School MUN Conference, OPMUNC, Manassas,
  Virginia, https://sites.google.com/site/ophsmodelun/
North Coast High School Conference, Lake Erie International Model United
  Nations (LEIMUN), Ashtabula, Ohio, http://leimun.com/nchsc.html
Metro Kansas City Model United Nations (MKCMUN), Johnson County
  Community College, Overland Park, Kansas, http://students.jccc.edu
  /orgs/un/mkcmun.htm
Oregon Model United Nations, Eugene, Oregon, http://oregonmun.org/
Hockaday Model United Nations (HOCKAMUN), Dallas, Texas
Southern Ontario Model United Nations Assembly (SOMA), Toronto, Canada,
  http://www.soma.on.ca/
UNA-USA Global Classrooms Houston (GC Houston), Houston, Texas,
  http://www.unausa.org/global-classrooms-model-un/model-un-conferences
  /model-un-city-conferences/houston

League of Creative Minds, Model United Nations (LCMMUN), San Francisco, California, http://www.creativedelegates.org/content-loader.php?page_key=index

University of Denver High School Model United Nations, Denver, Colorado, http://www.coloradomun.org/

Seton Hall University Model United Nations (SHUMUN), South Orange, New Jersey, http://www.shumun.com/?page_id=718

UNA-USA Global Classrooms Chicago (GC Chicago), Chicago, Illinois, http://www.unausa.org/global-classrooms-model-un/model-un-conferences /model-un-city-conferences/chicago

Princess Anne High School Model United Nations Conference (PAMUNC), Virginia Beach, Virginia, http://www.facebook.com/pages/P-A-M-U-N-C -Secretariat/264155076943598

May

UNA-USA Global Classrooms, Boston, Massachusetts, http://www.unausa.org /global-classrooms-model-un/model-un-conferences/model-un-city -conferences/bosto

BIMUN, Bishop Ireton High School, Alexandria, Virginia

UNA-USA MUN, New York, New York, http://www.unausa.org/global -classrooms-model-un/model-un-conferences/international-model-un -conference

UNA-USA Global Classrooms Minnesota, Hamline University, Minneapolis, Minnesota

UNA-USA Global Classrooms Tampa Bay (GC TB), Tampa, Florida, http://www .unausa.org/global-classrooms-model-un/model-un-conferences/model-un -city-conferences/tampa-bay

Washington State Model United Nations (WASMUN), Seattle, Washington, http://wasmun.org/

West Coast Invitational Model UN (WCIMUN), Century High School, Santa Ana, California, http://home.wcimun.com/category/news/

Trumbull Model United Nations Invitational (TMUNI), Trumbull, Connecticut

Canada International Model United Nations (CAIMUN), Vancouver, British Columbia, Canada, http://www.caimun.ca/

University of California, Irvine Model United Nations (UCIMUN), Irvine, California

Central Jersey Model United Nations, Watchung Hills, New Jersey, http://modelun.com/cjmun/

Davis Model United Nations (DMUNC), Davis, California

Maine Model United Nations Conference (MeMUNC), University of Southern
   Maine, Gorham, Maine, http://www.memunc.org/

You probably will not be able to attend more than one conference a month,
especially in your first year. Your conference schedule will depend in part on your
ability to recruit chaperones from among parents and teachers, funding, and testing schedules at your school (before you commit to attend a conference, be sure
to check with your school's testing coordinator to ensure that the MUN conference does not pose a conflict with scheduled testing). In addition, the roster of students traveling to overnight conferences should be vetted to ensure that students
with academic difficulties are identified well before the students depart for the
MUN conference.

When selecting conferences, what should you look for? The best matches are
those which cover **topics** and **UN committees** of interest to your students, and are
of a **size** and **competitive nature** that will challenge your students and excite them
about the sport without overwhelming them. A mix of different topics, types of
committees, sizes, and competitive levels will give them a good feeling for what is
out there, and what they can set as goals for future seasons. Conferences can last
from one to five days (most are limited to weekends) and vary in size, depending,
in general, upon the sponsor:

high school–sponsored	100 to 600 students
college-sponsored	300 to 2,000 students
international conferences	2,000 to 3,500 students

The latter conferences include the National High School MUN, with about
2,000 students; the North American Invitational MUN (NAIMUN) in Washington,
D.C., which is hosted by Georgetown University's International Relations
Association and is the largest in North America, at about 2,500+ students; and
The Hague International MUN (THIMUN), the world's largest high school con-
ference, with 3,500 students.

In general, the smaller conferences will tend to specialize in the smaller committees. You might find a conference of less than a hundred students that will have
several councils, including a **Security Council** (fifteen members, plus a few
observer delegations whose representation depends upon the topic being discussed,
e.g., Palestine Authority and Israel might be invited to a discussion of the Middle

East situation) and several General Assembly committees, with single or double delegations in each council.

The larger conferences will be able to model the 193-member **General Assembly (GA) committees**, either **standing committees** (e.g., Legal, Economic-Financial, Special Political, Social and Humanitarian, Disarmament and International Security) and/or **ad hoc committees** (e.g., special ad hoc committee on the situation in Iraq). Still-larger conferences can also offer experience with the **Economic and Social Council's (ECOSOC) committees**, and/or the **specialized agencies** (World Health Organization, International Atomic Energy Agency), **banks** (International Bank for Reconstruction and Development), **courts** (International Court of Justice, International Criminal Court), **regional organizations** (League of Arab States, African Union, OPEC, APEC, Organization of American States), or other organizations. Mid-size and large conferences may also have simulations of the **cabinets** of different countries, which may (or may not) interact with each other in handling an ongoing crisis written by the Secretariat. In these simulations, the students represent named individuals (e.g., Secretary of State John Kerry in the U.S. National Security Council; the Iranian Minister of Defense; the Venezuelan Minister of Labor) within a cabinet. Rules of procedure in the latter cabinet simulations are quite different—students are among colleagues, and are attempting to craft a national response to a fast-moving crisis by chatting with each other in an informal atmosphere, rather than by giving formal speeches in a parliamentary assembly. Simulations can also be held of **historic/future councils** (e.g., the League of Nations in 1939; the UN Security Council in 1994; the KGB and CIA during the Cuban Missile Crisis of October 1962; a UN Security Council, with various proposed UN reforms, in the year 2020).

The **competitive versus teaching** nature of conferences will vary. Some university-hosted conferences aim to be more of a learning experience, and while awards are given at the end of the conference, the Secretariat aims to teach as well as evaluate. At the competitive George Mason University (Fairfax, Virginia) and Salesianum School's DELMUN (Wilmington, Delaware) conferences, for example, it is not uncommon for Chairs to stop in the middle of a discussion to explain what a delegate has just done and why the speech or parliamentary motion was to be emulated by others. Other conferences are more aggressively competitive, and will have rules that forbid the use of cell phones, computers, and other electronic devices because they give an "unfair advantage" or that discourage teachers from providing suggestions to students. (Do not be deterred; your role is *always* to teach students, no matter what the venue.)

The **number of awards** given at conferences, even the competitive ones, will also differ. Some will give a first place (gavel), one or two second place awards (usually known as Outstanding Delegate, although this term is used by the Model Arab League group as a first place award), two or three third place awards (usually known as Honorable Mention, although the Model Arab Leagues refer to this as second place), and perhaps three Chair Commendations (fourth place, also known as Verbal Commendations—"attaboys" that do not include certificates). Other conferences will offer many more awards; some give awards to 70 percent of the participants. The latter conferences are especially good for your rookies to attend; they'll come back with a feeling of accomplishment, and an eagerness to try more challenging conferences. On rare occasions, awards will include a scholarship or cash (the Sarasota-Manatee UNA Chapter gave a $200 award to the Best Delegates at their conference).

You'll also need to consider whether you want/can afford to attend conferences that require **hotel/campus stays**. In some cases, you will be able to commute to conferences at which the out-of-towners will be staying in hotels. However, these larger conferences, as mentioned previously, also tend to have **midnight crisis sessions** for some of the smaller committees and cabinets. These sessions (which can start at midnight, 1 a.m., or sometimes 2 a.m.) usually last for three to four hours, and are meant to surprise the students. Nonetheless, if you are coaching a commuter school, you will want to find out from the Secretariat ahead of time which committees will have such sessions so that you can book hotel rooms. (We are not persuaded that crisis sessions in the wee hours have any more educational value over crisis sessions held at more reasonable hours, but you will run across these sessions in many venues, so be prepared!)

You will also on occasion be invited to virtual MUNs on the Internet, principally through list-servs.

What Countries/Councils Should We Represent?

Model UNing offers your students the opportunity to gain in-depth knowledge about nearly two hundred countries. The UN General Assembly currently has 193 governments represented; there are also several nonmember states (e.g., the Palestine Authority, the European Union, various NGOs, and on occasion news media), which you can choose to represent. Historic and future councils will further expand your choices with countries that have ceased to be, and countries that may someday come into existence.

Despite your initial impression that it's important for your school to represent one of the Big Five (the Security Council permanent members with vetoes—United

States, UK, France, China, and Russia) in order to be taken seriously and be heard on all issues, in MUNs, **it does not matter what country(ies) you represent. What matters is how well you represent them.** Chairs attempt to give every delegate a fair opportunity to be heard; after all, the UN General Assembly was designed to give every nation a forum. You have as good a chance to win with an island nation like Fiji as with a Big Five country. (You actually may have a better chance with a lesser-known country; fewer delegates and Chairs will complain that you are "out of policy" or "out of character," because they do not know your country's policies as well as they believe they know the policies of the more well-publicized nations.)

You may want to apply for countries of your **students' ethnic heritage**, if your school has a sizeable population of students who are foreign-born or who have family ties that connect to foreign nations. Such assignments lessen the amount of research the student has to do on the country they will represent, although you should still require them to conduct research on their government's positions. You should also encourage them to give their speeches, or at least part of their speeches, in their native language(s) and share a few words (greetings and key words) with other teammates who can use the terms in their committees.

At the larger conferences, you may have the opportunity to **send two students** to represent the same country in the same committee. You'll want to ensure there is good chemistry between the partners in these **double delegations**. When their nation is called upon to speak, both students approach the podium or microphone, and both speak in turn. (It doesn't happen like this at the UN, but be ready for this wrinkle at an MUN conference.)

You may also have the opportunity to send students to **single, smaller committees or cabinets**. This puts a premium on the self-confidence of the delegates chosen for those councils. The cabinets are a spinoff of the MUN format; most do not use parliamentary procedure, and the skills needed to win in these councils are somewhat different than those used in, say, a General Assembly. In the GAs, there is a premium on parliamentary skills, and in the formality of one's remarks. In the cabinets, students are being evaluated on their capacity for analysis, critical thinking, and creativity in developing responses to fast-breaking events. Although the students are representing named individuals, it does not matter which individual or which bureaucratic position they represent. They do not have to be the prime minister to win in small committees. What matters, as in the standard MUN formats, is how well the student represents that person. While it is essential that delegates in a crisis committee research the official they are representing, it also often does not matter how much they know about the policy positions of the person they are representing. Because they are being presented with hypothetical crisis situations, precisely how that person would react is inherently unknowable. What is important is that they get their ideas on the table, including their assessment of the problem presented, and that they are able to quickly craft a consensus to back their suggested solutions.

Who Should Go

If you have the opportunity to send students to both **large committees** and **small councils**, that is, if you have enough students for both, try to fill each council with at least one student. When it comes time for consideration for Best School awards, you want to have done well in as many councils/committees as possible; i.e., a gavel is a gavel, no matter whether you won it in a 193-member committee of the General Assembly or a 10-person French cabinet. That said, if some of your delegates—particularly your novices—are more comfortable having a partner, then assign them to one of the double delegations frequently found in the General Assembly committees.

When selecting **partners**, in addition to having the right chemistry, you should also consider **pairing a veteran with a rookie**. There is only so much that you can teach your novices in practices and through book and Internet research. Having a partner to show them the ropes in "battlefield conditions" is invaluable. (There are often novice-only committees at college-hosted conferences. Make sure that you abide by the rules of the conference—veterans are ineligible for awards in such committees.) Learning by doing is far more effective than all the lectures, videotapes, Internet sites, book-learning, etc., that you can provide. Even if they're dead silent in their first conference, the practice sessions that you hold will make more sense to them now that they've seen a real conference in operation.

It's your call on how you choose who gets what committee and what partner. In some cases, it's whoever raises their hand first when you announce what's available at a conference. (First choice should be given to students who attend practices and/or your own in-house training!) In other cases in which you are trying to win at a particularly challenging conference, you may wish to tap specific students for specific countries/committees. As your students develop substantive expertise, you might offer them the opportunity to be in committees or represent countries for which they have previous experience. For example, a student who has taken Advanced Placement (AP) or International Baccalaureate (IB) economics courses would seem to be a good match for assignments in the World Bank or as secretary of the treasury in a U.S. cabinet simulation. This lets your students build on what they already know, and lessens the burden of research. They can thus spend more time deciding how to package their research via writing position papers and crafting better speeches, rather than always conducting new research.

Once you have carefully considered all of the issues raised in this chapter, have developed your students' skills, and have put together the best team any conference has ever seen, your perfectly-crafted team will start to erode in about three days. Students will suddenly remember a band concert that conflicts with the upcoming MUN conference, have tons of homework that has suddenly come due, catch a cold, or have a family emergency. Only rarely will you see all of the students listed in the first draft of your MUN conference roster actually show up to a conference. High school is a dynamic place and the kids' priorities change. Your job is to be supportive of the students, to encourage them to manage their time wisely so that they can do MUN without compromising their studies, and offer them the opportunity to rejoin the team at a future point in time. Operate on the assumption that kids want to be active in MUN because they recognize its value to their intellectual and social development, and so keep the door open to their future participation.

5

The Triangle Offense and Defense

Overview of the Triangle System

As part of our MUN strategy, we use an adaptation of the Triangle Offense that Phil Jackson used with the NBA Chicago Bulls when Michael Jordan was a team member. We call it the Triangle Offense and Triangle Defense. There are three overall parts of the Triangle system that we'll explore: parliamentary procedure plays, public speaking styles and coalition formation in the Model UN context, and research.

Parliamentary Procedure

Most MUN conferences are conducted by parliamentary procedure (we'll put aside the cabinet simulations for this discussion). It's your key secret weapon. If used correctly, you can do absolutely anything you want, and your rivals will simply be frustrated and won't be able to respond.

Within the parliamentary procedure part of the Triangle, there are subtriangles:

- Diagrams/cheat sheets
- Triangle Offense plays
- Triangle Defense plays

Commentary on Rules: The first thing to do when you get materials from a conference organizer is to analyze their **rules of procedure**. (Robert's Rules, a set of parliamentary rules commonly used in many civic associations, are an example of parliamentary rules. However, they are *not* used in the UN or MUN, and they have absolutely no bearing on what you will be doing. All that matters is what the rules for that particular conference say. Each conference will have its own set of rules; every Secretariat or conference host believes they can write rules better than the UN did.) Rules can be only a page or can run multiple pages (the longest we've seen was seventy pages).

Read the rules a few times, and then **create a spreadsheet/chart** (see table 1). (Sometimes you'll get this from the conference organizers. Most often, you won't. Write your own anyway.) Along the side of the chart, figure out the order of precedence of the motions (things like motion to recess; motion to call the question—let's vote on this resolution; motion to amend; etc.) and points of procedure (these will be separate, and are things like Point of Order—your new best friend; Point of Personal Privilege; and the like). The order of precedence means that some things, when moved, have to be considered before what the group had been considering. For example, a motion to amend a resolution has to be voted upon before you vote on the resolution as a whole. Once you've figured out that precedence—and don't worry if it takes a while for you to get it just right; the folks who wrote this haven't worked all the bugs out of the system, and you'll find conflicts—write the following along the top of the spreadsheet: Name of Motion; Rule Number; Majority Required (some require a simple majority of those present, others require an absolute majority—every member of the group, no matter whether they are present or not—2/3 majority, majority of quorum, etc.); interrupt speaker (a simple yes/no); and oddities/special circumstances about the rule as to how it works in this conference (you'll find that sometimes the rule writer has unintentionally, or intentionally, thrown strange things into the rules). If you have a chance, try creating one of these "cheat sheets" for the rules that you'll find on the websites listed in this book. Creating these cheat sheets is an excellent exercise for your students in preparing for a conference. (See our lesson plans in appendix E for a sample exercise using long-form rules.)

A cheat sheet for the University of Virginia MUN Rules of Procedure is provided in table 1. Note that it comments on key rules in the order in which they appear in the overall Rules of Procedure. A different style cheat sheet would order the rules by their procedural precedence (see Rule 43 of the VAMUN rules for an example). The cheat sheet in table 1 is a short guide to the longer VAMUN Rules. Delegates should bring both the cheat sheet and the formal Rules of Procedure with them to every session of the meeting.

University of Virginia International Relations Organization (VAMUN Conference) Rules of Procedure (Long Form)

1. **SCOPE**: These rules for the General Assembly, the Economic and Social Councils, and the specialized agencies are self-sufficient, except for modifications provided by the Secretariat, and all shall be considered adopted in advance of the session. No other rules of procedure are applicable.

Table 1. University of Virginia Model United Nations Rules of Procedure—Short Form

RULE	MOTION	SPEAKERS	VOTE	COMMENT
15	Adoption of the agenda	2 for/2 against	Majority	Sets the order of topics to be discussed. The order of all committee topics must be specified.
17	Closing the Speakers' List	None	Majority	List may be closed at any time. When list is exhausted, debate ends and an immediate vote is taken on all resolutions before the committee.
24	Caucusing	None	Majority	Motion requires statement of purpose and establishment of time limit. Sometimes called "unmoderated caucus" or "moderated caucus."
26	Resolutions	Full discussion	Majority	Requires the signatures of 1/5 of the body and Chair for submission. (Some might be deemed "important questions" if there are UNGA resolutions on specific issues. See UN Charter and Rule 37 for definitions.)
27	Friendly amendments	None	None	If all sponsors of a resolution and the Chair agree, then the resolution stands amended.
27	Unfriendly amendments	Full discussion	Majority	Requires the signatures of 1/10 of the body and the Chair for submission.
36	Division of the question	2 for/2 against	Majority	If objection is made to the motion, then the division shall be voted on. If the motion is carried, then a substantive vote shall be taken on the divided parts. The approved parts will then be voted on as a whole.
39	Postponement of debate	2 for/2 against	2/3	Debate will move to the next topic area without voting on pending resolutions.
40	Closure of debate	2 against	2/3	If passed, the Speakers' List will be closed, and all pending resolutions will be voted on immediately.
PARLIAMENTARY POINTS				
21	Point of parliamentary inquiry	None	N/A	When delegates have a question about proper parliamentary procedure.
22	Point of personal privilege	None	N/A	When delegates wish to bring to the attention of the Chair some impairment that affects the operation of the committee (e.g., cannot hear the speaker).
23	Point of order	None	N/A	When delegates wish to bring to the attention of the Chair the improper use of parliamentary procedure.
18	Yields	None	N/A	Delegates may yield to questions, to another speaker, or to the Chair. Delegates who have been yielded to may not yield (i.e., no tertiary yields). Delegates may declare their yield at any time.

2. **DUTIES of the SECRETARY-GENERAL**: The Secretary-General shall act in that capacity in all meetings of the General Assembly and the Economic and Social Council, their committees and subcommittees. The Secretary-General may designate a member of the Secretariat to act in the place of the Secretary-General at these meetings. The Secretary-General shall provide and direct the staff required by the General Assembly, the Economic and Social Council, and any committees or subsidiary organs that they may establish. The term "Secretariat" refers collectively to those designated to act on behalf of the Secretary-General.

3. **STATEMENTS of the SECRETARIAT**: The Secretary-General, or a member of the Secretariat designated by the Secretary-General as his or her representative, may make, at any time, either oral or written statements to any plenary meeting or any committee or subcommittee.

4. **LANGUAGE**: English shall be the official and working language of the conference.

5. **DELEGATIONS**: The delegation of a Member State shall consist of no more than two representatives in any committee. Regardless of the number of representatives, a Member State has only one vote in each committee in which it is a member.

6. **CREDENTIALS**: The credentials of all delegations have been accepted upon registration. Actions relating to the modification of rights, privileges, or credentials of any member may not be initiated without the written consent of the Secretary-General. Any representative regarding whose admission a member objects shall be provisionally seated with the same rights as other representatives, pending a decision from the Secretary-General.

7. **PARTICIPATION of NON-MEMBERS**: Representatives of Accredited Observers shall have the same rights as those of full members, except that they may not sign or vote on resolutions or amendments. A representative of a state or organization that is not a member of the United Nations or an Accredited Observer may address a committee only with prior approval of the Chair.

8. **FUNCTIONS of the CHAIR**: The Chair shall declare the opening and closing of each meeting of the committee, direct its discussions, ensure observance of the rules of procedure, accord the right to speak, put questions, and announce decisions. The Chair shall rule on points of order and, subject to these rules, shall have complete control of the proceedings at any meeting and over the maintenance of order thereat. The Chair may, in

the course of the discussion of an item, propose to the committee the limitation of time to be allowed to speakers, the closure of the list of speakers, or the closure of debate. The Chair may also propose the suspension or adjournment of the meeting or the postponement of debate on the item under discussion. The Chair shall have discretionary powers to entertain a motion, or suggest to the body that a motion would be in order, or choose not to entertain a motion and suggest that it be withdrawn. The Chair may rule a motion out of order, thus disallowing that motion.

9. **ESTABLISHMENT of COMMITTEES and SUBCOMMITTEES**: The General Assembly and the Economic and Social Council may establish such committees as they deem necessary for the performance of their functions. Each committee may set up subcommittees.

10. **QUORUM**: The Chair may declare a committee open and permit debate to proceed when at least one quarter of the members of the committee are present. A member of the committee is a representative who is officially registered with the conference. The presence of a majority of the members shall be required for the vote on any substantive motion. Procedural votes refer to motions regarding the process of the discussion (e.g., motion for recess, or closure of the Speakers' List). Substantive votes address the substance of the topic under discussion (e.g., a vote on the contents of a resolution or amendment). A quorum shall be assumed to be present unless specifically challenged and shown to be absent. No roll-call vote is ever required to determine the presence of a quorum.

11. **ESTABLISHMENT of a PAGE**: A delegate may move that the committee establish a page, a volunteer from among the members represented, for the purpose of delivering messages between Members. The entertainment of this motion is entirely up to the Chair and his/her decision to entertain it is not debatable.

12. **SPEECHES**: No member may address a committee without having previously obtained the permission of the Chair. The Chair shall take a Speakers' List in the order in which the members signify their desire to speak. The Chair shall call a speaker to order if the speaker's remarks are not relevant to the subject under discussion. Members may speak as often as they wish; however, members must wait until they have already spoken before being placed on the Speakers' List again.

13. **TIME LIMIT on SPEECHES**: The Chair may, upon consultation with the committee or as a result of a motion by a member of the committee,

limit the time allowed to each speaker on any question. When debate is limited and a speaker exceeds the allotted time, the Chair shall call that speaker to order without delay.

14. **PROVISIONAL AGENDA**: The Provisional Agenda is the topic list provided by the Chair of the committee. The order of the topics does not imply the order of the agenda. The only topics to be discussed by the committee are these topics with exceptions allowed only under the direction of the Chair or the Secretariat.

15. **ADOPTION of the AGENDA**: Each committee shall order the provisional agenda provided by the Secretary-General. A proposed agenda shall include all topics provided in the provisional agenda. It requires a simple majority to approve an agenda order and proposed agenda shall be voted upon in the order in which they were proposed. A Speakers' List will be established for purposes of discussing the order of the agenda. After a sufficient number of speakers have spoken on the order of the agenda, a member may move that a particular agenda order be adopted. If the proposed agenda passes, debate on the order of the agenda will be deemed to have been closed, the Speakers' List will be discarded, and the committee will begin consideration of the first agenda topic.

16. **CHANGE of the AGENDA**: A committee may change the order in which it considers agenda topics. The Chair may entertain one speaker for, and one against, a motion to change the order. A simple majority vote is required to change the order in which agenda topics will be discussed. A motion to change the order of the agenda may only be removed after the substantive topic has been closed and all related resolutions and amendments have been put to a vote. A motion to change the agenda may not be moved during the substantive debate of any topic.

17. **CLOSING the SPEAKERS' LIST**: The Speakers' List may be closed at any time upon the majority vote of the members present and voting. When a closed Speakers' List is exhausted, debate automatically ends and an immediate vote is taken on all resolutions and amendments before the committee.

18. **REOPENING the SPEAKERS' LIST**: The Speakers' List may be reopened by a vote of the members provided that at least one speaker remains on the list at the time of the motion. One member may speak in favor of and one opposed to the motion.

19. **YIELDS**: When the time for speeches has been limited, a member recognized to speak on a substantive issue may yield his or her remaining time

to another member. The time may be yielded in one of three ways: to another delegate, to questions, or to the Chair. Only one yield is allowed: a speaker who is yielded to may not yield at all. A delegate may share his or her allotted time with another representative of the same member state and this shall not count as a yield. Yields are in order only on substantive speeches. A yield may be announced at any time before the speaker has left the floor. (NOTE: Questions and comments cannot be instituted at the end of timed speeches.)

a. **Yield to another delegate**: His remaining time shall be given to that delegate. The delegate who receives that yielded time may not, however, then yield to another delegate.

b. **Yield to questions**: The Chair shall select Questioners and limit them to one question each. The Chair shall have the right to call to order any delegate whose question is, in the opinion of the Chair, rhetorical and leading and not designed to elicit information. Only the speaker's answers to questions shall be deducted from the speaker's remaining time. The speaker may at any time determine that he or she will cease accepting questions and thus conclude his or her remarks.

c. **Yield to the Chair**: Such a yield should be made if the delegate does not wish to use the rest of his time for speaking on any other type of yield. The Chair shall then move to the next speaker.

d. **Yield to comments**: The Chair shall select any delegates, if the speaker has not enacted ANY of the above-mentioned yields, to comment on specific information contained in the previous speech. The number and time limit of comments are determined by the body before debate begins, along with the time limit for speeches in general.

20. **RIGHT of REPLY**: If a speaker has impugned the national integrity of another member state or observer, or the personal integrity of another representative, the Chair may accord that member or representative appropriate speaking time to exercise the right of reply. The right of reply is to be used to respond to the statements of the speaker. It may not be used to make corresponding, insulting remarks. It is granted at the discretion of the Chair and should only be requested at the conclusion of the speaker's remarks.

21. **POINT of PARLIAMENTARY INQUIRY**: A member may rise to a point of parliamentary inquiry when uncertain of the procedural setting of the committee. A member may not interrupt a speaker on a point of par-

liamentary inquiry. Representatives may use this point to have the Chair explain any procedural matter. A point of parliamentary inquiry may be raised during voting procedure. Points of Information do not exist.

22. **POINT of PERSONAL PRIVILEGE**: A member may rise to a point of personal privilege in order to bring to the attention of the Chair some physical discomfort that is disrupting the proper functioning of the committee. A point of personal privilege may interrupt a speaker. A representative may rise to a point of personal privilege when he or she is unable to hear the Chair or speaker or for some other physical reason that may impair the representative's ability to participate in or listen to the debate.

23. **POINT of ORDER**: During the discussion of any matter, a delegate may rise to a Point of Order to complain of improper parliamentary procedure. A Chair in accordance with these rules of procedure shall immediately decide the Point of Order. The Chair may rule out of order those points that are dilatory or improper; such a decision is not subject to appeal. A representative rising to a Point of Order may not speak on the substance of the matter under discussion. A Point of Order may only interrupt a speaker when the speech itself is not following proper parliamentary procedure.

24. **CAUCUSING**: A motion to caucus is in order at any time when the floor is open, prior to closure of debate. The delegate must briefly explain its purpose and specify a time limit for the caucus, not to exceed 20 minutes. The motion shall immediately be put to a vote. A majority of members present and voting is required for passage. The Chair may rule the motion out of order and his/her decision is not subject to appeal.

25. **MODERATED CAUCUS**: A motion for a moderate caucus is in order at any time when the floor is open, prior to the closure of debate. The delegate must briefly explain its purpose and specify a time limit for the caucus, not to exceed 20 minutes. The purpose of moderated caucus is to facilitate substantive debate at critical junctures in the discussion. With that goal in mind, the Chair will temporarily depart from the Speakers' List and call on delegates to speak at his/her discretion. Once raised, the motion shall be voted on immediately with a majority of the members present and voting required for passage. The Chair may rule the motion out of order and his/her decision is not subject to appeal.

26. **RESOLUTIONS and WORKING PAPERS**: Resolutions shall normally be submitted in writing to the Chair, who shall circulate copies to the members. No resolutions shall be voted upon unless copies of them have been made

available to all members. Any member may submit a resolution. Any member may be added to the list of sponsors of a resolution at any time before the resolution is put to a vote. Sponsorship indicates support of and agreement with a resolution. Because of the limited resources of the conference, it is necessary to ensure a minimum level of discussion of a resolution or amendment before it is produced for general distribution. Therefore, a resolution must have the signatures of one-fifth of the membership of the body. A "signature" does not indicate sponsorship or even agreement with a resolution. Rather, a signature is intended to mean that the member desires the opportunity to discuss the resolution. A less formal draft of a resolution, often referred to as a working paper, may also be submitted to the Chair for the purpose of making additional copies for wider distribution. The Chair will determine whether a working paper is copied and how many copies are made. Working papers are intended to aid the committee in its discussion and formulation of resolutions and need not be written in resolution format.

27. **AMENDMENTS**: Delegates may amend any resolution that has been introduced. All the sponsors of a resolution approve a friendly amendment. An unfriendly amendment, which is not approved by all the sponsors, must have the approval of the Chair and the signatures of one-tenth of the membership. An approved amendment may be introduced when the floor is open, but is not voted on until the committee moves into voting procedure for that topic area. When debate on the topic is closed, the committee shall vote on the amendments to a resolution before voting on the resolution itself. Amendments to amendments are out of order. Where the adoption of one amendment necessarily implies the rejection of another amendment, the latter amendment shall not be put to a vote.

28. **COMPETENCE**: Any motion calling for a decision on the competence of the committee to adopt a resolution or amendment submitted to it shall be put to the vote before a vote is taken on the resolution or amendment in question. The Secretary-General has approved the competence of each committee to discuss the topic areas included in the provisional agenda. This rule serves to prevent the exercise of powers reserved exclusively for the Security Council by the General Assembly or the Economic and Social Council. In this vote, an affirmative vote indicates that the body is NOT competent to pass the proposal and vice versa.

29. **WITHDRAWAL**: A motion, resolution, or amendment may be withdrawn by its mover or sponsor(s) at any time before voting on the motion,

resolution, or amendment has commenced. Any member may reintroduce a motion, resolution, or amendment thus withdrawn. A resolution may not be withdrawn after it has been amended. In order to withdraw a resolution or amendment, all sponsors must agree to the withdrawal.

30. **APPEAL**: A member may appeal a discretionary ruling of the Chair. The member may explain the appeal and the Chair may explain the basis of the ruling. The Chair's ruling will stand unless overruled by a majority of the members present and voting. The Chair's decision not to sign a resolution or amendment may not be appealed. Voting "yes" on this motion means a member wishes to overrule the decision of the Chair. Voting "no" means the member wishes to uphold the ruling.

31. **VOTING RIGHTS**: Each member of the United Nations shall have one vote. Observer delegations may not vote on substantive issues, but may vote on procedural motions. For the purpose of these rules, the phrase "members present and voting" means members casting an affirmative or negative vote. Members who abstain from voting are considered as not voting. There are no abstentions on procedural votes.

32. **CONDUCT DURING VOTING**: After the Chair has announced the beginning of voting, no member shall interrupt the voting except on a point of order in connection with the actual conduct of the voting or on a point of parliamentary inquiry. During a vote, representatives should maintain proper decorum; no caucusing should take place, no notes should be passed, and no representatives should enter or leave the room.

33. **METHOD of VOTING**: Decisions of committees on all questions shall be made by a majority of members present and voting except those specifically mentioned as requiring a two-thirds majority. If a vote is equally divided, the motion, resolution, or amendment fails.

34. **VOTING on RESOLUTIONS**: If two or more resolutions relate to the same question, the committee shall, unless it decides otherwise, vote on the resolutions in the order in which they have been submitted. The committee may, after each vote on a resolution, decide whether to vote on the next resolution. It requires a majority vote to change the order in which a committee considers resolutions.

35. **ROLL-CALL VOTING**: Committees shall normally vote by show of placards, but any member may request a roll-call vote on a resolution or amendment. The roll call shall be taken in English alphabetical order of the names of the members. The name of each member shall be called in

any roll call, and one of the member state's representatives shall reply "yes," "no," or "abstention." Members may pass in the order of a vote once per vote, but when called on later must vote "yes" or "no." The Chair may allow members to explain their vote after a roll-call vote. The Chair shall not permit the sponsors of a resolution or an amendment to explain their vote on their own resolution or amendment. The result of voting shall be inserted in the record in the English alphabetical order of the name of the members. The Chair may require that a motion for a roll-call vote be supported by as much as one-fifth of the committee. While abstentions do not count as votes for the purposes of determining majority, members abstaining from a vote may request the right to explain their abstention, provided that they were not the sponsor of the resolution or amendment. Roll-call votes may not be taken on procedural votes.

36. **DIVISION of the QUESTION**: After debate on any resolution or amendment has been closed, a delegate may move that the operative parts of the proposal be voted on separately. If an objection is made to the motion for division, the motion to divide shall be voted on. This is a procedural vote. Permission to speak on the motion for division may be granted to two speakers for and two speakers against. If the motion for division is carried, a substantive vote shall be taken on each of the divided parts. Those parts that are approved shall then be voted on as a whole. This shall be a substantive vote. If all the operative parts of the proposal are rejected, the proposal shall be considered to have been rejected as a whole. In the event of several motions for division, the Chair shall order the motions, selecting that motion which divides the resolution or amendment into the most parts first. A successful motion for division will supersede later conflicting motions.

37. **IMPORTANT QUESTIONS**: Decisions of the General Assembly on important questions shall be made by a two-thirds majority of the members present and voting. These questions shall include: recommendations with respect to the maintenance of international peace and security, the suspension of the rights and privileges of membership, the expulsion of members, questions relating to the operation of the trusteeship system, and budgetary questions. Any member may move to consider a resolution an important question. Two members may speak in favor of and two against the motion. It shall require a simple majority vote to consider a

resolution as an important question. Only when a resolution is in its final form may a motion be made to consider it an important question.

38. **RECONSIDERATION:** When a resolution has been adopted or rejected or when debate on a topic area has been postponed, it may not be reconsidered at the same session unless the committee, by a two-thirds majority of the members present and voting, so decides. Permission to speak on a motion to reconsider may be accorded only to one speaker in favor of the motion, and one opposing the motion, after which the motion immediately shall be put to the vote. This rule may be used to reconsider specific resolutions upon which an actual vote has been taken. It may not be used to reconsider entire topic areas upon which debate was closed and a vote was taken on the resolution(s). As a practical matter, a motion to reconsider a resolution should be made only by a member who voted with the originally prevailing side.

39. **POSTPONEMENT of DEBATE:** During the discussion of any matter, a member may move the postponement of the debate on the item under discussion. Two members may speak in favor of, and two against, the motion, after which the motion immediately shall be put to the vote. Postponement of debate is used to end discussion of a topic area. Postponement of debate is sometimes referred to as "tabling" debate on the topic area. When debate is postponed, the resolutions under that topic area are not voted on. A topic area that has been postponed may only be reconsidered in accordance with Rule 38.

40. **CLOSURE of DEBATE:** A member may at any time move the closure of the debate on the item under consideration, whether or not any other member has signified his or her wish to speak. Permission to speak on the closure of the debate shall be accorded only to two members opposing the closure, after which the motion shall be put immediately to the vote. If two-thirds of the committee is in favor of the closure, the Chair shall declare the closure of the debate. Closure of debate is used to end discussion of a topic area. When debate is closed, the committee must move to an immediate vote on the resolution(s) under that topic area. Motions for closure of debate are generally out of order until there has been full discussion of the issue by the committee. The Speakers' List will be discarded following passage of a motion to close debate. The Speakers' List will not be carried over for other substantive or procedural debate.

41. **SUSPENSION of the MEETING:** When the floor is open, a delegate may move the suspension of the meeting, to suspend all committee

functions until the next meeting. This motion may be ruled out of order by the Chair and is subject to appeal. This motion shall not be debatable but shall be immediately put to the vote and shall require a majority to pass.

42. **ADJOURNMENT of the MEETING**: A motion to adjourn the meeting is a motion to suspend all committee functions for the rest of the conference. This motion is out of order prior to the lapse of three-quarters of the time allotted for the last meeting of the committee.

43. **ORDER of PROCEDURAL MOTIONS**: The motions indicated below shall have precedence in the following order over all other proposals or motions before the committee:

    a. to suspend the meeting (Rule 41);
    b. to adjourn the meeting (Rule 42);
    c. to postpone debate on the item under discussion (Rule 39);
    d. to close debate on the item under discussion (Rule 40).

The Field of Play

The Secretariat staff (those who are running the conference) will be represented at the front of the room by up to four people:

- The Chair: usually the most outgoing person in the room, who keeps the meeting running, calls on people, etc. Unlike in the UN, this person is *not* a delegate, and does not have voting privileges. In rare instances, the Secretariat will give delegates the opportunity to chair a meeting for a few minutes. Your delegates should always volunteer for this chance to show their exceptional knowledge of the rules and their maturity to direct a committee's work.
- The Director: usually the best writer among the troop, and the person who handles the substantive topics and probably set the agenda and wrote the background guide for the topics to be discussed.
- The Parliamentarian: the person who wrote the rules and is going to chair the meeting next year.
- The Secretary/Rapporteur: the person who keeps tally of how votes went and who is usually the director in waiting.

The **delegates** can be sitting in a horseshoe arrangement (if it's a 15-member Security Council) facing the Secretariat team, or in an auditorium fashion (if it's a 193-member General Assembly).

What you are trying to do is influence *everyone* in that room—Secretariat and Delegates—but for different reasons.

The lifeblood of the sessions is the **consideration of the resolutions**, which have three parts:

- Sponsors/cosponsors;
- Preambular paragraphs (often written as "preambulatory" paragraphs; "Preambulatory" means "crawling" and is incorrect; do *not* make this mistake vocally, and do not complain if other delegates—or the Chair—make the error); and
- Operative paragraphs.

Sponsors wrote the resolutions. You'll find that, particularly for this early MUN experience, it's much easier to let someone else write the resolution, then offer to cosponsor it. (Some delegates will crassly "hijack" as many resolutions as they can, putting their names on everything considered by the committee in an attempt to "brand" themselves as the movers and shakers of the room.) What you'll want to do is get a copy of the resolutions, before the conference if you can, figure out which one(s) you can support, and contact the sponsor to offer to cosponsor it. It's important for you to be the first cosponsor, because this will increase the likelihood of you getting on the Speakers' List early.

What any delegation's job entails, in essence, is to ensure that the UN passes resolutions that we like, and does not pass resolutions we do not like. For our Triangle terminology, let's call trying to get resolutions passed as Offense, and trying to prevent passage as Defense.

Defense

The philosophy of the Defense is to **stop passage**. It does *not* necessarily mean that you want other delegations to directly kill the resolution. There are far more subtle ways to ensure that something doesn't pass than a direct frontal assault. You may well need the support of a sponsor of a hostile resolution a few votes from now, so let's not make them aware that you're in opposition directly. Try the following:

Stall Ball: The conferences have a very limited amount of time. If you're pretty sure that you have very few votes on your side on a substantive issue, period, then all you're trying to do is to kill the clock. You can do that by calling for:

- **Quorums**—this is usually good for about five minutes. The Secretariat has to read off the names of every delegation that could be there. You don't actually vote; nothing gets done, but the clock runs down.
- **Caucus time**—everyone likes to take a break from the formal sessions and schmooze with their friends, hit the restroom, get a sandwich, etc. If you're not too obvious about it, even the Secretariat will appreciate you doing this, because they're under stress and could use the break. Call for a ten-minute caucus—moderated or unmoderated. In either case, no voting will occur. Things never get started on time, and you'll have taken another twenty minutes off the clock.
- **A roll-call vote**—do this only if you have a prayer of possibly winning a vote. If it's going to be 192–1 against you, just accept the defeat gracefully.

Misdirection: This is the equivalent of saying "Hey, how 'bout them Yankees," or "look, a shiny object," in an effort to get out of an awkward social situation. Resolutions will be considered in the order in which the Secretariat sets them. Let's suppose that you don't like Resolution 1, are neutral on Resolution 2, but would support Resolutions 3 and 4. Rather than try to kill off Resolution 1, move to alter the agenda to consider Resolution 3 first. (If you can, try to get the sponsor of Resolution 3 to make this move. You thereby don't alienate the sponsor of Resolution 1, have gotten the sponsor of Resolution 3 to think you're with him/her, and have gotten what you want on the agenda. It's okay to second this motion. People will think you're just doing something minor in parliamentary procedure, but the sponsor of Resolution 3 will get the flak if this doesn't work.

Substitution: If misdirection doesn't work, try this. Move to substitute the entire text of Resolution 1 with the entire text of a resolution you like. (You might not want to substitute Resolution 3—you already know that you don't have the votes to do this, because your misdirection vote lost. Try it with Resolution 4. Again, if you can, try to get the sponsor of Resolution 4 to do this, with you seconding the motion. The reasoning behind this is the same as with misdirection.)

Salami Amending: If these plays don't work, try killing off individual offending paragraphs of the resolution with amendments that delete the paragraph entirely, water it down, substitute a better paragraph, or otherwise help your position. You can do this as many times as you want (assuming you haven't alienated the Chair and a majority of delegates by now) and pick apart the resolution. In some instances, you can actually get the original sponsor to try to withdraw the resolution in disgust. Check your rules to make sure they can do this. If the rules are written correctly, the resolution is the property of the committee, not the sponsor. There's no greater victory for the Defense than hacking up an offending resolution so badly that the sponsor is forced to vote against his/her own resolution!

Deleting sponsors and signatories: Sometimes rules of procedure require a set number of sponsors and signatories. If you can get a few of them to drop their sponsorship/signatory status before a vote takes place, the resolution can die without a formal vote. This is a fairly rare gadget play, but has a wonderful element of surprise and can confuse the Offense.

Get the resolution to be declared an **Important Question**. The UN Charter (Article 18) is very clear about what constitutes an Important Question— requiring a 2/3 majority, rather than a simple majority—in the UN General Assembly: budgetary questions, admission of new members, use of force, and the like. However, MUN rules of procedure often are not as clear. You can argue, "This is clearly an Important Question. What's not important about this issue?" Many delegates who have not done their research on the Charter can be swayed by such a specious argument. After all, they've put some work into writing their position papers and looking up the positions of their allies, so it's now emotionally important to them. If you obtain the simple majority needed to declare a resolution an Important Question, you've made it that much more difficult for the sponsors to get the resolution passed. Of course, if you're playing Offense, make sure that you argue vigorously that Important Question is irrelevant in this instance. You might also ask the Chair to rule that this is not an Important Question (and to rule that he/she cannot be appealed on this decision).

In all of these plays, it is important to have started to form **coalitions** with other delegates. You can't do all of this with just your vote. Coalition formation can begin even before the conference begins, when you phone or e-mail delegates from other schools that will be in your committee. As soon as you have your country/committee assignments for a particular conference, it is a good idea to register with hotmail.com, gmail.com, or other free e-mail provider so you can open a new account with an e-mail address that you can use just for that conference. I'd suggest creating names like hyltonmexicodisec1@hotmail.com so that you can chat with delegates from other schools ahead of time (but don't have to continue communications with them if things didn't go well—since you haven't given them your permanent e-mail address—after the conference).

At conference registration, it's up to the teacher/sponsor/coach/team parent to register the students. The delegates should not waste one second standing in lines. Rather, they should be making contacts with everyone, from giving the Chair and Parliamentarian copies of their cheat sheets and giving the Director a copy of their position paper, to cosponsoring resolutions, to establishing themselves as the leader of their regional caucus, to meeting all of the other delegates in the committee.

Offense

On Offense, you're trying to **move things along**. Your key weapon is the word "dilatory." You want to suggest to the Chair that a particular motion (in our parlance, "play") by the Defense is "dilatory"—that is, time-wasting, and should be declared by the Chair to be out of order. Such a decision helps you, because while most Defensive plays require a simple majority, in most sets of Rules it requires the Defense to get a 2/3 majority to overrule the Chair. (We've seen sessions of Georgetown's NAIMUN that required a unanimous vote to overrule the Chair.)

Parliamentary Procedure Playbook

Table 2 presents a simple **Parliamentary Procedure Playbook**. Remember that your country delegation's **goal** is *not* to solve a crisis, resolve issues, etc., but to **represent your country's position accurately** and get the best deal for your country that you can. You want to get your country's position in the limelight, and get your country mentioned favorably (and never negatively) as early and often as you can.

Plays mentioned early in the following discussion can be used at any time later, e.g., General Debate defensive plays can also be used when discussing the topic or discussing the resolution. Your use of them and their timing, however, depends on whether you're on Offense or Defense. Items that are centered mean that either Offense or Defense can use the tactic at that time.

Special Situations

Delegates on either side of an issue can use the following parliamentary points. Some may be missing from a conference's rules—make sure to ask about these at the start of a committee session. Sometimes a conference's rules let you do the same thing, but use different terminology. *Never* refer to another conference in arguing precedent for a rule that isn't specifically discussed in the current conference's rules. Instead, say "Can we do the following?" or "How do we do the following?"

Table 2. Parliamentary Procedure Playbook

OFFENSE	DEFENSE
Goal: Move things along. Get yes votes.	Goal: Stall, avoid voting, get no/abstentions.
Initial roll-call to establish quorum[1]	
General debate	
Get your speech in, and make sure that students from your school representing other countries also get heard; i.e., do not vote to end debate before they have spoken! You're also trying for a Best School award.	Get your speech in, keep debate going. You don't want any hostile resolutions introduced, much less voted upon.
Move to shorten speaking time; speak for it	Speak against shortening speaking time
Speak against lengthening speeches	Move to extend speaking time; speak for it
Move to close Speakers' List	Speak against it
Move to close debate	Speak against it
Right of reply	
Set agenda	
Move to set agenda topic	Fine, but not the offending topic; speak for it
Speak on your topic's importance	Argue that other topics are more important
	Comment on speech (if rules allow it)
	Get yields
	Ask questions
	Move for moderated caucus (informal debate)
	Move for unmoderated caucus (short recess)
Discuss topic	
	Stay on Speakers' List, give speech
	Get back on Speakers' List
	Get yields from other speakers
	Yield to questions; never to the Chair
Ask friendly question ("do you agree?")	Ask questions (cost, relevance, committee authority/competence)
Discuss resolution	
Get your resolution first on the agenda	Get anything else discussed first
	Point out typos
	Point of order (question whether sponsors/signatories agree with each friendly amendment by having Chair ask them individually)
	Try to get some sponsors/signatories to withdraw
	Move to recess early (e.g., lunch, etc.)

1 Do *not* say "present and voting"; just say "Present." "Present and voting" means that you cannot abstain. There is never a reason for you to throw away your option to abstain.

Table 2. Parliamentary Procedure Playbook (continued)

OFFENSE	DEFENSE
	Offer seemingly friendly amendments (poisoned apple)
	Move to amend (several times)
	Move to open Speakers' List on amendment
	Move to amend amendment (if it isn't yours, and if allowed by the rules)
	Move to substitute resolution
	Appeal Chair (on amending preambulars)
	Point of order (is there a quorum to vote?)
Voting	
Quick show of placards	Request roll-call vote
	Try to get others to pass, thereby killing time
	Use right of explanation
	Move to divide the question
	Move for Important Question
	Move to reconsider

Point of personal privilege—examples are "I can't hear," "it's too cold in here," "I don't have a copy of the resolution," "what's that amendment say again?"

Point of parliamentary inquiry—examples are "What are we voting on?" "What does a 'yes' vote mean in this instance?"

Credentials challenge—Most conferences assume that a delegate's/delegation's credentials have been accepted, and often so state in the rules of procedure and conference materials. While this is fine for whether the actual student is who he/she says he/she is, there might be instances in which the governmental authority is open to question (refusal by other governments to extend diplomatic recognition to a pariah regime, withdrawal of one's ambassadorial representation in a diplomatic spat, recent coup/change of regime under questionable circumstances). You might question the credentials of a delegate if he/she is representing a regime that has just been overthrown, is losing a civil war, etc.

Appeal of the Chair—Do *not* appeal the Chair often, but if you absolutely have to, make sure that you let the Chair know that you are not questioning the Chair's competence or knowledge, but rather underscore that the Chair had to make a ruling because the rules hamstrung him/her. No matter what your delegates may think of the Chair's abilities or personality quirks, they do not want to pick a fight with the Chair. The delegate will always lose. Delegates should leave it to their coaches to raise issues with the Secretariat; delegates should keep the Chair on their side, or at least not overtly hostile.

No abstentions on procedural motions are permitted. Mention this if you are playing Defense and want to move the Chair into taking a quick revote.

Long-term considerations—Even if you're on Offense right now, would it be in your best interest to kill time on this friendly topic, so that your committee never considers a hostile topic that puts you on defense?

Silly season—Toward the end of a conference, students and the Secretariat will be tired and want to blow off steam. This often leads to "silly season," in which all sorts of foolishness can occur. Experienced Chairs, be they college or high school students, do not allow this to happen. We tell our delegates to stay out of it. Period. No excuses.

The **Security Council** has slightly different voting rules. To pass a procedural motion (e.g., "let's have a caucus," "let's have lunch"), you need nine of the fifteen votes in favor. For a substantive motion ("let's pass this resolution," "let's pass this amendment"), you need nine "yes" votes, no matter how many of the fifteen members are actually in the room, *and* you need zero "no" votes from the permanent members (United States, UK, Russia, France, China). A permanent member can "veto" a resolution by voting "no" even if all fourteen other countries voted "yes." A permanent member does *not* veto with a "no" vote if there were not nine "yes" votes. (If you are a permanent member, you should determine whether a resolution you do not like is likely to have the requisite nine "yes" votes. If it has less than nine "yes" votes, there is no reason for you to vote "no." In this instance, an abstention is as good as a "no," because the rules require absolute majorities rather than relative majorities.)

The **delegate's responsibility**: While at a conference, it's acceptable for a student to call the coach on a cell phone, text them, or grab them in the corridors when they come into a situation they are not sure about. However, it's basically up to the students to call whatever plays they think are appropriate. The coach is not sending in plays from the sidelines, but should be there for students if they decide they need help.

MUN-Style Public Speaking

All the knowledge in the world regarding the UN, your country, and the issues in your committee does not matter if you don't put that knowledge to work. Students have to communicate that knowledge in their position papers, resolutions, and perhaps most importantly of all, public speaking, both substantively and procedurally.

Persuasive Speaking also has a triangle, and each point has a subtriangle. The key points of the triangle for students to remember are **style**, **research**, and **persuasion**.

For **style**, consider **character**—accurately representing the government of your country; costume (either native costume or business attire); and eye contact. Don't bother reading your speech; speak from notes. Keep in mind that you are no longer a student—you are the ambassador of a country. Most Chairs prefer that you do not use first-person pronouns. Rather than say "we believe" or "I think," try "the delegation of Ruritania wishes to underscore that. . . " or "the people and government of Ruritania believe . . ."

Have the students get comfortable with having the microphone an inch from their mouth at all times. Gesture often, but only with one hand, not both, if holding a microphone. Despite what you have seen other speakers do, do not tap the microphone. Do not blow into it. Microphones are very delicate instruments. If you want to test whether the microphone is working, just say something into it.

When students are initially learning public speaking, they will want to write out every word of their speech to make sure that they "get it right," and then want to keep their head down and read every word aloud. Try to get the students away from using this crutch as soon as you can. A successful speaker is not one who drones on from prepared texts. Effective speakers look the audience members in the eye. It's okay to bring up a short list of key talking points that the delegate wants to make, and to refer to them—quickly—as needed. If the student gets stuck for the correct word and loses his/her train of thought, he/she should *not* look up, down, or to the side. Rather, they should look a delegate in the back of the room in the eye to search for that word. These pauses look to the audience like the student is pausing for effect. While to the speaker this pause seems like minutes are passing by, this is not the impression that the audience gets. The pause gives the audience a chance to catch up to the thoughts the speaker is offering, and makes the speaker look thoughtful.

Students will find that their **speaking times are very short**. A comparatively long general debate speech might be limited by the rules or the committee to only three minutes; parliamentary procedure supporting speeches are usually between thirty and sixty seconds. Debate-trained students thus have a tendency to try to race through all of their arguments in an attempt to answer everything that's been put before the committee. Rather, the students should attempt to slow down and be memorable, focusing on no more than three facts and three key points they want to make. Trial attorneys will tell you that if they have ten great points they could offer to the jury, the jury will remember *none* of these points. So boil it down, make it simple, and make it memorable. What your team's delegates are trying to do is get the other delegations to cite a point your students made in their speech, "as the delegate from X so eloquently said," rather than hoping that the Chair will remember that the student covered fourteen points in thirty seconds.

Students should develop a certain **stage presence**, giving the impression that they are in charge of what's going on. "Taking over the room" requires the student to know in their heart of hearts that they are a great speaker, and to let that self-confidence flow into their speech. While most speeches will be run-of-the-mill, your student's will be the one that makes the audience cut short their private chats, sit up, and listen. Although some speakers have a certain native ability, stage presence can be developed, even among the most initially timid speakers.

One simple trick for these new speakers is to **project** their voice. We often invite the drama coach or singing coaches to visit our practices, and teach the students how to use their diaphragms in projecting their voices. One can easily be heard by an audience of two hundred, even without a microphone, with the proper projection techniques. The diaphragm allows volume; yelling from the throat merely tires out one's throat, and quickly causes hoarseness—as well as irritation on the part of the audience.

To give the students a feeling for how the diaphragm works, have them place one hand on their stomachs, and the other hand on the small of their back, then talk. They'll feel the vibrations of the diaphragm. Another technique is to have them pretend that they've just been punched in the gut. That forceful expulsion of air comes from the diaphragm, and has a different feel than expelling air from the voice box. They'll quickly get the idea.

To get students used to projecting once they've found their diaphragms, we do the following:

- Have half of the audience (the other students getting ready to give their speech) murmur to each other. In most MUN committees, easily half of the delegates are chatting with their friends, texting, talking about resolutions, etc., and not listening to the speaker. The rookie speaker should get used to being initially greeted with this din, and should develop projection techniques accordingly.

- Take the students to a cafeteria, an auditorium, or a hallway, with a fifty- to a hundred-foot gap between the two halves of the team. Speakers in turn give their speeches to the faraway team, with the distant teammates giving immediate feedback as to whether they can be heard. You'll need to do this often in practice, particularly with the quiet-spoken students, as well as with the otherwise outgoing students who will mistake projection for yelling.
- Require the students to speak while standing. Students should not speak while seated—it is difficult to get the full projection effect of one's diaphragm in such a position. Standing also commands more authority in your efforts to take over the room.
- Encourage students to get away from the lectern. Grabbing on to the sides of the lectern dissipates their energy into the furniture, and thereby erodes their projection. Standing to one side, or on occasion pacing, focuses their energy into their speech. It also makes it easier to gesture, which in turn adds to the energy and interest of the presentation.
- Urge students not to chew gum. While it may help relax your delegates, speaking with gum in one's mouth at an MUN conference conveys disrespect for the audience and an attitude of informality or even complacency.

Research

For **research**, look into the UN, your topic, and your country's position on that topic. A conference's background guides offer useful materials on where to look for information on the topics to be discussed in the committee. Consult appendix C of this book for an example of a background guide.

Here are a few **simple techniques** that the students can use in integrating their research to make the speech memorable (an example of how to do this is provided below).

First, the student is looking to be remembered by the Chair as being **well-researched**. To do this, the student should throw in at least **three facts** (hopefully, that are relevant to the country, committee, and issue at hand) in any given substantive speech. These can include specific citations to paragraphs from the UN Charter, treaties, previous UN resolutions, statistical notations, or quotations from major experts or statesmen.

Second, some facts are difficult to absorb intellectually and emotionally. Saying "a million people were made homeless by the tsunami" is difficult to envision. But **making it personal** by talking about the plight of one individual—perhaps a nine-year-old child, with a name and a backstory—and how he or she was affected by the disaster at hand will be far more effective. You can even pass out photographs of that child to make the presentation even more long-lasting.

Third, **parallel constructions**, echoing the same point after each sentence/paragraph, gives the audience something to take away from the speech.

You will often find that the substance of most of the delegates' speeches is lacking. Even the schools that can register dozens of people at the conference often do not have that much of substance to say. So state your research in *each* speech you give, and if you have only three facts, use those three facts *every* time you speak. Cite conventions, previous UN resolutions, the Charter, other facts you've found, and keep reminding them of how it affects that nine-year-old kid.

For persuasion, **always try to be the first speaker**. This gives you a chance to **frame the debate** for everyone else who follows you. You are creating powerful images for them, to which they'll respond. If you're following a speaker who tries a spread offense on you (giving a blizzard of arguments like an academic debater challenging you to answer each one in turn), ignore them. Instead, say "interesting presentation, but it fails to look at the larger picture. Let me provide you with the proper context, the proper perspective, which will help us to better frame these issues before us." By doing so, you just wiped out all of the other delegate's arguments without having to respond directly to the substance of each. Finally, don't worry about the long litany of things which are suggested in the "how to do public speaking" section of the MUN website handout. What you're trying to do is persuade people to vote with you, NOT impress them with your knowledge of your country's position, knowledge of the topic, knowledge of the UN's history, etc. Figure out what's in it for them, and tell them how voting with you gets them what they want. (Don't waste the research—make sure that you use it where appropriate, and be sure to incorporate it into your detailed position paper, which you will give to the Secretariat.)

In the opening minutes of a committee, the Chair will open the floor to the Speakers' List for general debate. Students should immediately raise their placards and try to be among the first delegations listed. In general, only the first ten or so delegations on the Speakers' List will actually get an opportunity to speak from the Speakers' List. Other interruptions—calls for moderated caucuses, motions to consider specific resolutions, to modify the agenda, etc.—will quickly divert the committee's consideration away from the Speakers' List. So while it's important to get on the List, even if you're Speaker #60, the students should assume that after about Speaker #10, they won't actually get called upon, and should resort to other tactics to be heard (such as using Comments, Yields, Questions, Moderated

Caucuses, Motions, and any other specialized actions allowable by the rules of the specific conference).

Here is an all-purpose general debate speech that can be adapted for any committee and country. Once you have your country/committee assignment, of course, you will wish to incorporate mentions of your country whenever possible. You may also wish to pepper it with names of the affected nine-year-olds, and offer more backstory. This is just a draft—students should make it their own by putting it into their own personal styles.

Thank you, Mr. Chairman, fellow delegates, and distinguished guests. [Author's Note: *All* speeches should begin with this politeness. Delegates should *not* immediately jump into the points they want to make. Chairs will remember this courtesy.]

Fellow delegates, it is an honor to be here today, to work with you on the issues facing the world. The history of peoples and governments coming together for the betterment of all has a long tradition. Going back to the end of World War I, governments thought they had fought the War to End All Wars, and joined together to create the UN's predecessor organization, the League of Nations. But we all know that differences between governments ultimately defeated that hope, and World War II dashed the League's chances for success. After World War II, people committed to peace against came together to form the United Nations, aiming to make the hopes of the world's peoples a reality.

I left my home early today to get to our meetings. Before I did, I looked in on my nine-year-old brother, who was asleep in his bed, dreaming. Perhaps he was dreaming of what he can become—a doctor, a lawyer, or maybe even the Secretary-General of the United Nations.

But other nine-year-old children around the world do not have such dreams. They only have nightmares—nightmares they face while asleep, and only too-real nightmares to which they awake.

A nine-year-old in Africa yesterday watched his mother die of AIDS, while his father, sister, and brother all lay in their beds, awaiting for death to take them from their sufferings from the ravages of AIDS. What will become of him? [Author's Note: Note the echoing "what will become of him" in the rest of this litany and the parallel construction of the opening part of each paragraph.]

A nine-year-old in Asia yesterday watched rebels break into his home and bludgeon his family to death. The child was then kidnapped from his home, force-marched to a rebel training camp, and will be taught how to kill, and maim, and take away the dreams of other children. What will become of him?

A nine-year-old villager in an island nation watched the destructive forces of el Niño whip up hurricanes that leveled his home, wiped out the local hospital, and deprived him of safe water and food. What will become of him?

A nine-year-old in the Middle East yearns to join his brothers who earlier became suicide bombers who killed other nine-year-olds. What will become of him?

Throughout the world, red alerts, orange alerts, the spread of chemical, biological, radiological, and nuclear weapons to terrorists, make nine-year-olds wonder if they will become the next victims of attacks. They all wonder: What will become of them?

The delegates of this committee, and our colleagues in other committees working on these issues and a multitude of others, can provide the answers those children long to hear. They ask only one thing of us: that we put aside our petty jealousies, our differing ideologies, our religious differences, and join together to let them enjoy the fruits of peace, human rights, and a better tomorrow. My country looks forward to working with you to erase those nightmares and make my brother's dreams a reality for all. Thank you, Mr. Chairman.

Practical Considerations

Partnering: In some conferences, you can have two delegates per country in each committee. When it comes time to speak, you can double up speakers at the microphone. In practices, students should get comfortable going solo as well as going with a partner. Both students are being evaluated by the Chair for delegation awards. Make sure both speak. And make sure they have worked out ahead of time who leads off, and who covers what issues. You don't want to look hesitant while at the microphone. Both should stride confidently, and continue that presence in their speechifying.

Other Substantive Speeches: In practices, you should get students used to writing resolutions and amendments, and bringing in "all purpose" amendments that you can tack on to pretty much anything. The speaking style for getting these adopted is the same as what you'll use on resolutions. Students speak to the specifics of the resolution, but can also bring in the facts that they had developed for their general debate presentations.

Getting Called on Outside of the Speakers' List: The Speakers' List is not the only time that the student will have an opportunity to speak. The delegates should use such techniques as getting yields, commenting, questioning, speaking in caucuses, and making parliamentary motions and speaking to them.

Yields: There are usually three types of yields: The speaker can yield time back to the **Chair** (*Never* do this. Always use your allotted time.), yield to **another speaker** (tertiary yields—A yields to B yields to C—are rarely permitted under most rules of procedure), and yielding to **questions**. Sometimes rules specify that delegates may yield to **comments**, although this more generally is either the option of the Chair or can be designated by the entire committee. Yielding to another (presumably like-minded) speaker gives the delegate more control than does yielding to comments.

A common refrain from your delegates will be "The Chair isn't calling on us. What can we do?" The delegates may quietly—outside of the formal session—ask the Chair to call on them more frequently. Sending a note to the Chair often works. Your delegates may do this *once* per conference. Doing it more than once will be perceived as whining, Chair-baiting, or both. You want to avoid this reputation.

Instead, the delegates can ask like-minded delegations to yield to them following their speeches. (Some rules require that speakers indicate before they speak how they will yield, if at all.) Delegates should be encouraged to get yields from other delegations. They can do so by chatting with them in unmoderated caucuses, or sending them notes or texts. (Unlike in school, texting and note-passing is permitted, and even encouraged. Most committees will have designated a page or two to facilitate communication by written notes. Students can write some of their notes—on delegation letterhead—ahead of the conference, merely filling in the name of their colleagues later. "Please yield to us. We agree with you on this issue," is something they can write ahead of time. Their notes might also suggest coordinating on friendly questions, and suggest language for resolutions and amendments.) Colleagues will expect the same consideration from them. While your delegates should of course agree to this horse-trading, and should announce at the beginning of their speech that they are yielding to a given country, they should make their points and still allow time for the yield. This may not always work. When the allotted time is exhausted, it's up to the Chair to announce that the yield is void, thus making the Chair, not your delegate, the bad guy in this play.

If your school is representing more than one country in a given committee, consider whether it would be in character for those countries to yield speaking time to each other. Failing that, consider whether it would be in character for them to serve as rivals to each other, giving each other a legitimate reason to be called upon by the Chair to address points made by the other. But danger lurks here:

when one of your country's delegates—say, Cuba—endorses a policy put forth by another of your country's delegates—say, the United States—there is a risk that Cuba's representative has just abandoned his/her role (gone "out of character"), and this will trigger a stern warning from an alert Chair.

Your multiple-country teams should also look carefully at the Speakers' List. If one of your school's delegations is soon to be called upon according to the Speaker's List, all other delegations should do what they can to ensure that the Speakers' List arrives undamaged at that point, and that your school's delegates get the opportunity to speak. They should *not* support efforts to close debate, and should speak against such motions (thereby getting an opportunity to speak themselves, and helping out their schoolmates). Students on multiple-country teams should also consider whether they can legitimately "second" motions made by other members of their school, and speak on them, when the rules of procedure require seconds. But again, alert your delegates to the pitfalls of going "out of character."

In many conferences, speakers can yield to questions. This gives your delegates terrific opportunities, as the questioner as well as the speaker. You can strategically ask questions of speakers:

- How does this proposal help the people of my region?
- What is this going to cost?
- How much money—give me a precise dollar/Euro figure—has your country given/will it pledge to give to fund this project? If you're not willing to fund it, why should we take this seriously?
- There are inconsistencies in the argument you've just presented. Here they are: _____. Which is correct?
- These paragraphs are vague. What precisely do you mean?

On the other hand, your delegates should offer to yield to questions. You can use shills in the audience who will ask friendly questions. (Although in general, Chairs, rather than the delegates, determine who asks the questions. But check your local rules for what will be the custom at your specific conference.)

Yielding to questions gives you yet another way to get your point across. Delegates should keep in mind, however, that they are trying to stay on point. A hostile question doesn't need to be answered directly. If there is no legitimate answer to a question, or it raises issues that you wish to brush aside, it is perfectly acceptable to rephrase the question, or answer the question that you wanted to answer. (Consider candidates in presidential debates. They always reframe the hostile question fired by the debate's moderator into something far more palatable—or they dismiss the question by attacking the underlying assumption as being false.) The rules generally prohibit follow-up questions or to-and-fros between interlocutors. You're there to frame the debate, not to respond to the agenda of others.

When a **resolution is introduced** by the cosponsors, there will usually be a **five-minute question-and-answer period**. In some instances, there will be two such periods, one for pointing out typos, and one for questioning the substantive merits of the resolution. When your delegate is sponsoring a resolution, he or she should answer *every* question asked, even if another sponsor has already adequately answered the question. This gives the impression that your delegation is the power-behind-the-throne, and actually in charge of the resolution. Your delegates should also be standing very near to the microphone so that they can throw in their two cents before the Chair turns to the next questioner.

In some cases, a conference's rules will permit **comments** immediately after a formal speech. The Chair will call for short (say, thirty-second) comments on the substance of a speech. This is an excellent opportunity for your delegates to leapfrog from the back of the Speakers' List and get in their main points. The rules usually call for comments to directly pertain to the speech just given, but Chairs generally give you some leeway.

Speaking for and against Parliamentary Motions also gives you the opportunity to be heard. In some judging criteria for awards, speeches regarding such motions are given the same weight as substantive speeches. Always take the opportunity to speak on these, and use all of the time allotted for your speech. Don't just say "we agree" in one sentence and be seated. You're still trying to be remembered as eloquent and to build coalitions. You can do this by referring with approval to the speeches of other delegations. Here's an example of a speech against closure of debate that does more than merely oppose the motion:

> The wish to come to closure—to get things done, to solve the world's problems—is a laudable one. However, it is one that we must resist, lest we rush to judgment without knowing all the facts and all the pitfalls. We have heard from only a handful of nations regarding this topic. Yet a look at the Speakers' List suggests that there is much wisdom left to be heard. The nations of W, X, Y, and Z we all know to have firsthand knowledge of the topic, and lessons that we can learn from their hard-won experiences. Their people have immediate concerns which deserve to be heard on the world stage. We owe it to ourselves, and to them, to hear them out. The problems we are discussing

today have festered for years. Surely we can wait for a few more minutes to make sure that we have considered all the angles before diving headlong into what might be shallow waters. John Stuart Mill referred to the marketplace of ideas as the preferred method for getting the best thoughts aired, and the best thoughts adopted by all. Closing debate this soon puts us in the five-items-or-fewer counter at the dollar store of ideas. Let us not make this mistake.

Other Tips for Speakers

In your speeches, **use your country's name often**. You're trying to keep your country's name at the forefront of discussions.

Don't be afraid to appeal the Chair's decision on caucusing, etc., but do so judiciously.

When you're introducing a resolution read an operative paragraph. Do not let just the principal drafter read the entire resolution to the audience. And make sure that if you aren't the principal drafter that you're standing right next to him or her, close to the microphone.

Even when using a microphone, project. (For some of the more soft-spoken students, this means "yell" in their terms. But see our earlier discussion of the difference between yelling from the voice box and projecting from the diaphragm.)

Most conferences discourage having polished resolutions handed in at the beginning of the conference. For these conferences, write the resolution out in longhand on-site, get the requisite signatures, incorporate other delegations' ideas and wording (so long as they do not conflict with your country's position), and then hand it in, perhaps an hour after the session begins.

Some conferences—few and far between—expect delegates to write resolutions before the conference, and to hand them in to the Chair along with your position paper. This can lead to you having to face dozens of virtually duplicate resolutions on the same topic, and wasting time getting the agenda just right. Try to meld your resolution with those of others who had the same ideas—but make sure that your name is the first in the list of cosponsors, so that delegations refer to it as *your* resolution.

In your opening speeches, and any others, be sure to include sentiments to the effect of "we look forward to working with you on your resolution. Please contact us if you're looking for sponsors."

Consider putting together one **briefing board and/or prop** per topic in your committee. Very few speakers think of doing this, but it is very effective—recall U.S. secretary of state Colin Powell's 2003 presentation before the United Nations regarding the situation in Iraq, in which he used overhead photography, video, charts, audiotapes, and other media. It gets you noticed and remembered. Schools have won awards using that technique.

Make sure that the first thing you do when you walk into the committee is to introduce yourself to the Secretariat members on the dais. The second thing to do is sit in front of them, so they can easily see you when they're setting up the Speakers' List, etc. It makes it much easier for you to get to the front of the room quickly, so that you can "take over the room," rather than trudging from the back of the room. Much of what you are trying to do in this style of public speaking is to give the impression that you're in charge of what's going on. Being in front also allows you to easily move from your seat to schmooze with others in the room. If you're in an auditorium-style seating arrangement, get in the front row, or at worst, on the aisles, so that you're not trapped in place by others. You want to be able to move around the room easily during unmoderated caucuses, and you want others to be able to access you as well.

6

Special Topics and Research

What to Research

Most conferences will provide you and your delegates with **background guides**—the Secretariat's view of what the important issues that face your UN committee are. (See Appendix C for an example of a recent **background guide**.) They will usually cover the two to three topics the Secretariat has deemed appropriate and timely for your committee. Often, they will include suggestions—and even offer citations—for further research, and offer questions that the delegates might consider in formulating their country's position on these issues. Be sure to cite these items in the bibliography accompanying your position papers. The backgrounders will vary in length—some can cover twenty to thirty pages (particularly true at the larger college-hosted or national-level conferences); others can be just a page or two, if they are offered at all. The backgrounders should be considered as a starting point in research, not the end point.

Another starting point for research in advance of any MUN conference is the United Nations Charter and the Universal Declaration of Human Rights. These two documents are the basis of United Nations authority. They set forth the roles of the General Assembly and the Security Council and they lay down their respective roles and responsibilities and those of member states. These two documents should be part of every delegate's portfolio and should be consulted as necessary during conferences.

Backgrounders will usually arrive a few weeks or, unfortunately, even a few days before the beginning of the conference. Delegates should not wait for the committee background guides to arrive—or for the backgrounder's drafter(s) to clarify ambiguities you will inevitably discover—before beginning their own research. Delegates should strive to be better-prepared on the topics at hand than the Secretariat members who wrote the background guide.

Packaging Your Research

Position papers are only sometimes required by conferences, but are always worth writing. Most college-hosted MUN conferences require them, as do some of the best high school conferences. To ensure that delegates are serious about their responsibilities to prepare for MUN conferences, many MUN coaches and club advisors make them a requirement. Position papers are simply concise overviews of your assigned country, its views on the topics you'll be discussing, and what the country's delegation hopes to get out of the UN session. They do not need to be especially long, and the requirement for your students to draft them should not be considered especially burdensome. It helps direct your delegates' research efforts efficiently. They are typically turned in to the committee chairs at the opening of the conference. They are most often read by the Secretariat and can influence decisions on awards.

As with all assigned student work prepared outside the classroom, the position paper must meet the standards for academic integrity. Ideas and text borrowed from print or Internet sources—whether from a book, online journal, a diplomat's speech, or a nation's UN mission website—demand citations. At the University of Virginia's VAMUN conference and at TechMUN, the spring conference hosted by the Thomas Jefferson High School for Science and Technology, plagiarism in position papers will be brought to the attention of the offending delegate's MUN Club sponsor and it will disqualify the student from awards. A "word to the wise" delivered by MUN Club advisors to their MUN delegates ahead of the conference is often sufficient.

Let's walk through an example of a simple five-paragraph position paper for a delegation representing the Republic of Fiji:

Paragraph 1 addresses where Fiji stands in the world, making the following points: Fiji, while at first blush a small, seemingly insignificant island nation, instead is a model of what it means to live in an interdependent world. Our economy is buffeted by what is going on in the rest of the world, not just in our region. We are heavily dependent upon tourism as our primary source of foreign exchange. Tourism, in turn, depends upon our being able to provide a haven, an area of carefree recreation, in a safe environment. When that safety is threatened by manmade disasters, drug trafficking, terrorism (witness what one terrorist attack did to our neighbors a few thousand miles away in Bali), we need to react. The threat of nuclear war in the region—the Koreas or the South Asian continent—could affect not only the flow of tourists (who might be war casualties), but also our environment. When we are threatened by El Niño or other natural disasters, we need international help. We thus have been very active in the United Nations, and even put our sons and daughters in harm's way, sending hundreds of troops on UN peacekeeping missions. We have shed blood with the UNIFIL contingent in Lebanon. We stand ready to work with other like-minded, like-situated nations, be they from island nations, Asia, the Third World, or from other situations similar to ours, on issues of key interest to us.

The **second, third, and fourth paragraphs would discuss some background on the topics in your committee**, noting how those topics affect Fiji's interests.

If you're going to sponsor a resolution, explain in general terms how the legislation will look at the problem. If you don't have a solution, but can think of who your natural allies and/or enemies are, mention it. In some instances (for example, George Mason University-sponsored conferences), you will be required to write an "**internal**" and an "**external**" version of your position paper. The "internal" version is a no-holds-barred explanation of what your policy truly is, and what the reasoning is behind it. This is to be shared only with the Chair/Secretariat. The "external" version is a shortened, and perhaps less-sensitive, version, which can be distributed to the other delegations as a part of your public diplomacy initiatives. Be sure you clearly mark your position papers as "external" and "internal" and that you are fairly sure that the Chairs can be counted upon not to leak your "internal" paper. Despite Secretariat entreaties that you can be up front with them in these essays, be judicious. You do not want to be embarrassed by leaks—intentional by pot-stirring, ill-meaning Secretariat members or inadvertent by well-meaning but inept staffers.

The **final paragraph will talk some about your overall strategy**, looking at parliamentary procedure.

Just say that you're going to work on getting your interests taken care of by, among other things, conducting e-caucuses and text-caucuses with like-minded delegations before the conference. This preparation begins via various social media, working in hallway/corridor conversations ("unmoderated and informal caucuses"), heavily using notes during committee sessions, taking leadership roles in regional and affinity (say, island nations) groups, and cosponsoring resolutions/amendments. You'll also use the rules of procedure to your advantage, drawing from the playbook to get things done (or stop things that aren't in your interest). You might include: "Our activities will begin before the conference, via extensive e-mailing and blogging with other delegations attending the conference. This will give us the opportunity to solidify our leadership in our regional coalition as well as reach out to like-minded nations on our topics. We also will aim to draft resolutions with our e-colleagues and secure signatures/sponsorships, thereby saving conference time and permitting more substantive, focused debate. At the conference, we will continue working with our colleagues, both in formal and moderated debate as well as behind the scenes via leadership in unmoderated fora, sending notes and texts, informally meeting outside the conference rooms, and caucusing between meetings."

Some conferences, such as the National High School Model United Nations, will include in their background guides extensive questions that the delegate is expected to answer in their position papers. The answers do not need to be in a question-and-answer format, but be sure that your delegates cover each question somehow.

In addition to the position paper, for each conference, your delegate should create a briefing book with tabs:

- **Tab 1** will be the **position paper**.
- **Tabs 2–4** will be the material that you've read on each of your three **topics**.
- **Tab 5** will be the material you collect on your **country**. Be sure to print out the material from the *CIA World Factbook* and the U.S. Department of State's background notes. If you can find anything from the country's UN mission's site, or get anything else from the country's embassy and/or UN mission, throw it in.
- **Tab 6** can include any **resolutions** you want to have, such as texts of previous UN resolutions, notes on what to include in a new resolution at the conference, parliamentary procedure notes, etc.

Be creative. If there are other tabs you want to throw in, do so. (For example, you could include tabs that have **voting records** of other countries on your topics, a list of e-addresses of the delegates you've been schmoozing with, etc.) When you're doing this research, be sure that you're sharing this material with everyone else in your school's delegation. Even if a delegate's committee does not have a particular topic on its preset agenda, they should be aware of their country's position on every issue in the country—they could be surprised in debate, or in crisis sessions, by the introduction of these topics with little warning by opposing delegations and/or by the Secretariat. You might include the following language:

- **Conference strategy**: This would be boilerplate on how we go about getting what we want at the conference. Don't use precisely this language, but be sure to include something like this: "The Delegation of (country name) to (name of Model UN conference) will use a three-pronged strategy, concentrating on coalition formation to pass our resolutions, engaging in targeted public speaking at appropriate times, and strategically using parliamentary procedure to move things along."

- **Public speaking**: "We will concentrate on tailoring the results of our research to offer more in-depth, substantive speeches. In addition to illustrating our points with research on the general topics, we will personalize our arguments with stories of how individuals are affected by the crisis under discussion. We will use the Question periods to provide friendly questions to like-minded colleagues, and quizzing unsupportive delegations on inconsistencies in their arguments and evidence."
- **Parliamentary procedure**: "Using the summary sheet (see separate tab on this briefing book) we will use offensive and defensive tactics to move along debate to get our resolutions adopted, and be of assistance to the Chair."

The briefing books—a superset of the position papers—demonstrate to the Chair and the rest of the Secretariat the extent of your research. You should make two copies of the briefing books—one to **give to the Chair** right before the beginning of the committee's deliberations, and one to keep. (We've often seen Chairs refer to our briefing books during sessions. You can win a special research and/or writing award strictly on the basis of the strength of your written research.) It's fine to have a copy on your laptop or other PDA, but make sure that you have a physical copy to visually demonstrate your research and organizational skills.

Beyond simple textual treatments of the topics, consider including charts, graphics, and maps to illustrate your points. Delegates should also consider making presentation-size graphics to aid their speeches.

Appendix D provides an example of a particularly well-crafted position paper, written by a Marshall High School team in preparation for the National High School Model UN conference.

The topics listed in the positions papers above and in the appendix—overview of one's country, topics, positions on the topics, and tactics—are not the only things that will require research. Your delegates should also conduct "competitor intelligence," examining:

- The **organization and committee** in which you will serve: There are differences between the General Assembly standing and ad hoc committees, Economic and Social Council (ECOSOC) committees, specialized agencies, the Security Council, Cabinets, European Union, NATO, League of Arab States, the Organization of American States, the African Union, the Organization of Petroleum Exporting Countries, historic organizations, and notional future organizations. Make sure your delegates know the mission, composition, and powers of these organizations.

- **The rules of procedure**: You are guaranteed to see a different set of rules for each conference. Every Secretariat believes that they can write rules better than the UN did, and certainly better than the organizers of competing conferences. They will alter rules to respond to the needs of the conference, and the abilities of their Chairs. The rules will range from one page to seventy pages to "just use *Robert's Rules of Order.*" You should carefully examine every word of every rule—there are always oddities (unintentional loopholes) in rules that you can exploit. Look carefully at the discretionary powers of the Chair, and make sure that you understand how the individual Chair interprets rules. Committees—and the experience of your delegates and ultimately, their enjoyment of that experience—will differ according to the personality, competence, and interpretations of the Chair. If the conference offers a pre-convocation session on the rules of procedure, attend it. It doesn't matter if you've created your own cheat sheets and can cite chapter and verse of the rules, you have to know how the Chair understands and interprets the rules. When coaching, make sure to visit every committee room in which you have delegates to get a feeling for whether there are differential rules interpretations by Chairs. If you spot such inconsistencies, raise it with senior Secretariat members.

- **The conference**: There is a distinct "look and feel" to every conference. Certain things "just aren't done"; other ways of doing things are expected. For example, you should know ahead of time whether "prewritten" (written before the conference convenes) resolutions are expected, or are taboo. You should know if computers and other electronic devices are permitted within the committee rooms. Does the conference consider itself "friendly, noncompetitive, offering a learning atmosphere," or is it strictly aimed at awards? Is native costume, including additions to formal Western business attire, permitted? Does the Secretariat reserve the right to meddle in the language of the resolutions and amendments, no matter whether the requisite sponsors and signatures have been obtained? How will the Secretariat react to attempts to start Silly Season antics—harshly or will they egg on the delegates or even join in? Some of this conference atmospherics material will be mentioned in the rules of procedure and/or other conference preparatory materials—but some will not. You should contact the Secretariat—and other delegations that have had experience with this conference—regarding any issues that will affect your team's performance.

- The **Chair** and the **Secretariat**: Oftentimes, the Chair and committee Director will include in their background guides information about their likes, dislikes (both substantive regarding the issues before the committee, as well as outside interests), hobbies, etc. The Secretariat members may have posted similar information on social media. You will also want to know whether the Chair likes extensively researched position papers, whether they speak the language of your adoptive country, whether they have had chairing experience, and the like. Make sure to research social media—not just the conference website—to find out useful information about the interests and preferences of your Secretariat members, especially those running the committees.

- **Other delegations**: You can chat with fellow delegates at several websites. You can ask the Secretariat for the names of the schools attending, and what countries they will be representing. The best conferences will include this information in their conference programs. This transparency also discourages delegations tempted to act out of character. It's useful to know whether you will be facing schools that will throw more than a hundred students your way, or whether the conference participants are comparative rookies with little experience.

- The **language** of your adoptive country: The Secretariat will not expect you to give fluent articulations of your country's policy in a native language, but knowing a few phrases, even if it's the level of "good morning, fellow delegates," makes you stand out that much more. If a conference permits it, your delegates should consider giving their speeches in the native language, with the speaker's partner providing immediate (either simultaneous or consecutive) translations. In some cases, you can double your allotted speaking time by using this technique. Note, however, that some rules of procedure specify English as the only permissible language. At least try to use one of the other official languages

(Chinese, Russian, Spanish, French, or Arabic) of the UN, and cite the UN Charter if challenged. It will at least establish that you know the UN's intricacies.

7
Care and Feeding
of Your Website

Websites offer you all manners of publicizing your team's efforts, keeping in touch with your delegates, and pointing them to useful research locales. You might consider including the following features:

- A general **calendar** of events that the team will attend. The calendar should have the following:
  - A link to the **website of each conference** mentioned.
  - A list of the **delegates** attending that conference, by committee. This list should include the text of their position papers. It can also be used to keep track of whether the student has paid the relevant fee(s) for the conference, is assigned to a carpool, etc.
  - The **award** won by that student in that committee.
- **Photos** from conferences.
- An **archive** of position papers and background guides from previous conferences, searchable by conference, committee, topic, and country.
- **Press clippings** regarding your team, including items from the PTSA and Boosters newsletters, your high school's newspaper, the high school's website, and any local newspaper, radio, blog, and television coverage.
- Generic general debate and parliamentary procedure speech.
- Generic language to use in resolutions.
- A roster of all team members, including names, addresses, e-mail addresses, and phone numbers (home and cell). Maps to their homes are helpful if you are carpooling. This section should be password protected.
- A **schedule of practice sessions**. Any teaching notes from each session— including lessons learned from conferences—should be posted there.
- Your **playbook**.
- A **discussion database**, similar to those available on Facebook, livejournal.com, and yahoo.com, but specific to your team's discussions.

- Links to useful **research sites** (see appendix F for a starter kit).
- Links to other sites. We like the following:[1]
  - UN Cyber Schoolbus: http://www.un.org/cyberschoolbus/
  - UN Association of the United States of America: http://www.unausa.org /global-classrooms-model-un.
  - Iowa High School UN: https://sites.google.com/site/ihsmun0uni/
  - Lock Haven University MUN: Criteria for Judging: http://www.lhup.edu/lfarley/muncrite.htm
  - TJ Model UN: http://www.tjhsst.edu/mun
  - UN Online Information Service: http://www.unol.org/resource.shtml
  - MUN of the University of Chicago: Preparation: http://www.munuc.org/preparation/positionpapers
  - CIA: http://www.cia.gov
  - U.S. Department of State: International Organizations: http://www.state.gov/j/ct/intl/io/
  - Best Delegate: Model UN Research: http://bestdelegate.com/research/
  - MUNmatters on Twitter: https://twitter.com/MUNmatters
  - International MUN Association: http://www.imuna.org
  - Harvard University: World MUN 101: http://www.worldmun.org/upload/WorldMUN_101.pdf
  - MUN Development Organization: http://www.model-un.net
  - Wikipedia: MUN: http://en.wikipedia.org/wiki/Model_United_Nations

Also look at the sites mentioned elsewhere in this guide, and the sites of the major conferences hosted by high schools, universities, and national/international groups.

You might also want to keep records of how your team has done and how your students have done individually. With this information in hand, you are prepared to present an oral report to your school's leadership team and to the parent-teacher organization, a potential source of financial support for your MUN club. You'll want to password-protect information posted on your club's website. For example, here's how we keep track of how we've done as a team for a given semester:

---

[1] If you get errors on any of these sites, go to the main page and search for the MUN subpage from there. If that does not work, run the name of the conference in your favorite search engine. Some variant of the original URL will pop up. Conferences frequently change URLs; we do not guarantee that those listed will still be live by the time you are ready to use them.

George C. Marshall High School MUN Calendar

September 18: "My First MUN" Training Conference, hosted by Marshall High School, Falls Church, Virginia

October 1–2: George Mason High School—19 students attended (plus one research director), 2 Gavels, 5 Outstanding, 2 Honorable Mention, Best Small School

October 15–16: Fairfax High School—8 students attended, 1 Gavel, 2 Honorable Mentions, 4 Verbal Commendations, runner-up Small School

November 12–14: Princeton University—13 students attended, 5 Outstanding, 1 Honorable Mention, 2 Chair Commendations (one for use of Spanish), Outstanding Small School

November 19–21: University of Virginia—17 students attended, 3 Gavels, 1 Outstanding, 6 Chair Commendations, Best Small School

December 10–11: Hylton High School, Woodbridge, Virginia—12 students attended, 2 Gavels, 1 Outstanding, 2 Chair Commendations, Best School-Research

December 11: DELMUN, Salesianum School, Wilmington, Delaware— 5 students attended, 2 Gavels, 2 Outstanding, 1 Honorable Mention

When you're trying to figure out Most Valuable awards at the end of the year, here's one way to tally their performance. (This does **not** include the intangibles, such as helping with fund-raising, critiquing speeches in practice, helping with research, etc.) You may also believe that a conference Chair overlooked your student's performance in determining awards, and give your student an asterisk for a good performance that didn't win. This system gives you an idea of how many students are attending conferences, and how many are just seeking to add another activity to their resume. The following is a notional listing of our fall semester rankings, with the points given for various levels of participation and awards:

1: attended the conference and/or provided research assistance (two points if it results in an award)

2: member of a team that won Best School or a team research award, or individually won a Verbal Commendation

3: Honorable Mention

4: Outstanding Delegate

5: Gavel, Best Delegate

* Should have received an award

25* Alyssa

Mason High School: Gavel, School Award

Fairfax High School: Honorable Mention

Princeton: Outstanding, School Award

UVA: School Award*

Hylton: Gavel, School Award

16 Kate

Mason High School: Honorable Mention

UVA: Gavel, School Award

Hylton: Verbal, School Award

14 Prashanth

Fairfax: Gavel, Verbal

UVA: Gavel, School Award

12 Bryan

Mason High School: Outstanding, School Award

Princeton: Outstanding, School Award

12 Brent

Mason High School: Outstanding, School Award

UVA: Outstanding, School Award

11 Ramy

Fairfax High School: Verbal

UVA: School Award

Hylton: Gavel, School Award

11 Patrick

Princeton: Outstanding, School Award

DELMUN: Gavel

11 Nassim

Mason High School: Gavel, School Award

UVA: Verbal, School Award

10* Sravya

Mason High School: School Award*

UVA: Verbal, School Award

DELMUN: Outstanding

9 Betty

Fairfax: Honorable Mention

Princeton: Outstanding, School Award

9 Arjun
  UVA: Verbal, School Award
  DELMUN: Gavel
8* Melanie
  Mason High School: Outstanding, School Award
  Princeton: School Award*
8 Steven
  Mason High School: Outstanding, School Award
  UVA: School Award
7* Jason
  Fairfax: Attend*
  UVA: School Award
  DELMUN: Outstanding
7* Salma
  Mason High School: Honorable Mention, School Award
  Hylton: School Award*
7 Julia
  UVA: Gavel, School Award
6* Jeff
  Mason High School: School Award
  UVA: School Award*
  Hylton: School Award
6 Dema
  Hylton: Outstanding, School Award
6 Julian
  Mason High School: School Award
  UVA: Verbal, School Award
6 Tishan
  Princeton: Outstanding, School Award
6 Pari
  Mason High School: Oustanding, School Award
5* Sophia
  UVA: School Award
  DELMUN: Honorable Mention*
5 Red
  Princeton: Honorable Mention, School Award

4 Maya
  Princeton: Verbal (for Spanish), School Award
4 Catherine
  Hylton: Verbal, School Award
4 Tom
  Mason High School: School Award
  Fairfax: Verbal
4 Sabrina
  Mason High School: School Award (research director)
  Princeton: School Award
4 Stacey
  Princeton: Verbal, School Award
4 Asif
  UVA: Verbal, School Award
4 Taesung
  UVA: Verbal, School Award
4 Litic
  Mason High School: School Award
  UVA: School Award
3* Saleh
  Mason High School: School Award
  Fairfax: Attend*
2 Gwen
  Fairfax: Verbal
2* Aparna
  Mason High School: School Award*
2* Kira
  Princeton: School Award*
2* Alena
  Princeton: School Award*
2* Johanna
  Hylton: School Award*
2* Natalie
  Hylton: School Award*
2* Lia
  Hylton: School Award*

2* Elfadil
   Hylton: School Award*
2 Madhav
   Hylton: School Award
2 Maddie
   Mason High School: School Award
2 Nora
   Mason High School: School Award
2 Lauren
   Princeton: School Award
2 Aruna
   Mason High School: School Award

8

What to Do at a Conference

All of this preparation—practice and research—comes together at the actual conference, when your students get to try out their newly honed skills.

When debarking from your buses or vans, your students should already be in your **team uniform**—Western business attire and/or formal business costume for your adoptive country. We prefer black suits for our women, dark suits for our men. A flag lapel pin of your adoptive country is a nice touch. An excellent selection can be found by calling Abe Lincoln Flags, 8634 Lee Highway, Fairfax, Virginia, 22031, 703-201-1116. Once one of our delegates has won an award, we give them a bronze gavel pin, available from Anderson's, P.O. Box 1151, Minneapolis, Minnesota, 55440-1151, 1-800-848-0258.

At **registration**, the sponsor should register the delegation, pick up badges and packets, which usually contain schedules, rules of procedure, school maps, lunch coupons, etc. Your delegates should not be lined up with you at the registration line. Rather, they should immediately begin chatting with the members of the Secretariat who will affect their committees (not just the Chairs and others on the dais, but other senior Secretariat members who might from time to time stop by, or are in charge of printing documents, etc.), and with the delegates from other schools who will be on their committees. Team members should have their "game face" on—they are no longer high schoolers, they are dedicated ambassadors from their country. Until they get back on the bus, they should never "break character." They are *always* being evaluated at the conference.

Part of how Michael Jordan became a winner is being the first in the gym and the last to leave. You should use the same mind-set: get there earlier than any other delegation and be the last delegation to leave. Your delegates can always be talking to somebody—staff, other delegates, coaches, each other, etc. *Most* of the work of MUNs—and parliamentary bodies in general—is conducted in corridors, not in formal sessions.

Some conferences will host pre-kickoff **parliamentary procedure workshops**, to explain how rules of procedure work. If these sessions are offered, no matter how well-coached and experienced your delegates are regarding these particular rules, every one of your delegates (and you) should attend. You will learn how the Chairs have been told to interpret rules, have an opportunity to ask questions about ambiguous phrasing of the rules (you are virtually guaranteed to find loopholes), and get a chance to meet with the Chairs ahead of time.

Team members may wish to print individualized **business cards** and delegation **stationery**. The former can have their name, school, country name, committee assignment, cell phone number, website(s), and e-mail addresses printed. The stationery is useful for the informal notes they will be passing to their colleagues. They may wish to write some notes ahead of time and fill in the name of the recipient delegation at the conference.

As soon as you have finished with registration and have handed out badges, information packets, room keys, etc., you should do the following:

- Huddle with your delegates to go over **last-minute coaching hints** (including any changes you note in the rules of procedure that you just received, versus the rules that you saw on their website or received via mail or in an e-mail).
- Discuss what oddities in the **rules** your delegates should raise at the start of the committee meeting.
- Discuss whether your delegates should call for a **Moment of Silence** at the beginning of the committee session to memorialize someone mentioned in the news that week (it could be a major international figure, individuals killed by terrorists, individuals victimized by natural disasters, etc.) or to note the anniversary of such an event.
- Send your delegates to their **committee rooms**, where they should establish their territory. They should sit in the center chairs in the front row of the room or on the edges of the rows, but still in front. As mentioned earlier, the Chair can see them easier and thus call on them and have colloquies with them. It is easier for your delegates to run off for hallway caucusing from that position. It is also easier for your delegates to host an informal caucus of their region from that location. And you can find them easily in case of emergencies. Find out whether there are dead spots for cell phone reception, find out whether the room has dead spots for the Wi-Fi computer network provided by the host school or hotel (be sure to check whether the Wi-Fi is free or involves a fee), find power outlets for their laptops and printers, and get a feeling for the acoustics of the room.

9

Line of March

Conferences usually begin with a **plenary session** in an auditorium, cafeteria, or some other large meeting room. The Secretariat members will introduce themselves, various functionaries from the host school or organization will welcome the delegates, and a guest speaker may give a presentation. Your delegation should sit at the back of this room. This makes it easier to exit the room when it's time to leave and get to the committee rooms.

Once your delegates are in the committee room, the Secretariat members will arrive, and the scene will revert to the following **field of play**:

The Front Desk:	Director, Chair, Parliamentarian, Rapporteur, Page
Rows of Delegates:	X X O O O O O O O O O X X X X X X X X X X O O O O O O O X X
	X X O O O O O O O O O O O O O O O O O O O O O O O O O X X
Os: other schools' delegates	X X O O O O O O O O O O O O O O O O O O O O O O O O O X X
Xs: your delegates	O O O O O O O O O O O O O O O O O O O O O O O O O O O O O
Ys: likely yields (see below)	O O O O O O O O O O O O O O O O O O O O O O O O O O O O O
	Y Y Y Y Y Y Y Y Y Y Y Y Y Y Y Y Y Y Y Y Y Y Y Y Y Y Y Y Y
	Y Y Y Y Y Y Y Y Y Y Y Y Y Y Y Y Y Y Y Y Y Y Y Y Y Y Y Y Y

The Director is the substantive leader of the Secretariat team in that committee, approving all resolutions and amendments. The Chair keeps the meeting moving by calling on delegates and ruling on parliamentary procedure. The Parliamentarian assists the Chair regarding the interpretation of the rules. The Rapporteur assists the Director, tallying votes. The Page serves as a courier for notes between delegates and between delegates and the Chair. (Chairs may sometimes ask delegates to volunteer to serve as pages. Your students should **never** volunteer to be pages. Your students are there to compete, not to carry others' papers. Chairs may also ask for delegates to volunteer to be Chairs. Your delegates should jump at the chance.)

Your delegates should immediately **introduce themselves to the Chair** and the rest of the denizens of the dais and turn in their position papers and briefing books (notebooks that contain printed materials related to the topic). At this point, they can tell the Chair that if he/she needs to take a break, just look your way and you'll move for a five-minute unmoderated caucus. You can also ask the Chair to announce that the meeting of your regional or affinity bloc will take place at your desk(s) during the unmoderated caucus.

Your students should then **introduce themselves to everyone else in the room**. They will be able to quickly read the room regarding which other students are likely to be active, and who will most likely be uninvolved. In general, the activists will be in the front and middle seats. The students who are not there to win, but rather are there to enjoy the experience, talk with their friends from other schools, hit on other delegates, etc., will huddle in the back. The latter students are your best friends. They dread being called upon, but know that their sponsors will be looking in from time to time to see if they are on the Speakers' List. Your students should simply offer them a deal—they get on the Speakers' List, but when actually called upon, they yield to your students, who will do the heavy lifting regarding public speaking, parliamentary procedure, etc.

General Debate, Caucuses—Moderated and Unmoderated, and Setting the Agenda

The Line of March will then be as mentioned in our discussion of the Playbook. Your students will have an opportunity to get on the Speakers' List for the General Debate on the topics selected earlier by the Secretariat. After a while, students lower on the Speakers' List will give up hope of the queue ever reaching them, and move for a Moderated Caucus, in which the rules—and, more importantly, the Speakers' List—will be suspended, and they'll have a better chance of getting recognized to speak. Once back into formal session, a delegate will move to set the agenda. After debate has begun on a topic, resolutions will begin to be formulated.

Resolutions

Resolutions are the lifeblood of the committee, the only way that the UN can formally get anything done. They are similar to bills in national parliamentary bodies. Resolutions begin as working papers and after having met the required number of sponsors and signatories and other format requirements, they are assigned a number and become a resolution.

Resolutions begin with the name of the committee/body and include the names of the sponsors and signatories. In any committee, there will be a certain number of sponsors required for the resolution to be considered by the committee. A separate number of signatories may also be required. **Sponsors** are delegations that had a hand in drafting the resolution, and/or agree to vote for it. **Signatories** are delegations that agree that it would be an interesting issue to discuss, but make no promises about actually supporting the proposed legislation.

The resolution is written in most MUN conferences (although not in the UN in some special cases) as a single sentence. It begins with what in national parliaments are the "whereas" clauses, called preambular (often misnamed "preambulatory") clauses, which describe the situation on the ground that the resolution is designed to remedy. Once the preamble has established this scene setting, the resolution then offers its solution, in the form of numbered operative paragraphs. **Amendments** alter something in the resolutions. (The rules usually stipulate that the preamble cannot be amended. This custom makes little sense, but get used to it.)

Typical **preambular phrases** include (and to these you can usually add deeply, further, gravely, with approval, with deep concern, with regret, and other breathless modifiers):

Affirming	Expressing its	Reaffirming
Alarmed by	appreciation	Realizing
Approving	(or satisfaction	Recalling
Aware	or wish)	Recognizing
Bearing in mind	Fulfilling	Referring
Believing	Fully aware (or	Regretting
Concerned	believing, etc.)	Reiterating
Confident	Guided by	Seeking
Conscious	Having adopted	Taking into account
Considering also	Having considered	Taking into
Contemplating	Having devoted	consideration
Convinced	attention to	Taking note
Declaring	Having examined	Viewing with
Deploring	Having heard	appreciation
Desiring	Having received	Welcoming
Disturbed	Having studied	
Emphasizing	Keeping in mind	
Expecting	Noting	
	Observing	

Typical **operative phrases** include (and accordingly, you may also use such modifiers as further, solemnly, strongly, among others) the following active verbs:

Accepts	Deplores	Regrets
Affirms	Designates	Reminds
Appeals	Draws the attention of	Renews
Approves	Emphasizes	Requests
Authorizes	Encourages	Resolves
Calls	Endorses	Supports
Commends	Expresses its	Takes note of
Condemns	appreciation	Transmits
Confirms	(or hope)	Trusts
Congratulates	Invites	Urges
Considers	Notes	
Declares accordingly	Offers	
Demands (usually	Proclaims	
used only by the	Reaffirms	
Security Council)	Recommends	

These are only suggestions of terms that can be used. Students should not assume that if a term isn't on this list, that it cannot be used. Similarly, they should not take a "one-from-column-A-", "one-from-column-B-" approach to writing resolutions either.

Here's an example of a resolution. Your resolutions do not need to be this detailed, or this long.

Sponsors: Egypt, Syria, Qatar

Signatories: Russian Federation, Fiji, United States, Cameroon, Mexico, Zimbabwe

Topic: North African Regional Trade and Development

Committee: SOCHUM (Social, Humanitarian and Cultural Committee, a.k.a. The Third Committee)

The General Assembly,

Noting the past action of the United Nations to further Regional Trade,

Recognizing the benefits to all North African nations of increased regional trade,

Cognizant of the barriers to trade that exist today,

Resolving to develop and improve the standards of living of North African citizens through increased trade;

1. **Recommends** the immediate lowering of trade barriers in North African nations from major exports such as:

a. Crude oil and petroleum products
b. Natural gas
c. Cotton and cotton products
d. Chemical products, including phosphates and hydrocarbons
e. Sesame
f. Cattle
g. Ore and minerals
h. Agricultural products;

2. **Encourages** the following plan of regional tariff reduction:
   a. A 5 percent reduction of tariffs on goods produced within the region for a year
   b. A 2-percent reduction of tariffs on goods produced within the region for the next three years
   c. A 1-percent reduction of tariffs on goods produced within the region for the next seven years;

3. **Requests** the use of Confidence Building Measures to demonstrate regional stability and increase foreign investment, specifically:
   a. The recognition of territorial claims, such as, but not limited to:
      i. The Moroccan claim to the Western Sahara
      ii. The Egyptian claim to the Hala'ib Triangle
   b. The immediate resumption of talks between governments and insurgent groups in troubled countries;

4. **Further requests** the use of Confidence Building Measures by the North African governments to increase tourism revenues;

5. **Suggests** that governments allow an open dialogue between engineers and scientists to increase the level of regional development, especially in the areas of:
   a. Efficient agriculture
   b. Water sanitation and recycling
   c. Education
   d. Infrastructure development;

6. **Endorses** increased tariff and non-tariff barriers to protect regional industries from nonregional competitors, such as:
   a. Protective tariffs on the important of goods produced by developing industries
   b. Quotas on the amount of protected goods that can be imported from nonregional sources

   c. More stringent safety and quality standards for importation of protected goods;

7. **Encourages** cooperation with other regional bodies, such as the OAU and LAS in forming and maintaining the North African free trade zone;

8. **Recommends** that intra-region trade should be limited to:
   a. Agricultural products
   b. Equipment designed to develop the deficient industries of North African nations
   c. Copyrighted or otherwise protected machinery and technology
   d. Other goods essential to the creation and maintenance of an efficient infrastructure;

9. **Requests** that North African nations expand their existing international means of transportation, such as highways, to expedite trade and lower shipping costs;

10. **Suggests** that credit organizations operating within any of the North African nations widen their operations to all North African nations to:
    a. Facilitate the free flow of capital throughout the region
    b. Provide available and stable loans to new industries throughout the region;

11. **Further suggests** the creation of a regional banking group made up of banks from all North African nations to improve the people's access to capital;

12. **Encourages** North African nations to offer Free Zones to foreign investment that would allow foreign investors to invest their money at reduced tax levels; and

13. **Resolves** to remain actively sized on the issue.

The rest of the "line of march" progresses as described in the Playbook section.

Voting

When it comes time for voting, sometimes the rules will call for all talking to cease, and the doors to be locked, with no one permitted to exit or enter. Make sure to make abundantly clear to the Chair and the rest of the Secretariat that this stricture does not apply to you, the sponsor/coach of the school. You are legally responsible for the health, safety, and welfare of the students on your delegation, and you *must* have access to your students at all times. Furthermore, locking the doors could be a fire-safety violation. You should never relinquish your authority and responsibility regarding your delegates to the Secretariat. You should treat this as a deal breaker and be willing to pull your delegation from the conference if a Chair persists.

10
The Coach's Role at the Conference

You are there as a **facilitator**, an **educator**, and an **inspiration** to your students. You are there to get them to believe in themselves—that they can succeed at a rather unnatural endeavor: speaking to hundreds, sometimes thousands, of people and persuading them to their point of view. You're there to praise, to start them believing in themselves by being the first to believe in them, to always cheerlead for them. No matter how poorly they believe they are doing in their committees—and there are always dead spots in the committees, even for your stars, when they believe they cannot get called upon no matter what they try—you are there to tell them to never give up on themselves. (We have often pulled out victories in the last hours of a conference, despite having a terrible beginning.) Their self-confidence starts with you, and no matter what happens, you are the touchstone to their success.

When you get to the conference, you will usually find a **faculty lounge** or some other hospitality suite that has been made available to the other sponsors, and has been declared generally off-limits to the students, although the occasional Secretariat member will stop by with announcements and to get feedback from you. Most of the sponsors—teachers—will be loaded down with essays, tests, lesson plans, etc., they hope to catch up on. Looking at only your role as coach—do not do as they do. You are there for your students, period. Make contacts with the other faculty members, get their addresses, hand out brochures for your conference, find allies for the short-term (the conference) and long-term (upcoming conferences), grab a donut, and get out of there.

Visit all of the committee rooms in which you have students. Although there may be some committees that are intellectually interesting a priori, if you don't have a student in those rooms, ignore them. You're there for your students. They want to see you in the back, quietly cheering them on, and available to them when they have questions about strategy, tactics, and facts.

You might also find it helpful to "**bench coach**" from the sidelines. This can take the form of simply sending notes via the pages to your students, giving them "attaboys" for well-argued presentations, suggestions on potential allies based upon your discussions with the other coaches, insights on how the debate is going and what arguments they might use to supplement their cause, etc. Some conferences have a "no coaching" rule. Ignore it. You are an educator and the students are there to learn. Many students learn much more efficiently in experiential settings. No MUN Secretariat is going to deny that they are fostering an educational setting. And once they grant that part of the argument, they have to grant you leave to come and go as your needs dictate.

The Secretariat will want **feedback** from the sponsors on the conference's proceedings, and will often host plenary sessions, usually in the faculty lounge, with all of the teachers. In these sessions, publicly praise the Secretariat. Any complaints should be made privately. Do not embarrass the Secretariat members, who may remember your thoughtfulness and cooperative spirit.

You are there, however, to **back your students** if the need arises, but pick your battles. It is acceptable to point out to the Undersecretary General for personnel that the committee Chairs are inconsistent among themselves in their interpretations of the rules. It is acceptable to advise the Secretariat when "silly season"—usually and hopefully limited to "superlatives" (best tie, best accent, etc.) during the final minutes of a conference—is detracting from the educational process, especially when it begins early or crosses the line on propriety. You might even want to mention that another delegation is hopelessly "out of policy/out of character" (not representing the real-world government's political views). You do not want to use up political capital by complaining that your students are not being called upon, and it is never acceptable to argue awards decisions. You can privately raise rules interpretation issues with the Chairs; your students should avoid irritating the Chair with the same observations.

You are also in loco parentis and are there to ensure discipline and safety. This means, inter alia, that your students will not participate in "silly season," a period at the end of the conference when Chairs lose control and discipline is apt to break down. Always ask—would a parent be proud of his/her student at this moment? If the answer is "no," complain to the Secretariat.

Once it's time for awards to be given, sit on the sidelines and cheer on your students. If they win Best School, have either the delegation Chair pick it up, or a delegation member whom you believe should have won an individual award, but did not. Be gracious in victory. Do not gloat. Likewise, if your delegation did not receive the accolades you believe they deserved, save your assessment for after the conference. Remember that awards decisions always involve a degree of subjectivity. Learn from every experience and use what you learn for the future.

And now it's time to start the process all over again, with a "hot wash" practice meeting to discuss how you did, what you learned, what could have been done better, and whether you want to return to the conference next year, etc.

11

How Students Can Help Your Team Outside the Conference

When you're not actually researching, practicing, or performing, there are a host of other tasks you can take on that will help everyone. There are some tasks that an individual member of the team can take care of for everyone on the team. For example, not everyone needs to visit the same website to look up a particular topic—one check by one person for everyone will do. With that in mind, here are some individual tasks for which students can volunteer, many of which can be performed even before you have country and topic assignments:

- **Supplies**: One student can make sure everyone brings their briefing books, position papers, lapel pins, and everything else to school on the day of a conference. You'll be using them from Hour One.
- Getting **letterhead** printed with your adoptive country's name and flag (skip including your school's name—you don't want to remind other schools' students that you're ultimately their competition). You'll be amazed how much scrap paper you go through in sending notes to other delegations. Might as well have good-looking paper!
- **Finding e-mail addresses** of other delegates to a conference you'll attend. You'll want to "do your homework," which in terms of politicking at meetings, means knowing others' positions, how they will behave, and who will support you before you even walk into the room. (Talking to them before the conference does this for you.)
- **Being the rainmaker**: The fund-raising leader who organizes the car washes, contacts potential corporate sponsors, schedules presentations to the Boosters and PTSA, etc.
- Obtaining team/country/gavel **lapel pins**. (These are usually a dollar or so in bulk and are little details that help create the character you're portraying.)
- **Contacting the embassy/consulate, UN mission, foreign ministry, or website** of your adoptive government. It would be a fine idea if you could

visit the embassy/mission of the country you're portraying. You'll want to contact the political counselor, public affairs counselor, or sometimes—for the smaller embassies/missions—the Ambassador.

- Contacting the appropriate **U.S. Department of State desk officer**. Try the International Organizations bureau as well as the specific country desk. The State Department's website also has material of use to MUNers. If you're visiting Washington, D.C., try to get an appointment to talk to the State officers.

- Contacting the **UN Information Center**, 1775 K Street, NW, Suite 400, Washington, D.C. 20006, 202-331-8670. The Center is the only official UN information center in the United States. Its library contains stacks of printed materials, including copies of UN resolutions and UN Charters (every delegate should have their own well-thumbed copy). You will also find liaison offices for the UN Development Program, UN Environmental Program, and International Fund for Agriculture.

- Checking out information on your country(ies) in the CIA's **World Factbook** (http://www.cia.gov) and the U.S. Department of State's **country profiles** on http://www.state.gov. One person can **write the introductory paragraph** on your country, which each of your students can use in their introductions for their committee-specific position papers.

- Getting **UN Charters** from UNA-USA, the UN depository libraries, or other sources.

- **Creating the rules cheat sheet**. (This is an easy-to-use graphic organizer of the main rules of the conference. It's usually found in a plastic sheet protector. Novices should carry one at all times during their first conference, just so everyone will know how to use it.)

- Getting a desk-size **country flag** (these are about 4x6 inches) to establish your presence in the conference room.

- Creating **business cards** (this is really helpful when you're at a hotel conference, and you want other delegations to be able to contact you. Just write your room extension on the card that already has "Delegation of _____ to the _____ MUN, Committee Name, your name" printed on it. (Again, skip the school identifiers.) If any student has computer graphics skills, there's a simple business card program that will do this; all you provide is the paper stock.

- **Splitting up research on the committee topics**. For example, one person in the country delegation handling World Health Organization matters could research malaria; the other could be the primary expert on HIV/AIDS. If you're primary on the topic, you'll be doing most of the speaking when that topic is being debated, while your partner is busily schmoozing the other delegations and helping to draft resolutions or amendments.

- **Pooling research** on a particular topic/committee, regardless of country.

12

Diversity

Perhaps the most apparent item of 1950s technology that reveals the cultural diversity residing within the Great Hall where delegates to the General Assembly convene is the beige plastic earpiece that adorns the delegation desks that carry each nation's name. There are six official languages spoken at the United Nations, each simultaneously translated so that every speaker's voice can be heard and understood in Arabic, Chinese, English, French, Russian, or Spanish. Beyond the official languages at the UN, one can easily overhear countless other languages and dialects in the hallways of the UN.

That is certainly the trend in American high schools, where children of immigrant families as well as diplomats posted in the United States bring a rich cacophony of the spoken word into the classroom. It is the most audible evidence that high schools are experiencing the challenges and benefits of a society that values cultural diversity.

The MUN coach's protest at the 2003 NAIMUN conference over students speaking Arabic was an appeal for fairness rather than an indictment of those students whose voices, representing the Kingdom of Jordan, had found a safe harbor in which to be heard. In this instance, the coach was urging fair play in an MUN conference setting where English is usually the only language spoken. He and other advisors understood the advantage of foreign language abilities that are demonstrated in a competitive setting like Model UN. Curiously, most high school–sponsored and college-hosted Model UN conference rules do not outlaw languages other than English. They presume, probably incorrectly, that students come to MUN conferences unprepared to speak any other language, even if they are representing non-English-speaking nations.

There is a strange asymmetry at play here. Universities, whose international relations graduates are among the most highly sought after by elite international commercial institutions and government agencies including the U.S. State Department, often make minimal effort to showcase their cultural diversity at MUN conferences. By offering no or only token opportunities to engage high school students in a language other than English, they are sending a too-telling signal. It is interesting to contemplate the reverberations of a high powered university hosting an MUN conference where all delegates were offered the opportunity to engage in negotiations and debate in Arabic, Chinese, Farsi, French, German, Hindi, Russian, and Spanish sessions, and yes, even one reserved for English.

The multiplicity of languages and dialects spoken at the UN is mirrored by the variety of languages spoken today in many American high schools—languages that number well beyond those precious few taught there. While since 9/11 many school systems have made strides in expanding language offerings to include Arabic and Chinese, others have done well in difficult financial times to retain the Romance languages in their academic offerings. To the extent that students strive to retain their cultural identity through the use of their native language, especially when that language (and its literature and culture) is not among a school's language offerings, Model UN offers these students an outlet to use their language skills in addressing international issues. We should not be wasting this opportunity.

Some college Model UN organizations have recognized this situation as an opportunity to enrich the high school conferences they sponsor. Three examples at the collegiate level and two other high school-sponsored conferences merit attention, in part because they are rare but also because they are well-run and serve as examples to other colleges and high schools hosting MUN conferences of what can be done. The Princeton Model UN (PMUNC) has consistently offered at least one such "bilingual" committee, often a "crisis committee" dealing with a complex political or military threat, where the delegates are expected to speak in either French or Spanish. At NAIMUN, hosted by Georgetown University, a recent simulation of the Hugo Chavez cabinet in Venezuela offered students fluent in Spanish an engaging and authentic crisis where linguistic skills came into play in crafting nuanced policy statements and news releases. The Secondary Schools UN Symposium Simulation (SSUNS) run by students at McGill University in Montreal offered Canadian, American, and other high school students the opportunity to serve as ministers in the Quebec cabinet where French language skills melded with an understanding of Quebec's history and politics to produce an exciting real-world experience. The high school conference that consistently offered similar bilingual opportunities in French and Spanish for Model UN delegations was the International Baccalaureate Mid-Atlantic Regional Consortium Conference hosted by Gar-Field Senior High School in Woodbridge, Virginia. For reasons that are not altogether clear, the Consortium ended its sponsorship of the conference in 2010. Sadly, these French and Spanish language committees are too isolated and too often limited—limited to a single committee at a conference where there are a dozen or more committees operating, and rarely venturing beyond French or Spanish. But other high schools are stepping in to fill the void: In 2012 the PWMUN Conference, hosted by C.D. Hylton Senior High School in Woodbridge, Virginia, offered a crisis committee in which the status of Puerto Rico was debated in Spanish.

Perhaps the scarcity of committee offerings in Chinese, Arabic, German, Hindi, Farsi, Russian, or other languages in high demand by the U.S. Foreign Service is further evidence of how far American academic institutions have to travel to meet our country's need for well-trained and linguistically versatile Foreign Service, military, and intelligence officers. High school MUN teachers/advisors can affect this paucity of offerings by being wise shoppers—rewarding those conferences that do offer linguistic diversity with their registration dollars, and by urging other conference hosts, especially college and university-hosted conferences, to introduce such offerings.

Many of MUN's success stories originate not only among the top AP and IB students but also from the ranks of students with an Individualized Education Program (IEP) or a 504 Plan—protections provided by the Americans with Disabilities Act (ADA) and Section 504 of the Rehabilitation Act. On stage at MUN conferences, students with disabilities often come to discover hidden talents as persuasive advocates. MUN coaches and club sponsors who fall victim to the myth that MUN is only for the gifted and talented are missing an opportunity to watch students develop highly prized skills that often do not emerge in the traditional classroom setting.

13

The Ethical Dimension of MUN

She left her [paper] on the chair, and someone took it and submitted it with their name on it.
—MUN advisor from First Colonial High School during the Harvard Model United Nations conference in 2008[1]

A delegate has taken ideas from the document we are working on and . . . submitted them as their own.
—Delegate in the UN Environmental Policy Committee[2]

I snagged an idea from France. I helped him create the idea and then I didn't like what he was doing, so I took it and went off on my own. He got pretty mad about that; he called me a cheater. I would have felt guilty about stealing his idea, but he wasn't the nicest person about it so I really don't.
—World Health Organization delegate[3]

By its very nature, diplomacy—as practiced both in the real world and in Model United Nations—conjures up a rigorous competition of ideas and strategy. And for most MUNers and their teacher-advisors, playing by the rules fits the expected norm. The difference between modern diplomacy in the real world and what takes place in its scholastic counterpart is, of course, the educational purpose of MUN. Learning to play by the rules, fostering the idea of nations working cooperatively to understand each others' views, and crafting language that reflects a consensus of nations' views—those are essential elements to Model UN.

Upholding the educational purpose of Model UN and fostering its ethical dimension is in large part the responsibility of adult teacher-advisors who, by their words and actions, are able to ensure that the proper message reaches their student audience: namely, that "winning" in Model UN—however it may be measured, whether by writing working papers and position papers or getting resolutions to the floor and passed—does not justify unethical practices. Unfortunately, sometimes

---

1 Jessica Levine, "HMUN Delegates Play Dirty," Conference Newspaper, Harvard Model UN Conference, 2009, 1.
2 Ibid.
3 Ibid.

the wrong message or an inconsistent message—or no message at all—is what students receive. With win-at-any-cost motivation and AWOL ethical standards, competition crowds out the hard work of understanding multiple perspectives and seeking consensus, and for some delegates the thrill of victory or the fear of defeat becomes a driving force fueling students who resort to deceitful practices. But the burden of promoting best practices and policing violations does not rest solely with teacher-advisors. Conference sponsors also have a responsibility to set high ethical standards, promote and publicize them, and stand by them. The role of high school MUN coaches and sponsors should be to reward conferences that uphold ethical standards and bypass those that do not. Just as some high school MUN teams gain reputations among MUN faculty sponsors and advisors for poor ethical practices, so do conference sponsors, both at the college and high school levels. Repairing those reputations once gained is an almost-impossible task.

Too often, ethical practice goes unmentioned in preconference materials prepared by conference sponsors, especially at the college level where one might reasonably expect to see the issue of ethical practices highlighted. Then at the conference, harried Secretaries-General and their staffs listen patiently to protests by students and/or teacher-advisors and then plead ignorance or "it's your word against theirs, what am I supposed to do?" Bringing together the complaining party and the accused may not resolve the immediate issue, but it would put everyone on notice that unethical behavior is inconsistent with the purposes of Model UN, and that any further examples of such behavior would have consequences. Making it clear ahead of the conference that unethical practices will cause delegations to be removed from award contention would go a long way to discouraging such behavior. For example, the Montreal Secondary Schools United Nations Symposium (SSUNS) Model UN Conference run by students from McGill University includes among its rules the right to sanction delegations whose votes or support for resolutions is at variance with its national policies. Such rules are effective in limiting the occasions in which two country delegations from the same high school end up supporting each other or the same resolution when their national policies are in opposition. For example, Cuba might agree to support a U.S.-sponsored resolution cracking down on drug smuggling in the Caribbean but it is highly unlikely that Cuba would support a U.S.-sponsored resolution calling for a trade embargo against a left-wing Latin American government that was threatening to nationalize private land holdings of an American corporation. The McGill rule is an effective deterrent to such unethical actions.

In a conference setting where awards reinforce competition among schools and delegations—or in the case of MUN classes, where an award translates into a higher course grade—the bulk of the responsibility for keeping ethical practices front and center for students rests squarely with teacher-advisors. Taking advantage of "teachable moments"—reacting to ethical lapses—is certainly called for. However, a more effective practice is found in school-based training sessions for students seeking to understand how MUN works. For example, many Model UN clubs require delegates to do research and prepare position papers in advance of conferences. Some clubs use the position paper as a passport to the conference, something we regard as a must-do. This approach offers many advantages, most importantly, developing delegates who are well versed on the topics they will be debating. Students who are knowledgeable on their country and its position on the assigned topics come to conferences with a solid knowledge base and have no reason to steal the ideas of others.

Teacher-advisors are uniquely positioned to apply academic integrity standards when it comes to writing position papers. By their nature, these student-drafted position papers are expected to state the policy position of an assigned country and a rationale and supporting evidence, be it demographic, cultural, historical, geographic, security, resource-driven, etc. References in a position paper to specific ideas that belong to that country's president, prime minister, ambassador, or other source require footnotes acknowledging the origin of the idea or quoted text. Requiring citations in position papers sends an important message to the students: Integrity demands that ideas and text borrowed from others be attributed to the rightful source. Footnotes and a bibliography do not diminish the gravitas of a position paper; rather they enhance the writer's authority and credibility. Unfortunately, too many conference organizers do a poor job of policing the quality of position papers, or lack the time to even read them and offer constructive criticism. Some conference organizers (for example, the McGill University conference) set aside separate awards for writing, which allows recognition of well-written, well-organized, and well-cited position papers. But even those few conference sponsors who take this approach often do not make clear in advance their expectations for citing sources. The result—students adopt a "why bother" approach to citing sources when conference organizers hand out awards to delegations and schools whose position papers exhibit little regard for the rules against plagiarism. The remedy—teacher-sponsors who make explicit their expectations for citing sources reinforcing the message students are getting in the classroom—good analytical and evidence-backed writing requires citations. MUN teacher-advisors whose school districts have access to programs or services (e.g., Turnitin.com or Blackboard's SafeAssign) that check for plagiarism in student work is one way to reinforce rules on citations.

Beyond taking steps to professionalize students' position papers, teacher-advisors should include in their MUN training for new and veteran students a discussion of what constitutes an ethical strategy. Is it acceptable to engage in behavior that involves deceit, theft of ideas, sabotage of another delegate's working paper, resolution or amendment to a resolution?

Every MUN conference has a set of rules that guide the conduct of the conference, including debate. Virtually no two conferences, particularly at the college level, use the same rules. Teacher-advisors who have any desire to see their students do well should carefully read the rules well ahead of the conference date and seek clarification of rules that appear vague. Most quality conferences will set aside time for a Q&A session to explain the rules. Teacher-advisors should take advantage of this opportunity to raise questions and secure a broad agreement on the rules of the game. If, for example, the rules permit the committee chair to allow only one working paper on a particular subject to go forward to become a resolution, then it needs to be widely understood that multiple resolutions taking the same approach to solving an international problem will be racing each other to enlist sufficient support and to fit the required resolution format, and that redundant resolutions arriving after the first will die without a vote. Thus, knowing and understanding the rules before the conference chair bangs the gavel and calls the conference to order is essential.

APPENDIX A:
UN FACTSHEET

FACT SHEET ON THE UNITED NATIONS ORGANIZATION AND MISSION

Attempting to wade through the mountains of information available on the United Nations can quickly erode your time for researching anything else. The following article was prepared by the State Department for its website, and provides virtually everything your students should know about the actual organization in order to adequately prepare for their MUN experience:

UN Factsheet
Bureau of International Organization Affairs
Washington, D.C.

UNITED NATIONS
Profile of United Nations: Beginnings, Purpose, and Structure

In 1942, President Franklin Roosevelt, flanked by the leaders of twenty-six Allied countries, first coined the term "United Nations" to describe the continued fight against the Axis Powers. Following World War II, the allies adopted the term to define a worldwide body of nations. On June 26, 1945, fifty nations signed the United Nations Charter in San Francisco, California. The United Nations came into effect on October 24, 1945. October 24 is now celebrated around the globe as UN Day.

The United Nations' aims are set out in the preamble to the UN Charter: to maintain international peace and security; to develop friendly relations among nations; to achieve international cooperation in solving economic, social, cultural, and humanitarian problems and in promoting respect for human rights and fundamental freedoms; and to be a center for harmonizing the actions of nations in attaining these common ends.

The principal organs of the United Nations include the Security Council, the General Assembly, the Economic and Social Council (ECOSOC), the International Court of Justice, and the Secretariat. (The Trusteeship Council, an original principal organ, suspended operations in 1994 when it fulfilled its function by overseeing the independence of the UN's last remaining trust territory.)

In addition to its principal organs, the United Nations system is made up of a complex mix of commissions and funds created by the General Assembly, such as UNICEF (UN Children's Fund) and the World Food Program; specialized agencies, such as the World Health Organization and the International Monetary Fund; and other UN entities, such as the Office of the High Commissioner for Human Rights and the peacekeeping missions established by the Security Council.

The headquarters of the United Nations is located in New York City. The General Assembly building and the Secretariat were built in 1949 and 1950 on land donated by the Rockefeller family. The property is now considered international territory. Under special agreement with the United States, certain diplomatic privileges and immunities have been granted, but generally the laws of New York, New York, and the United States apply.

The General Assembly approved the biennial UN program budget for 2012–2013 in the amount of US$ 5.152 billion (Resolution 66/248), including US$ 1.083 billion for political missions that are expected to be extended or approved during the course of the biennium. Areas of increased expenditure—a direct result of additional commitments and priorities set by UN member states—include disarmament and initiatives to strengthen the Office of the High Commissioner for Human Rights and the Rule of Law activities. Among the UN's major program areas are political affairs (25.9%), overall policymaking direction and coordination (14%), and regional cooperation for development (10.3%). The most substantial increase in the UN's program budget over the past decade has resulted from increased requirements for special political missions, growing from US$ 198.4 million 10 years ago to US$ 1.083 billion for 2012–2013. UN staffing for 2012–2013 increased to 10,336 positions, up from 10,307 in 2010–2011. The United States is the major donor to the UN budget, contributing 22% in 2011, followed by Japan (12.53%), Germany (8.018%), and the United Kingdom (6.604%).

The United States and other major UN contributors continue to press for budgetary and administrative reform to make the UN as efficient as possible. In 1999, the United States Government legislated the "Helms-Biden" provision, which authorized the payment of U.S. arrears to the UN and other international organizations upon certification of the Secretary of State that a number of reform goals had been achieved in the UN and major specialized agencies. Between 1999 and 2002, the UN met all required certifications. As a result, the United States cleared over $900 million in arrears to the UN and other organizations. The

Secretary-General submitted a further round of reform initiatives in late 2002, and the United States is advocating and closely monitoring their implementation.

The United Nations currently has 193 member states. The official languages of the United Nations are Arabic, Chinese, English, French, Russian, and Spanish. More information about the UN is available on its website at http://www.un.org.

PRINCIPAL ORGANS
Security Council—New York

The Security Council has five permanent members (China, France, Russia, the United Kingdom, and the U.S.—informally known as the P-5), each with the right to veto, and ten nonpermanent members elected by the General Assembly for two-year terms. Five nonpermanent members are elected from Africa and Asia combined, one nonpermanent member comes from Eastern Europe, two from Latin America, and two from Western Europe and other areas. The 2013–2014 nonpermanent members, elected for two-year terms by the General Assembly, are with end of term date: Argentina (2014); Azerbaijan (2013); Australia (2014); Guatemala (2013); Luxembourg (2014); Morocco (2013); Pakistan (2013); Republic of Korea (2014); Rwanda (2014); and Togo (2013). Over seventy United Nations member states have never been Members of the Security Council. A country that is a Member of the United Nations but not of the Security Council may participate, without a vote, in its discussions when the Council thinks that that country's interests are affected. Both UNSC members and nonmembers of the United Nations, if they are parties to a dispute being considered by the Council, may be invited to take part, without a vote, in the Council's discussions; the Council sets the conditions for participation by a nonmember state. The president (or chair) of the Council rotates monthly in English alphabetical order of the members.

Under the UN Charter, the Security Council has "primary responsibility for the maintenance of international peace and security," and all UN members "agree to accept and carry out the decisions of the Security Council in accordance with the present Charter." Other organs of the UN make recommendations to member governments. The Security Council, however, has the power under the Charter to make decisions that member states must carry out. Unlike other representative bodies, the Security Council is always in session. A representative of each Council member must always be available so that the Council can meet at any time.

Decisions in the 15-member Security Council on all substantive matters require the affirmative votes of nine members, including the support of all five permanent members. A negative vote by a permanent member (also known as a veto) prevents adoption of a proposal that has received the required number of affirmative votes. Abstention is not regarded as a veto.

Under Chapter IV of the Charter, "Pacific Settlement of Disputes," the Security Council "may investigate any dispute, or any situation which might lead to international friction or give rise to a dispute." The Council may "recommend appropriate procedures or methods of adjustment" if it determines that the situation might endanger international peace and security. These recommendations are not binding on UN members.

Under Chapter VII, the Council has broader power to decide what measures are to be taken in situations involving "threats to the peace, breaches of the peace, or acts or aggression." In such situations, the Council is not limited to recommendations but may take action, including the use of armed force "to maintain or restore international peace and security." Decisions taken under Chapter VII, both with regard to military action and to economic sanctions, are binding on all UN member states.

Starting with the UN Truce Supervision Organization (UNTSO) in 1948, the Security Council has dispatched peacekeeping missions to the world's conflicts. These missions have helped prevent or limit many outbreaks of international violence from growing into wider conflicts.

In the wake of the September 11, 2001, attacks on the United States, the Security Council, acting under Chapter VII of the UN Charter, adopted Resolution 1373, which obliges all member states to take action against international terrorism. The resolution also established the Counter-Terrorism Committee within the Council to monitor progress in the war against terrorism and implementation of the resolution.

General Assembly—New York

All UN member states are members of the General Assembly. The Assembly has six main committees: Disarmament and International Security; Economic and Financial; Social, Humanitarian, and Cultural; Special Political and Decolonization; Administrative and Budgetary; and Legal. Other committees address UN procedures, membership, and specific issues, including peacekeeping, outer space, and UN Charter reform.

The General Assembly meets in regular session once a year under a president elected from among the representatives. The regular session usually begins in mid-September and ends in mid-December. Special sessions can be convened at the request of the Security Council, a majority of UN members, or, if the majority concurs, a single member. A special session was held in October 1995 at the head of government level to commemorate the UN's 50th anniversary.

Voting in the General Assembly on important questions is by a two-thirds majority of those present and voting. Voting questions may include recommendations on peace and security; election of members to organs; admission, suspension, and expulsion of members; and budgetary matters. Other questions are decided by majority vote. Each member state has one vote. Apart from the approval of budgetary matters, including the adoption of a scale of assessment, General Assembly resolutions are not binding on the members. The Assembly may make recommendations on any matter within the scope of the UN, except on matters of peace and security under Security Council consideration. Since the late 1980s, virtually all budgetary decisions at the UN have been taken by consensus.

As the only UN organ in which all members are represented, the Assembly serves as a forum for members to launch initiatives on international questions of peace, economic progress, and human rights. It can initiate studies; make recommendations; develop and codify international law; promote human rights; and advance international economic, social, cultural, and educational programs.

The Assembly may take action on maintaining international peace if the Security Council is unable to exercise its primary responsibility, usually due to disagreement among the permanent members. The "Uniting for Peace" resolutions, adopted in 1950, empower the Assembly to convene in emergency special sessions to recommend collective measures—including the use of armed force—in the case of a breach of the peace or act of aggression. Two-thirds of the members must approve any such recommendation. Emergency special sessions under this procedure have been held on ten occasions, most recently in 1997.

Developing countries constitute a majority among the UN's 193 members. Because of their numbers, developing countries are often able to determine the agenda of the Assembly, the character of its debates, and the nature of its decisions. For many developing countries, the UN General Assembly is the source of much of their diplomatic influence and the principal forum for their foreign relations initiatives.

When an issue is considered particularly important, the General Assembly may convene an international conference to focus global attention and build a consensus for consolidated action. High-level U.S. delegations use these opportunities to promote U.S. policy viewpoints and develop international agreements on future activities. Recent examples include

- Under the auspices of ECOSOC, the United States participated in the World Summit on Sustainable Development held in Johannesburg, South Africa, in 2002.

- The UN Conference on Financing for Development, held in Monterrey, Mexico, on March 2002, broke new ground in development discussions with the United States calling for a "new compact for development" defined by greater accountability for rich and poor nations alike.

The General Assembly has also been active in the fight against terrorism. On September 12, 2001, it adopted a resolution condemning the terrorist attacks against the United States. In its 56th and 57th Sessions, the General Assembly also passed resolutions calling on all states to prevent terrorism and to strengthen international cooperation in fighting terrorism.

Economic and Social Council—New York

The General Assembly elects the fifty-four members of the Economic and Social Council (ECOSOC). Eighteen are elected each year for three-year terms. The United States has always been a member.

Under the UN Charter, ECOSOC is responsible for identifying solutions to international economic, social, and health problems, as well as facilitating international cultural and education cooperation and encouraging respect for human rights. ECOSOC meets for one annual four-week session and for shorter ad hoc, procedural, or special meetings. Voting is by simple majority.

ECOSOC coordinates the work of fourteen specialized UN agencies, ten functional commissions, and five regional commissions. Through much of its history, ECOSOC had served primarily as a discussion vehicle. ECOSOC had little authority to force action, which a number of member states felt marginalized the agency's utility. However, beginning in 1992, the United States and other nations began an effort to make ECOSOC more relevant by strengthening its policy responsibilities in economic, social, and related fields, particularly in the area of development.

The resulting reform made ECOSOC the oversight and policy-setting body for UN operational development activities and established smaller executive boards for the UN Development Program (UNDP), UN Population Fund (UNFPA), and UN Children's Fund (UNICEF). The creation of an oversight body and smaller executive boards provides those agencies with operating guidance and promotes more effective management. The reform also gave ECOSOC a strong hand in ensuring that UN agencies coordinated their work on issues of common interest, such as narcotics control, human rights, the alleviation of poverty, and the prevention of HIV/AIDS.

One positive impact of this reform was the manner in which the UN development system began to respond more coherently and efficiently to humanitarian crises around the world. Former General Kofi Annan's reform initiatives have attached considerable importance to further strengthening coordination among relief agencies.

Another positive reform outcome was the ECOSOC decision in 1994 to authorize the creation of the Joint United Nations Program on HIV/AIDS (UNAIDS). This Program acts as the main advocate for worldwide action against HIV/AIDS and has brought together into one consolidated global program the AIDS-related resources and expertise of UNICEF, UNDP, UNFPA, UNESCO, the UN International Drug Control Program, the World Health Organization, the International Labor Organization, and the World Bank. UNAIDS has been instrumental in the expanded global response to HIV/AIDS, eliminating duplication among agencies and enhancing the ability of member states to respond effectively to the AIDS pandemic. UNAIDS began operating in January 1996.

International Court of Justice—The Hague, Netherlands

The International Court of Justice (ICJ) is the principal judicial organ of the UN. It was established in June 1945 by the Charter of the United Nations and began work in April 1946.

The seat of the Court is at the Peace Palace in The Hague (Netherlands). Of the six principal organs of the United Nations, it is the only one not located in New York (United States of America).

The Court's role is to settle, in accordance with international law, legal disputes submitted to it by States and to give advisory opinions on legal questions referred to it by authorized United Nations organs and specialized agencies.

The Court is composed of fifteen judges, who are elected for terms of office of nine years by the United Nations General Assembly and the Security Council. It is assisted by a Registry, its administrative organ. Its official languages are English and French.

Judges serve for nine years and may be reelected. No two may be nationals of the same country. One-third of the Court is elected every three years. A U.S. citizen has always been a member of the Court. Questions before the Court are decided by a majority of judges present.

Only states may be parties in cases before the International Court of Justice. This requirement does not preclude private interests from being the subject of proceedings if one state brings a case against another. Jurisdiction of the Court is based on the consent of each UN member state to comply with an ICJ decision in a case to which it is a party. Any judgments reached are binding. If a party fails to perform its obligations under an ICJ decision, the other party may seek recourse in the Security Council.

Among the ICJ's most contentious cases in recent years were disputes between Nicaragua and Costa Rica over construction of a road along the San Juan River (2011), between Cambodia and Thailand over interpretation of an ICJ ruling of June 1962 involving the Temple of Preah Vihear (2011), and between Australia and Japan over whaling in the Antarctic (2010).

The US has also been party of ICJ adjudicated disputes, including the following:

- A complaint by the U.S. in 1980 that Iran was detaining American diplomats in Tehran in violation of international law.
- A complaint filed by Iran in 1992 alleging that the United States violated a treaty obligation by attacking three Iranian oil platforms. The U.S. filed a counter-claim with respect to Iranian attacks on U.S. shipping interests in the Persian Gulf.
- A dispute over the course of the maritime boundary dividing the U.S. and Canada in the Gulf of Maine area, filed in 1981, judgment in 1984.

Secretariat—New York

The Secretariat is composed of international civil servants who carry out the daily tasks of the United Nations. It provides studies, information, and facilities needed by UN bodies for their meetings. It also carries out tasks as directed by the Security Council, the General Assembly, the Economic and Social Council, and other UN bodies. The Charter provides that the staff be chosen by application of the "highest standards of efficiency, competence, and integrity," with due regard for the importance of recruiting on a wide geographical basis.

The Charter provides that the staff shall not seek or receive instructions from any authority other than the UN. Each UN member is obligated to respect the international character of the Secretariat and not seek to influence its staff.

Under the UN Charter, the chief administrative officer of the UN and the head of the Secretariat is the Secretary-General of the United Nations, appointed to a five-year term by the General Assembly on the recommendation of the Security Council. On January 1, 2007, Ban Ki-moon of the Republic of Korea became the eighth Secretary-General of the United Nations, bringing to his post thirty-seven years of service both in government and on the global stage. On June 21, 2011, he was unanimously reelected by the General Assembly and will continue to serve until December 31, 2016.

The Secretary-General's duties include helping resolve international disputes, administering peacekeeping operations, organizing international conferences, gathering information on the implementation of Security Council decisions, and consulting with member governments regarding various initiatives. The Secretary-General may bring to the attention of the Security Council any matter that, in his or her opinion, may threaten international peace and security. The Secretary-General also appoints Special Representatives and Envoys to mediate conflict in the world's trouble spots.

Trusteeship Council

The UN Charter established the Trusteeship Council and assigned it the task of supervising the administration of Trust Territories placed under the System. All the territories attained self-government or independence by October 1994. The Trusteeship Council therefore suspended operation on November 1, 1994.

THE UN FAMILY

In addition to the principal UN organs, the UN family includes over sixty programs or specialized agencies, often headquartered in one of the UN offices around the world. Some agencies existed prior to UN creation and are related to it by agreement. Others were established by the General Assembly. Each provides expertise in a specific area. Some of those programs and agencies (with the location of their headquarters) are described below. A diagram of the entire UN system can be found at http://www.un.org/en/aboutun/structure/org_chart.shtml

Funds and Programs

UN Children's Fund (UNICEF). New York City. UNICEF provides long-term humanitarian and developmental assistance to children and mothers in developing countries. UNICEF relies on contributions from governments and private donors. Its programs emphasize developing community-level services to promote the health and well being of children. UNICEF was awarded the Nobel Peace Prize in 1965.

UN Development Program (UNDP). New York City. UNDP is the largest multilateral source of grant technical assistance in the world. Voluntarily funded, it provides expert advice, training, and limited equipment to developing countries, with increasing emphasis on assistance to the poorest countries. It focuses on six areas of assistance: democratic governance, poverty reduction, crisis prevention and recovery, energy and the environment, information technology, and HIV/AIDS.

UN Environment Program (UNEP). Nairobi, Kenya. UNEP coordinates UN environmental activities, assisting developing countries in implementing environmentally sound policies. UNEP has developed guidelines and treaties on issues such as the international transport of potentially harmful chemicals, transboundary air pollution, and the contamination of international waterways.

The UN High Commissioner for Refugees (UNHCR). Geneva, Switzerland. UNHCR protects and supports refugees at the request of a government or the UN and assists in their return or resettlement. UNHCR was awarded the Nobel Peace Prize in 1954 and 1981.

World Food Program (WFP). Rome, Italy. The WFP distributes food commodities to long-term refugees and displaced persons, and provides emergency food assistance during natural and man-made disasters. In addition, the World Food Program's Purchase for Progress (P4P) has expanded to twenty countries since its launch in 2008, bringing together demand, supply, credit, and policy actors to support the development of small farmer organizations, providing them with technical expertise as well as credits. Over 193,000 farmers, agricultural technicians, warehouse operators and small and medium traders have received training from WFP and partners in improved agricultural production, postharvest handling, quality assurance, group marketing, agricultural finance, and contracting with WFP. Almost 300,000 metric tons of food valued at US$ 115 million has been contracted, either directly from farmers' organizations and small and medium traders or through innovative marketing platforms such as Commodity Exchanges and Warehouse Receipt Systems.

Specialized Agencies

Food and Agriculture Organization (FAO). Rome, Italy. FAO programs seek to raise levels of nutrition and standards of living; to improve agricultural productivity, to promote rural development; and, by these means, to provide access of all people at all times to the food they need for an active and healthy life.

International Civil Aviation Organization (ICAO). Montreal, Canada. ICAO develops the principles and techniques of international air navigation and fosters the planning and development of international air transport to ensure safe and orderly growth. The ICAO Council adopts standards and makes recommendations concerning air navigation, the prevention of unlawful interference, and the facilitation of border-crossing procedures for international civil aviation.

International Labour Organization (ILO). Geneva, Switzerland. The ILO seeks to strengthen worker rights, improve working and living conditions, create employment, and provide information and training opportunities. ILO programs include the occupational safety and health hazard alert system and the labor standards and human rights programs.

International Maritime Organization (IMO). London, England. The IMO's main objective is to facilitate cooperation among governments on technical matters affecting international shipping to achieve the highest possible degree of maritime safety and navigational efficiency. It also attempts to improve the marine environment through the prevention of pollution caused by ships and other craft and deals with legal matters connected with international shipping.

International Monetary Fund (IMF). Washington, D.C. The purposes of the IMF are to promote international monetary cooperation through consultation and collaboration, to promote exchange stability and orderly exchange arrangements, and to assist in the establishment of a multilateral system of payments and the elimination of foreign exchange restrictions.

International Telecommunication Union (ITU). Geneva, Switzerland. The ITU brings together governments to coordinate the establishment and operation of global communication networks and services, including telegraph, telephone, radio communications, Internet, and the information society. It fosters cooperation and partnership among its members and offers technical assistance in this area.

UN Educational, Scientific and Cultural Organization (UNESCO). Paris, France. UNESCO's purpose is to contribute to peace and security by promoting cooperation among nations through education, science, culture, and communication to further universal respect for justice, the rule of law, human rights, and fundamental freedoms without distinction of race, sex, language, or religion.

Universal Postal Union (UPU). Bern, Switzerland. The UPU attempts to secure the organization and improvement of the postal services, to promote international collaboration, and provide technical assistance in this area. The member countries constitute a single postal territory.

World Intellectual Property Organization (WIPO). Geneva, Switzerland. The purpose of WIPO is to promote international cooperation in the field of intellectual property rights. It works in the areas of both industrial and literary-artistic property.

World Meteorological Organization (WMO). Geneva, Switzerland. WMO coordinates global scientific activity to allow increasingly prompt and accurate weather prediction and other services for public, private, and commercial use.

World Health Organization (WHO). Geneva, Switzerland. WHO acts as a coordinating authority on pressing global public health issues. WHO's objective, as set out in its Constitution, is the attainment of all peoples of the highest possible level of health.

Other Related Bodies

World Bank. Washington, D.C. The World Bank is one of the world's main sources of development assistance. It focuses on the poorest people in the poorest countries.

International Atomic Energy Agency (IAEA). Vienna, Austria. The roles of IAEA are to promote the contribution of atomic energy for peace, health, and prosperity throughout the world and to enhance the safety and security of radioactive materials and nuclear facilities worldwide. It has the responsibility of creating and implementing the safeguard provisions of various nuclear non-proliferation and nuclear free zone treaties.

U.S. Representation

The U.S. Permanent Mission to the UN in New York is headed by the U.S. Representative to the UN, with the rank of Ambassador Extraordinary and Plenipotentiary. Samantha Power has been named to serve in that position. The mission acts as the channel of communication for the U.S. Government with the UN organs, agencies, and commissions at the UN headquarters and with the other permanent missions accredited to the UN and the nonmember observer missions. The U.S. mission has a professional staff made up largely of career Foreign Service officers, including specialists in political, economic, social, financial, legal, and military issues.

The United States also maintains missions to international organizations in Geneva, Rome, Vienna, Nairobi, Montreal, and Paris. These missions report to the Department of State and receive guidance on questions of policy from the President, through the Secretary of State. The Assistant Secretary of State for International Organization Affairs coordinates relations with the UN and its family of agencies.

The U.S. Mission to the United Nations is located at 140 E. 45th Street, New York, NY 10017 (212-415-4000). More information about the U.S. Mission to the UN is available on the mission's website at http://www.un.int/usa.

APPENDIX B:
AWARDS CRITERIA

Although many conferences attempt to give the impression that awards are not important and that the key reason for the conference's existence is education, solving the world's problems, etc., virtually all of them actually give awards to individuals and sometimes to schools. So you might as well compete for them.

Judging for awards can be conducted by the chairs of the committees, other members of the Secretariat, outside experts, faculty members, the sponsors of the participating schools, or even the participants. School awards are usually based on summing the performances of all of the delegations from a participating school, with weight given for the more senior awards. Sometimes the absolute number of awards, weighted or unweighted, is considered, sometimes it is divided by the number of students attending. (One unique method, used in the past by the National Model Arab League, gives individual awards, even to paired delegations. It is thus possible for partners to get different awards. We are not persuaded that putting partners in competition with each other is the best way to go.) Each method has its benefits and disadvantages. Make sure you know who is judging your students before you arrive.

In addition to delegates, sometimes conferences will give awards to Chairs (determined by vote by the coaches who have visited all of the committees) and to coaches. Criteria for the latter can include attempts by the Secretariat to make up for grave administrative errors in treating a school, in addition to criteria you might otherwise expect. In some instances, you can nominate colleagues for the best coach award.

Some conferences will admit their competitive nature up front, and will provide discussions of their awards criteria. One of the most complete awards guidelines we have seen is from the Prince William MUN, hosted by C.D. Hylton Senior High School in Woodbridge, Virginia. The conference is one of the largest high school-hosted MUNs on the east coast, with some eight hundred students and faculty members attending. Here's what the PWMUN Secretariat tells its participants:

PRINCE WILLIAM (PWMUN—C.D. HYLTON SR. HIGH SCHOOL) JUDGING CRITERIA

Judging criteria have elicited tremendous debate among both the student-delegates and the faculty. We therefore establish the following and strongly urge the adherence of these guidelines.

All decisions on recognition of outstanding performance will be made by the committee staff assigned to that particular committee. For each committee, there shall be two delegation awards: a best delegation and an outstanding delegation. Each committee is recommended to have no more than two honorable mentions, but these are not mandatory. The use of honorable mentions is under the discretion of the Chair. For the PWMUN Conference there will be three Secretariat awards: The Secretary General's Award for Best Delegation, the Director General's Award for Merit, and the Director General's Award for Honor. In order to be fair to all participating schools, the Secretariat awards shall be decided by overall performance of country delegations. The award will be given to the school with the best country delegation.

The following criteria are listed in order of importance:

1. **The ability of a delegate to accurately and knowledgeably follow his or her country's policies on the issues under discussion**
   Accurate policy representation is a must if realism is to be achieved. However, if a delegate is representing a country that rarely speaks in the UN, the delegate should not do that during the simulation. All delegates should actively participate in all debates and caucusing whether or not their country would do so in the actual UN.

2. **Realistic and characteristic role-play as a diplomat and delegate to the UN**
   Compromise and negotiation should be the goal of each delegate. (*Authors' Note:* We believe that the purpose of a delegation is to express the views of the government of their country, and to get the best deal they can. Certain pariah countries' policies are inherently nonnegotiable. Your Chairs will understand that.) Those who display these qualities will make the proper impression. Team delegations will be evaluated on how well they cooperate in fulfilling the delegations' responsibilities. There should not be an aggressive, bullying style of diplomacy during speaking or caucusing. Of course, there is a proper time for a delegate to speak with force, deep conviction, or even anger; there will, and should be, intense debate. Delegates should use proper diplomatic language at all times, avoid histrionics, and assuredly engage in no name-calling or other derogatory or prejudicial remarks.

3. **Caucusing Ability**

   Delegates will be noted for their participation in and constructive contributions to the caucuses. It is not necessary to be the "leader" of the caucus, but to be actively involved.

4. **Use of the Rules of Procedure**

   All delegates should have a good working knowledge of the rules. Such use of the rules that contribute to the smooth workings of the committee will be rewarded; obstructive use of the rules will result in unfavorable judging.

5. **Speaking Ability**

   This criterion is of lesser importance. All delegates, however, regardless of their level of eloquence, should actively participate in giving speeches.

6. **Proper Attire**

   Delegates must at a minimum be in proper business attire; at least a shirt and tie for men and a dress (or the equivalent) for women.

7. **Policy Papers**

   PWMUN does not require a policy paper. Country delegation papers are, however, strongly encouraged, and they should be handed in at the registration desk. Papers should express an extensive knowledge of the country being represented and should include a policy statement on each issue being addressed in the committees to which the country is assigned. There will be an award presented to the country delegation with the best delegation policy paper. Also, the presence of a policy paper could be a determining factor for the Secretariat awards should there be a tie.

It is important that all delegates be aware of these criteria and understand what we expect of them at the conference. The key to a successful conference is cooperation, negotiation, and proper diplomatic behavior. Furthermore, no delegate or delegation will be judged by the number of resolutions it introduces or sponsors. Resolutions should be the result of caucusing and be the product of several nations.

Authors' Note: You should keep in mind that the priorities articulated in the judging criteria documents of a conference might not be the same as what the judges actually use. Personal preferences on the criteria may well differ across committee chairs, as well as the ability of the Chairs to know whether a delegation is actually in character. One cannot expect high school-level Secretariat members to know the positions of every member of the 193 UN members on every issue in each committee, yet that is precisely what the judging criteria you may see will require of the chairs in order to make a fair evaluation for awards. It is also logistically difficult for the chair to be aware of how effective a delegate is in corridor caucusing while the chair is running the meeting in the conference room. You'll note that the *quality* of one's speeches does not appear in the aforementioned criteria. In some instances, chairs will simply tally every time a delegate speaks, regardless of length, substance, or eloquence of the address; a "let's recess" speech may well have the same weight as a well-argued general debate speech. What this means to you is that you will often disagree with a chair's decisions on awards.

What ultimately matters is whether you—the coach—believe that your students deserved the awards, no matter what the chairs announced. If you're proud of their performance, let them know it, loudly. Your support will mean more to them in the long run than a trophy case full of gavels. In your postconference meeting with your students, get them to reflect on what they observed that impressed them—both the good and the not so good. And of course share with them the positive things you observed and get them to reflect on how they can improve their performances. They are often their own harshest critics. You should be their biggest booster.

APPENDIX C:
SAMPLE BACKGROUND GUIDE

Background Guide

Earlier background guides can be found at www.potomacbooksinc.com:

BACKGROUND GUIDE: CYBER SECURITY/CYBER WARFARE
By Taruni Paleru and Manjari Kumarappan

My First MUN IX Training Conference
Saturday, Oct. 13, 2012

George C. Marshall High School
7731 Leesburg Pike
Falls Church, Virginia

Table of Contents
Welcome Delegates!
Introduction to Model United Nations: What is MUN? What Is a Background
    Guide, and How Do I Use It?
Introduction to Cyber Security and History of Cyber Warfare
Current State of Cyber Warfare

WELCOME DELEGATES!

Welcome to "My First MUN IX." For most of you, this MUN Training Conference will be your introduction to Model United Nations, an academic simulation of the United Nations that aims to educate participants about current events, topics in international relations, diplomacy, and the United Nations agenda. Because "My First MUN IX" is a training conference for novice MUNers, there is only one topic up for discussion—cyber security/cyber warfare. As Model UN delegates, you will role-play as a diplomat representing either one of the UN's 193-member countries, or as the leader of an international corporation.

At the conference, you will represent your country (or corporation) in a simulated UN committee session of the General Assembly. In advance of the conference, we ask that you do four things: (1) research your assigned country or corporation (your faculty advisor will know the countries/corporations assigned to your school); (2) write a one-minute statement of your country/corporation's position on the topic (cyber security/cyber warfare) and bring it with you to the conference; (3) dress the part—western business attire (shirt and tie for young men and skirt and blouse/dress/pants suit for young women); and (4) come prepared to learn and practice the essential MUN skills of Internet research, writing position papers and resolutions, and public speaking.

This conference consists of two main parts. The morning session consists of large group instruction on the essential knowledge and skills needed to do well at future MUN conferences. These morning sessions are presented by veterans of MUN, history and government teachers at Marshall High School, and experts in the field of foreign policy. The afternoon committee sessions will simulate what delegates can expect to encounter at competitive MUN conferences. Each delegate will represent a country or international corporation active in the field of cyber security. These small group sessions will be chaired by students active in the University of Virginia's International Relations Organization (IRO). These sessions will operate under procedural rules developed for the IRO's annual VAMUN high school conference.

Led by Secretaries-General Monika Bapna and Jasmine Oo, the Steering Committee and its faculty advisors began work on this conference last May in hopes that it would encourage your successful participation in future MUN conferences.

In taking on the challenge of a topic as complex as cyber security, the Steering Committee held firm to the idea that it was not beyond the comprehension of high school and middle school students. We have included in this background guide a glossary and a set of general and country-specific websites to aid in your research. We trust you will find them helpful. We hope your active participation in the afternoon simulations will bear out our confidence that this topic is a timely and interesting one. And finally, if we have inspired in you an excitement and enthusiasm for MUN, then we will judge this conference a success.

Sincerely,

Assistant Secretaries-General for Policy,

Taruni Paleru

Manjari Kumarappan

SECTION 1—INTRODUCTION TO MODEL UNITED NATIONS
What is MUN?[1] What is a Background Guide, and how do I use it?

Q: What is Model United Nations?

A: Model United Nations is an authentic simulation of the UN General Assembly and other multilateral bodies.

Q: How did Model UN begin?

A: Simulating international organizations began even before the birth of the United Nations, when students held a series of Model League of Nations in the 1920s. The Model UN Program is a successor to a student-directed simulation of what preceded the UN itself, but it is not documented exactly how the Model UN began.

Q: Who participates in Model United Nations?

A: The popularity of Model UN continues to grow, and today more than 400,000 middle school, high school, and college/university students worldwide participate every year. Many of today's leaders in law, government, business, and the arts participated in Model UN during their academic careers—from U.S. Supreme Court Justice Stephen Breyer and former World Court Justice

---

1 United Nations Cyberschoolbus, http://cyberschoolbus.un.org/modelun/faq.html.

Stephen M. Schwebel to actor Samuel L. Jackson. Former first daughter Chelsea Clinton is a Model UN veteran as well.

Q: What is a Model United Nations conference?

A: Some Model UN exercises take place in the classroom and others are schoolwide. Still others are regional, national, or even international. These are called conferences, and the events are much larger, with participants from all over the United States and the world. More than one million people have participated in MUN conferences around the world since the conferences became popular over 50 years ago. Today there are more than 400 conferences that take place in 35 countries. Depending on the location, the average conference can have as few as 30 students or as many as 2,000.

Q: Where and when are Model United Nations conferences held?

A: There are an estimated 400 Model UN conferences held annually worldwide. These conferences take place virtually every month throughout the school year, but there are few events in the summer and even fewer around times of standardized testing such as the SAT.

Q: What is a Model United Nations delegate?

A: A Model UN delegate is a student who assumes the role of an ambassador to the United Nations at a Model UN event. A Model UN delegate does not have to have experience in international relations. Anyone can participate in Model UN, so long as they have the ambition to learn something new, and to work with people to try and make a difference in the world. Model UN students tend to go on to become great leaders in politics, law, business, education, and even medicine.

Q: Why should I participate in Model United Nations?

A: You should participate in Model UN because it promotes student and teacher interest in international relations and related subjects, increases the capacity for students to engage in problem solving, teaches aspects of conflict resolution, research skills, and communication skills, and creates the opportunity to meet new people and make new friends.

Q: What are some of the educational benefits of Model United Nations?

A: For over 50 years now, teachers and students have benefited from and enjoyed this interactive learning experience. It not only involves young people in the study and discussion of global issues, but also encourages the development of skills useful throughout their lives, such as research, writing, public speaking, problem solving, consensus building, conflict resolution, and compromise and cooperation.

Q: What is a Background Guide? And how is it used?

A: An MUN Background Guide is the document issued by the organization hosting an MUN Conference. It is intended to serve as an introduction to the conference and, more importantly, to the topic that the committee to which you have been assigned will take up. The Background Guide will typically include Questions to Consider, background information on the topic itself, and sources to consult—these are usually websites that have been prescreened by the conference organizers and have been determined to be authoritative and relevant to the topic. These sources may present a particular point of view so do not regard them as unbiased.

For this conference, because it is a learning conference, we have also provided two Internet sources for each assigned country/corporation—one from the government/corporate and one from a nongovernment source. You will find them listed in the Resource Guide. Use the background guide to help you identify your country/corporation's position on cyber security/cyber warfare. We have also provided a glossary at the back of this Background Guide to aid in your understanding of key terms related to the topic. When these terms appear in the text, they will appear in **boldface**. That is your cue to search them out in the glossary.

SECTION 2—INTRODUCTION TO CYBER SECURITY AND HISTORY OF CYBER WARFARE

The worldwide community of Internet users—including individuals, governments, business interests, and institutions—view the Internet as essential to modern life, a means not only for private and business communications, but also as a network used continuously by governments and corporations. Computer-based systems operating over the Internet are used to transact business and run vital infrastructure, including electric power grids, transportation and communication systems, and financial networks. This infrastructure includes in-country computer networks, such as those that control airports, train and commuter rail operations, cell telephone systems, stock exchanges, and power supply stations. But computer-based systems extend as well to international infrastructure that serves markets well beyond a single nation state. For that reason, the development, stability, and security of cyber systems has generated heightened interest among not only the governments of nation states, but also corporations operating within them and regionally or internationally. "Malicious activities, such as denial of service attacks, spam, viruses, phishing scams, and other fraudulent activities, abuse the freedoms of the Internet. Such activities can cause damage to others and interfere with the right of everyone to a safe and rewarding online environment."[2]

Efforts to secure the World Wide Web against malicious activities—whether generated by hackers, terrorists, private profit-driven interests engaged in espionage directed against business interests or governments, or by agencies of nation states engaged in cyber warfare—are proving difficult in part because of the nature of the Internet. While efforts to protect individual computer users from service interruptions generally enjoy broad public support in the developed world, solutions to Internet security problems are not so easily agreed upon. Solutions that are proportionate to the problem and that do not diminish the potential for the Internet to improve the quality of life for people around the world appear to hold the most promise.

This Background Guide (and the conference it supports) focuses on two aspects of cyber security. The first are the threats posed to critical national and international infrastructure—communications, power systems, transportation, and financial networks—and what constructive role the United Nations can play in promoting actions by its 193-member nation states to advance the security of this vital infrastructure. The second arises from events of recent years that have seen the development of cyber weapons used by one or more states against other states. This opening of a new battlefield for state-against-state conflict—conflict that could lead to retaliatory conventional warfare—would seem to make obvious the need for the United Nations to take on an expanded peacekeeping role.

Understanding the current state of cyber security and the threat posed to vital national and international infrastructure by cyber attacks, including cyber warfare, requires an acquaintance with the history of cyber threats, which follows below. This Background Guide also examines the current state of cyber warfare and actions taken or proposed by the United Nations to address threats posed by those who would use the Internet for destructive or other illegal purposes. And finally, this guide raises for delegates to this training conference a number of questions to consider as you research and develop your respective country's (or corporation's) position on how best to secure the Internet and prevent cyber conflict and its destructive consequences.

History of Cyber Warfare

Cyber warfare is "the digital warfare against digital infrastructure."[3] A nation-state can attack another nation-state's power grids, communication networks, govern-

---

2 The Internet Society, September 5, 2012, http://www.internetsociety.org

3 Michael Aguilar, *2010 General Assembly First Committee*. n.d. National Model United Nations. Washington D.C., 2010.

ment websites and servers, and other assets through computers. The attack can be initiated by a nation-state, a nonstate actor such as a terrorist or criminal group, and sometimes a terrorist or criminal group representing a nation-state.

The start of Cyber Warfare dates back to the 1970s when John Shoch, an engineer at Palo Alto Research Center, created a program called "tapeworm," which was developed to find idle computers, boot up a host machine through the network and replicate by sending copies of itself to other machines and to remain in contact with the replicated worms.[4] This program was accidentally leaked and what had started as an attempt to save time led to a release of similar **worms** across the world with the motive of gaining information and control. Today these "ancestor worms" have evolved into highly sophisticated weapons for cyber warfare. In the early twenty-first century they were able to compromise computers and create **Botnet farms**. The ability to gain information through the use of cyber warfare influenced the creation of Internet Mafias, such as the Russian Business Network (RBN), throughout the world. In 2005, allegations were made against hackers in China for attacking computers in the United States.[5] On August 13, 2006, Microsoft was attacked by **Botnet Herders** using worms known as **Bagles**. Once the Herders had spotted **wormholes**, they installed their bot program and created a network of one million **"zombie" computers**. By downloading their program, herders were able to control specific systems and obtained information without Microsoft's knowledge. There were also attacks spreading internationally such as the Lethic **Botnet**, which at its most successful time was responsible for 8 to 10 percent of all the spam sent worldwide. In response to the increased number of Botnet farms, the U.S. Federal Bureau of Investigation created an operation known as **"Bot Roast."** Even with the FBI's operation, NASA confirmed that laptops in the International Space Station had been detected with the worm.

In 2003, what appears to have been the first in a series of coordinated attacks on a nation's computer system was launched against companies and government agencies in the United States. Known today as **Titan Rain**, the attacks persisted for at least three years. The attacks were labeled as Chinese in origin, although their precise nature, e.g., state-sponsored espionage, corporate espionage, or random hacker attacks, and their real identities—masked by proxy, zombie computer, spyware/virus infected—remains unknown but has been classified as an **Advanced**

---

4 Craig Fosnock, *Computer Worms: Past, Present, and Future*. n.d., East Carolina University.

5 "The History of Cyber Warfare." *Lewis University Online*. Lewis University, n.d. Web. September 7, 2012, http://online.lewisu.edu/the-history-of-cyber-warfare.asp.

Persistent Threat or APT. In early December 2005, the director of the SANS Institute, a security institute in the United States, said that the attacks were "most likely the result of Chinese military hackers attempting to gather information on U.S. systems."[6] Titan Rain hackers gained access to many U.S. defense contractor computer networks, including those at Lockheed Martin, Sandia National Laboratories, Redstone Arsenal, and NASA.

The first all-out attack on a single country's Internet infrastructure occurred in April 2007. The target was the tiny Eastern European nation of Estonia, a country with a reputation as being the most "wired" in the world. Cyber attacks there swamped websites of Estonian organizations, including the nation's parliament, banks, ministries, newspapers, and broadcasters. It occurred at the same time as the country's dispute with neighboring Russia about the relocation of a World War II bronze statue, an ornate Soviet-era grave marker. Most of the attacks affecting the Estonian public were **Distributed Denial of Service** attacks ranging from single individuals using various methods to large-scale **spamming** and the use of botnets. Many experts reckoned that the onslaught on Estonia was of a level of sophistication not seen before. The attack on Estonia's Internet infrastructure has been studied intensively by many countries and military planners. At the time it occurred, it appears to have been one of the largest instances of state-sponsored cyber warfare, second only to the Titan Rain attack on U.S. infrastructure. The Estonian foreign minister accused the Kremlin of direct involvement in the cyber attacks, but on September 6, 2007, Estonia's defense minister admitted he had no evidence linking cyber attacks to Russian authorities.[7]

In late 2008, international predators hacked both the State Bank of India and the Pentagon; the hackers are supposedly from Pakistan and Russia respectively.[8] On January 8, 2009, pro-Hamas websites were targeted by Israeli students who developed a program to attack citizens' computers. In the summer of 2009, Russian software costing approximately $26 succeeded in compromising U.S. drones and intercepting live video feeds.[9] A **zero-day attack** was launched in December 2009 and companies in the United States such as Google were hacked. An unknown country stole intellectual property, and China denied any involvement with this attack.

---

6 "Titan Rain," Wikipedia, September 7, 2012.

7 Wikipedia, "2007 cyberattacks on Estonia," http://en.wikipedia.org/wiki/2007_cyberattacks_on_Estonia.

8 "The History of Cyber Warfare."

9 Ibid.

SECTION 3—CURRENT STATE OF CYBER WARFARE

Cyber Warfare entered the major headlines with the Distributed Denial of Service attack against Estonia, a small but intensively "Internet wired" Baltic nation in 2007 and again in 2008 during the Georgian-Russian War.[10]

In June 2010, Iran took center stage as victim of **Stuxnet**, a computer virus found in power plants, traffic control systems, and factories around the world. Its vast capabilities include the ability to increase the pressure inside nuclear reactors and switch off oil pipelines while still indicating to system operators that everything was normal. Stuxnet is much more complex than the average virus, apparently through its exploitation of twenty zero days.[11] The code within Stuxnet was targeted at the centrifuges that isolate uranium in Iran's enrichment facilities. The Washington Institute for Science and International Security (ISIS) believes that Stuxnet resulted in physical damage in 2010 to a thousand centrifuges at Natanz, Iran's main enrichment facility.[12]

The Iranian government acknowledged that the virus's infection of its unfinished Bushehr Nuclear Facility could lead to a national electricity blackout, if turned on. In response, Iran called for hackers to join the Iranian Revolutionary Guard, which supposedly is the second-largest online army in the world. In June 2012, the *New York Times* reported that from his first months in office, U.S. president Barack Obama secretly ordered increasingly sophisticated attacks on the computer systems that run Iran's main nuclear enrichment facilities, significantly expanding America's first sustained use of cyber weapons. Mr. Obama decided to accelerate the attacks—begun in the Bush administration and code-named Olympic Games—even after an element of the program accidentally became public in the summer of 2010 because of a programming error that allowed it to escape Iran's Natanz plant and sent it around the world on the Internet. Computer security experts who began studying the worm, which had been developed by the United States and Israel, gave it a name: Stuxnet.[13]

Flame is another computer virus. It was discovered in 2012, but the exact date of the release of the virus is unknown. This program was identified by the MAHER Center of Iranian National CERT, the Russian Kaspersky Lab, and the Laboratory

---

10 "Special Event on Cybersecurity and Development," *ECOSOC.* United Nations, December 9, 2011, September 10, 2012, http://www.un.org/en/ecosoc/cybersecurity/summary.pdf.

11 Patrick Clair, "Stuxnet: the first weapon made out of code," n.d., http://www.patrickclair.com/2011/06/stuxnet-anatomy-of-computer-virus-from.html, accessed September 7, 2012.

12 Ibid

13 David E. Sanger, "Obama Order Sped Up Wave of Cyberattacks Against Iran" *New York Times*, June 12, 2012, http://www.nytimes.com/2012/06/01/world/middleeast/obama-ordered-wave-of-cyberattacks-against-iran.html?pagewanted=all&_moc.semityn.

of Cryptography and System Security of the Budapest University of Technology and Economics. The discovery was made after the United Nations International Telecommunications Union asked Kaspersky Lab to investigate the virus infecting Iranian Oil Ministry computers. In the investigation, the Lab found a virus with a filename of MD5# on only customer machines from Middle Eastern nations. The initial point of entry of Flame is unknown, but it is capable of spreading through USB drives to local networks. Its main goal is to gather information by revealing hidden passwords, recording audio through attached microphones, capturing screenshots of important programs such as instant messaging services, and collecting information from nearby Bluetooth devices. Flame will then upload this information to command and control servers.

The Kaspersky Lab also discovered the latest cyber surveillance virus called Gauss, and Kaspersky officials believe that it was made by the same laboratories as Stuxnet and is related to Flame and Duqu (another computer worm found in 2011).[14] Gauss can spy on banking transactions and steal usernames and passwords. It has infected more than 2,500 personal computers, with the majority of victims in Lebanon, Israel, and the Palestinian territories.

SECTION 4—UN ACTIONS AGAINST CYBER WARFARE
UN involvement:

Both the United Nations Economic and Social Council (ECOSOC) and the UN's Department of Economic and Social Affairs (DESA) address issues regarding cyber security and cyber warfare. The ECOSOC's objective on this matter is to build international awareness of cyber security issues and influence international policymaking. It also wants to observe regional policies and initiatives around the world and find a strong global response to cyber warfare. ECOSOC created an intergovernmental expert group on identity-related crime in 2004. Within the ECOSOC is the United Nations Commission on Science and Technology for Development (CSTD). CSTD is aware of the increasing cyber attacks and emphasizes the need for a new proficient team to combat them. The International Telecommunications Union (ITU) is a UN agency that has been taking the lead role in addressing cyber security and cyber warfare. The ITU set up a high-level expert group that created the cyber security agenda in 2007 and plays a crucial role in combating cybercrime, building capacity, and child online protection with other committees of the UN.

---

14 "Gauss Virus: Stuxnet-like Cyberweapon Hits Middle East Banks," GE Investigations Blog. N.p., n.d., September 10, 2012, http://geinvestigations.com/blog/2012/08/gauss-virus-stuxnet-like-cyberweapon-hits-middle-east-banks/.

In 1998, the Russian government introduced a resolution in the First Committee of the General Assembly (GA)—known more commonly as DISEC or the Disarmament and International Security Committee—which deals with disarmament and related international security questions. This resolution coincided with the year in which there was a significant increase in the threat level of Internet hosts.[15] The United States objected to the resolution, but in 2010, a Group of Governmental Experts (GGE) had convened under DISEC, revealing that the United States had reversed its position on the resolution and for the first time has cosponsored a draft resolution on cyber security.[16] In September 2011, Russia joined with China, Tajikistan, and Uzbekistan in proposing an "international code of conduct for information security."

A UN-sponsored World Conference on International Telecommunications is scheduled to be held in December (December 3–14) of 2012 in Dubai, United Arab Emirates. It is expected to involve a referendum on several Internet governance policy initiatives such as cyber security, regulation of traffic routing, spam, and data protection.[17]

UN General Assembly Resolution A/Res/64/211 of March 17, 2010— "Creation of a global culture of cybersecurity and taking stock of national efforts to protect critical information Infrastructures"—http://daccess-dds-ny.un.org/doc /UNDOC/GEN/N09/474/49/PDF/N0947449.pdf?OpenElement.

This resolution reviews all past actions taken by the General Assembly since 2000 to advance cyber security. Passed by the General Assembly in March 2010, this Resolution affirms the right of each country to determine its own critical information infrastructures. It also:

- Calls for enhanced efforts to close the digital divide in order to achieve universal access to information and communications technologies and to protect critical information infrastructures by facilitating the transfer of information technology and capacity-building to developing countries; and . . .
- Recognizes national efforts should be supported by international information-sharing and collaboration, so as to effectively confront the increasingly transnational nature of such [cyber] threats; and . . .

15 Tim Maurer, "Cyber Norm Emergence at the United Nations—An Analysis of the Activities at the UN Regarding Cyber-security," Harvard Kennedy School - Belfer Center for Science and International Affairs, http://belfer-center.ksg.harvard.edu/files/maurer-cyber norm-dp-2011-11-final.pdf. Accessed September 10, 2012.

16 "TSG IntelBrief: The Evolution of Cyber Governance," http://www.soufangroup.com/briefs/details/?Article _Id=330, accessed September 7, 2012.

17 Ibid.

- Calls for public-private cooperation, specifically, information sharing among nation states and all other stakeholders to address common challenges among both critical infrastructure participants and private-sector actors mutually dependent on the same interconnected infrastructure; and . . .
- Identify networks and processes of international cooperation that may enhance incident response and contingency planning, identifying partners and arrangements for bilateral and multilateral cooperation, where appropriate.

UN conventions:

Proposal for Cyber Weapons Convention

http://www.ccdcoe.org/articles/2010/Geers_CyberWeaponsConvention.pdf

Kenneth Geers, PhD is the U.S. Naval Criminal Investigative Service (NCIS) Cyber Subject Matter Expert. Geers has been a student in six countries, served as an intelligence analyst, a French and Russian linguist, and a computer programmer in support of arms control initiatives. Geers was the first U.S. Representative to the Cooperative Cyber Defence Centre of Excellence in Tallinn, Estonia. Geers is widely published on the relationship between information technology and national security, and is the author of *Strategic Cyber Security*, now a free download: http://ccdcoe.org/278.html.

His book argues that world leaders are beginning to look beyond temporary fixes to the challenge of securing the Internet. One possible solution may be an international arms control treaty for cyberspace. The 1997 Chemical Weapons Convention (CWC) provides national security planners with a useful model. The CWC has been ratified by 98 percent of the world's governments, and encompasses 95 percent of the world's population. It compels signatories not to produce or to use chemical weapons (CW), and they must destroy existing CW stockpiles. As a means and method of war, CW have now almost completely lost their legitimacy. This article examines the aspects of CWC that could help to contain conflict in cyberspace.

Special Event on Cyber Security and Development

http://www.un.org/en/ecosoc/cybersecurity/summary.pdf

The General Assembly adopted a resolution on cyber security at their 64th session on December 21, 2009. The General Assembly adopted Resolution 211 of 2009, entitled "Creation of a global culture of cyber security and taking stock of national efforts to protect critical information infrastructures," without a roll-call vote. It emphasized the need for regional and international information-sharing and collaboration to support national efforts because of the global reach of cyber threats. Key points of Resolution 211 include suggesting voluntary self-assessment tools for each nation to protect critical digital infrastructures, emphasizing the cooperation between governmental and non-governmental organizations, and recommending initiatives regarding the investigation and prosecution of cybercrime. An account of UN action can be found at http://www.un.org/News/Press/docs /2009/ga10907.doc.htm.

A complete documentation of General Assembly Resolution 64/211 of 2009 can be found through this link: http://daccess-dds-ny.un.org/doc/UNDOC /GEN/N09/474/49/PDF/N0947449.pdf?OpenElement.

Twelfth United Nations Congress on Crime Prevention and Criminal Justice
http://www.cybercrimelaw.net/documents/UN_12th_Crime_Congress.pdf

The United Nations Congress on Crime Prevention and Criminal Justice established an open-ended intergovernmental expert group on cybercrime in 2010. The UN Congress, which was assembled to prevent crime in the cyberspace, believed cyberspace to be the fifth Common Space for warfare after land, sea, air, and outer space. Due to the significant power cyberspace holds, the countries represented at the UN Congress asserted that coordination among nations was required to protect themselves from criminals who exploit vulnerabilities and attack countries' critical infrastructure.

SECTION 5—QUESTIONS TO CONSIDER

As you research your country/corporation's concerns with cyber security and as you begin to develop a statement of your country's or corporation's position, you may wish to consider the following questions:

- Has your country or corporation been the victim of a cyber attack? What networks or computer systems were targeted, and is it possible to know where or by whom the attack originated?
- What national systems are in place in your country to address the threat of cyber attack? If they exist, have they proven to be effective?
- Does your country or corporation support increased sharing of information among UN member states and between member states and private corporations as ways to protect the Internet against cyber attacks?
- To what extent are your computer systems vulnerable to attacks by states or nonstate actors?

- What does your country or corporation believe should be done to contain cyber warfare and to prevent cyber attacks from leading to conventional warfare?
- What measures can the UN take to contain cyber warfare within the digital world and prevent escalation of that conflict to conventional warfare?
- Under what conditions or circumstances would it be appropriate for the United Nations to consider sanctions against countries that initiate cyber attacks that result in disruption of, damage to, or destruction of a nation's critical infrastructure?
- Under what conditions or circumstances would it be appropriate for the UN to get involved in regulating its member nations' use of the Internet without infringing on its member states' national sovereignty?
- What constitutes an act of war in the digital world?

SECTION 6—GENERAL SOURCES TO CONSULT

The sources listed below (unlike those country- or corporation-specific sources listed in the Resource Guide) address cyber security from a global perspective and a developed nations' perspective (G20) and should be consulted as an aid in understanding the general context of the international condition of Internet security, especially from the perspective of the most developed countries.

1. Booz Allen Hamilton and the *Economist* Intelligence Unit produced "The Cyber Hub" in January 2012. This digital report provides a comprehensive overview of the digital arena, using a "cyber power index" to evaluate the strengths and weaknesses of nations that are members of the G20 group, including the **United States, the U.K., European Union, Germany, Canada, France, Japan, Italy, Brazil, Mexico, Argentina, China, Russia, Turkey, Saudi Arabia, South Africa, South Korea, India, Indonesia,** and **Australia.** http://www.cyberhub.com/

2. United Nations DESA, "Cybersecurity: A global issue demanding a global approach," New York, NY, December 12, 2011. "Cybersecurity is a complex transnational issue that requires global cooperation for ensuring a safe Internet," according to the UN Economic and Social Council. According to a 2011 Norton study, threats to cyberspace have increased dramatically in the past year afflicting 431 million adult victims globally—or fourteen adult victims every second, one million cybercrime victims every day. Cybercrime has now become a business which exceeds a trillion dollars a

year in online fraud, identity theft, and lost intellectual property, affecting millions of people around the world, as well as countless businesses and the governments of every nation. To address the issues and challenges around cybersecurity and cybercrime, the United Nations Economic and Social Council (ECOSOC) held a Special Event on "Cybersecurity and Development," organized jointly by the Department of Economic and Social Affairs (DESA) and the International Telecommunication Union (ITU) on December 9, 2011, in New York. http://www.un.org/en/development /desa/news/ecosoc/cybersecurity-demands-global-approach.html.

3. Isaac Porche III, "Stuxnet is the world's problem," *Bulletin of the Atomic Scientists*, December 9, 2010.

4. Josh Smith, "McCaul, Langevin Raise Fears of UN Internet Regulation," *National Journal*, March 27, 2012.

5. Jim Finkle, "UN agency plans major warning on Flame virus risk," Reuters News Service, May 30, 2012.

6. Joshua Pollack, "Is the cyber threat a weapon of mass destruction?," *Bulletin of the Atomic Scientists*, January 20, 2010.

7. R. Scott Kemp, "Cyberweapons: Bold step in a digital darkness," Bulletin of the Atomic Scientists, June 7, 2012.

8. Rebecca Greenfield, "A Complete Guide to Flame, the Malicious Computer Virus Ravaging Iran," *National Journal*, May 30, 2012.

9. Josh Smith, "House Panel: Iran Preparing for Cyberwar Against US, Allies," *National Journal*, April 26, 2012.

10. Allya Sternstein, "US and Russia Among 22 Nations Supporting Cybersecurity Resolution," *National Journal*, July 6, 2011.

11. Josh Smith, "Unresolved Questions Dog International Cybersecurity Policies," *National Journal*, November 7, 2011.

12. UN News Service, "World's largest security body vows to boost cooperation with UN," February 15, 2011.

13. Josh Smith, "Study: UK, US Wield Most 'Cyber Power,'" *National Journal*, January 13, 2012.

14. Booz Allen Hamilton, "The Cyber Hub," January 2012, http://www .cyberhub.com/Home/About/.

15. "U.S. official says cyberattacks can trigger self-defense rule," *Washington Post*, September 18, 2012. "Cyberattacks can amount to armed attacks triggering the right of self-defense and are subject to international laws of war, the State Department's top lawyer said Tuesday. Spelling out the U.S.

government's position on the rules governing cyberwarfare, Harold Koh, the department's legal adviser, said a cyber-operation that results in death, injury or significant destruction would probably be seen as a use of force in violation of international law."

16. Associated Press News Summary: "Panetta talks cyber issues with Chinese; experts see no decline in attacks," *Washington Post*, September 20, 2012. "U.S. Defense Secretary Leon Panetta repeatedly raised the issue of aggressive cyberattacks against American companies and the government during meetings with Chinese military and civilian leaders, but left with little more than agreements to talk again. Panetta has warned that cyberattacks and cyberwarfare could set off the next war, although experts say the main threats are intelligence espionage and theft of corporate and high-tech data. A key concern is an attack against critical infrastructure, including the electric grid, power plants or financial networks that could plunge the U.S. into crisis. Chinese officials have denied the cyberattacks, saying they also are victims. But the U.S. has accused China of systematically stealing American high-tech data for its own economic gain. U.S. officials and security experts say government and private industry systems are constantly being probed, breached and attacked, in particular critical oil, gas and energy companies."

17. Andrei Soldatov, "Vladimir Putin's Cyber Warriors: The Kremlin's Hamhanded Effort to Squelch Online Dissent," *Foreign Affairs*, December 9, 2011, www.foreignaffairs.com/print/134010.

18. Andrew J. Nathan, "Cybersecurity and US-China Relations," *Foreign Affairs*, September/October 2012. This report considers how hacking, cyber-espionage, and the threat of cyberwarfare affect US-Chinese relations. http://www.foreignaffairs.com/print/135226.

19. Wesley K. Clark and Peter L. Levin, "Securing the Information Highway: How to Enhance the United States' Electronic Defenses," *Foreign Affairs*, November/December 2009. This opinion piece argues that the United States must diversify the country's digital infrastructure. "Generations of public- and private-sector systems operators have—in an attempt to keep costs down and increase control—exposed the country to a potential catastrophe." http://www.foreignaffairs.com/print/65622.

20. Ellen Nakashima, "Pentagon seeks more powers for cyberdefense," *Washington Post*, August 10, 2012. "The Pentagon has proposed that military cyber-specialists be given permission to take action outside its com-

puter networks to defend critical U.S. computer systems—a move that officials say would set a significant precedent."

21. "Malware is linked to Stuxnet, Flame, Software steals bank, PayPal data, 2 related viruses attacked Iran's nuclear program," *Washington Post*, August 10, 2012. "Researchers said Thursday that they have identified a new kind of malicious software that appears to be the creation of the same state-sponsored program that produced the viruses known as Stuxnet and Flame."

22. "The Enterprise Threat Landscape," *PC Today*, May 2012. "The security threat landscape is in constant flux, requiring regular maintenance and oversight of security protection. . . . Social networking is a new area where threats are becoming prevalent."

SECTION 7—COUNTRY/CORPORATION LINKS

Ireland

- **Government Link**: http://www.enisa.europa.eu/activities/cert/background /inv/certs-by-country/ireland. This URL is the official website for the European Network and Information Security Agency. It gives the links to the contact information of different CERT (Computer Emergency Readiness Team) departments including the address, phone number, and official website of each of the different departments. There are also links in the side bar that tell you what new events are happening in CERT, what CERT is, etc.

- **Non-Government Link**: http://www.irishtimes.com/newspaper/finance /2012/0329/1224314044188.html. This link goes to the *Irish Times* website and it features an article on 440 Irish firms hit by cybercrime. The article primarily talks about the amount of cyber crime that occurred against Ireland in 2011, who was attacked, and what was done in response to the attacks. It also talks about what kinds of cyber attacks occur, and different types of hackers, such as politically motivated hackers or financially motivated hackers.

Chile

- **Government Link**: http://www.defense.gov/news/newsarticle.aspx?id =116102. The link goes to an article on the official U.S. Department of Defense website. It talks about a pact between Chile and the United States, made in 2012, on issues such as cyber security and military defense; the official transcript is available at the bottom of the page.

- **Non-Government Link**: http://www.bnamericas.com/news/technology /government-aims-for-personal-information-protection-law-by-2014. This link goes to an article from bnamericas.com about a bill for a personal information protection law. It has entered the lower house and will put pressure on companies to invest in IT security.

Argentina

- **Government Link**: http://www.sans.org/reading_room/whitepapers/basics /argentina-preparing-security-violation_598. This link goes to the SANS Institute webpage on Argentina preparing for a security violation. It mentions court cases, punishments, and ways to prevent breaches of security.
- **Non-Government Link**: http://www.ibls.com/internet_law_news_portal _view.aspx?s=latestnews&id=2090. This article is from IBLS about an Internet law that was updated to include punishment for information technology crimes. It provides information such as the new name of the law and tells what actions would violate this law.

Libya

- **Government Link**: http://nationalcybersecurity.net/anonymous-the-truth -about-the-war-on-libya/. This web article shows the structure of the Libyan electronic infrastructure and its relevance to national security and the relationship to Libya's government and its place in the Arab state. This article also provides the threats to Libya's electronic infrastructure and can be used in reference to other Arab-spring-affected areas.
- **Non-Government Link**: http://cybersecurity.byu.edu/cyberdawnlibya ?destination=node/29. This link is a report on Libya's online structure. This shows the conflict that occurs in Libyan cyberspace.

Bhutan

- **Government Link**: http://www.bhutan.gov.bt/government/ministries .php?min_id=2. This is the portal to the government of Bhutan. Here you can find the individual policies on information and technology. Bhutan's information is very neatly organized into the individual areas of policy.

- **Non-Government Link**: http://www.unodc.org/documents/treaties /organized_crime/EGM_cybercrime_2011/Presentations/ITU_Cybercrime _EGMJan2011.pdf. This PowerPoint slide gives you the basic structure of cyber security around the world. This site then talks about the measures of different countries including Bhutan and less developed countries on cyber security.

CISCO Corporation

- **Corporate Link**: http://www.cisco.com/web/strategy/government /defense_cybersecurity.html. This is CISCO's main portal, where corporate policy and security reports from this year can be found. In them CISCO describes details of security and its threats to security presently on the CISCO information network. This paper shows the vulnerabilities of network communication and broadband tools, and how CISCO is working to secure information transactions.
- **Non-Government Link**: http://www.computerworld.com/s/article /9228584/GOP_Senators_revise_cybersecurity_bill. This article shows hardline defense measures purposed by the U.S. Congress to stop cyber threats. This article allows the reader to gain a perspective on the direction that the U.S. government wants to pursue.

Italy

- **Government Link**: http://www.ict.go.ug/index.php?option=com_content &view=article&id=112:cyber-security-at-itu-forum-&catid=35:ict-news &Itemid=74. This is the Ministry of Foreign Affairs' website. It can be used to look up foreign policies.
- **Non-Government Link**: http://thenextweb.com/eu/2011/07/05 /anonymous-suspects-arrested-in-italian-police-raids/. This article references several attacks on Italy by the hacker organization known as Anonymous.
- **Non-Government Link**: http://www.infowar.it/slides/IWC_2011 -BLITZBLAU_1.pdf. This is a study on how cyber warfare affects Italy.

Australia

- **Government Link**: http://australia.gov.au/topics/it-and-communications /cyber-security. This is located on Australia's official government website. There are several links pertaining to the topic of cybersecurity in Australia at this URL.

- **Non-Government Link**: http://www.defensenews.com/article/20110914
  /DEFSECT04/109140304/U-S-Australia-Treaty-Will-Cover-
  Cyberwarfare. Australia and the United States created a treaty that also
  covers cyber warfare. Through the article, it is possible to learn the
  Australian government's stance on cyber warfare and cyber security.

Brazil

- **Government Link**: http://www.cert.br/en/. This is the official website of
  the Brazilian National Computer Emergency Response Team.
- **Non-Government Link**: http://cyberwarzone.com/cyberwarfare/brazil
  -prepares-cyber-war. An article concerning Brazil's preparations for a new
  technological age and the possible viruses that would accompany cyber
  warfare.

South Africa

- **Government Link**: http://kganyago.org/2012/05/18/cybersecurity-agenda
  -how-are-we-doing-in-south-africa/. This links to the information security
  discussion by Microsoft's South African security advisor. The article is a
  thorough report of the conference and South Africa's current state in cyber
  security threats and other various types of media piracy.
- **Non-Government Link**: http://www.technologytrends.co.za/2012-trends
  /cyber-security/cyber-security-policy-framework-cyber-security-south
  -africa/. The website is an article that overviews cyber security in South
  Africa.

Austria

- **Government Link**: http://www.euractiv.com/energy/cyber-attacks-feared
  -eu-energy-t-news-501547. Keeping in mind that Austria is a member of
  the European Union, this link provides a background on the emerging
  threat of cyber crime against the EU.
- **Non-Government Link**: http://www.tomsguide.com/us/austria-cyber
  -crime-cyber-defense-secret-service,news-11077.html. This is an article
  about Austria's concerns regarding cyber threats. The article goes further on
  how the government sees Austria more vulnerable to cyber threats than
  physical military attacks.

Belgium

- **Government Link**: http://www.b-ccentre.be/. This site links to the Belgian Cybercrime Centre of Excellence organization that collaborates and coordinates with cyber crime matters in Belgium. It lists their strategies and further plans against cyber warfare.
- **Non-Government Link**: http://www.enisa.europa.eu/activities/stakeholder-relations/files/country-reports/Belgium.pdf. This links to Belgium's Country Report which states Belgium's national strategy against cyber warfare from pages 5 to 8.

Pakistan

- **Government Link**: http://202.83.164.25/wps/portal. The government website with information on different departments of governments.
- **Non-Government Link**: http://thehackernews.com/2011/05/pakistan-cyber-army-pca-owner-shak.html. A blog regarding cyber security and hacking around the world. Has specific information on the Pakistan Cyber Army (PCA).

Germany

- **Government Link**: http://www.cio.bund.de/SharedDocs/Publikationen/DE/Strategische-Themen/css_engl_download.pdf?__blob=publicationFile. A government published document regarding Germany's cyber security policies.
- **Non-Government Link**: http://kingsofwar.org.uk/2011/03/germanys-cyber-security-strategy/. This is a non-government online newspaper devoted to topics such as cyber security. This specific article discusses Germany's new cyber security strategy ("Nationale Cyber-Sicherheitsstrategie").

France

- **Government Link**: http://www.diplomatie.gouv.fr/en/country-files/united-kingdom/events-3313/article/internet-and-its-governance-third; http://www.securite-informatique.gouv.fr/gp_article158.html. The French Ministry of Public Affairs website provides links to France's news and global issues including the country's condition in terms of defense and security. The second link is to the French national security agency. The second website is only available in French. You can easily translate the

website using google chrome (here's how: http://support.google.com
/chrome/bin/answer.py?hl=en&answer=173424) or you can just stick to
the first link.

- **Non-Government Link**: http://www.afp.com/en/search/site/cyber
%20security. This is the Agence France-Presse (AFP)'s website in English.
AFP is one of the world's largest news agencies. You can easily search
articles pertaining to topics like cyber security.

China

- **Government Link**: http://ndn.org/blog/2012/03/foreign-policy-chat
-%E2%80%93-managing-china%E2%80%99s-cyber-threat. This website
of NDN, a U.S.-based consulting firm, offers a U.S. corporate perspective
on "Managing China's Cyber Threat." This is a summary of a report of
China's cyber capabilities and how it can serve as a threat to other nations.
- **Non-Government Link**: http://www.atimes.com/atimes/China
/NC15Ad01.html. This links to an article in the *Asia Times* on China's
capacity for cyber war. The article expands on the history of cyber security
in China as well as the current issues China is currently facing.

India

- **Government Link**: http://www.cybersecurity-india.com/Event.aspx?id
=548338. Developed with direct support of the Indian Armed Forces, this
links to the Cyber Security India conference, which provides an
opportunity to engage in discussions by cyber officials in the Indian Armed
Forces.
- **Non-Government Link**: http://articles.timesofindia.indiatimes.com/2010
-07-19/internet/28273582_1_cyber-security-cyber-warfare-cryptographic
-controls. This article from *The Times of India* provides an evaluation of
how the Indian Army has advanced in electronic warfare. Related articles
listed on the site can also inform on issues regarding India's experience with
cyber warfare.

Russia

- **Government Link**: http://defensetech.org/2009/01/30/russia-now-3-and
-0-in-cyber-warfare/. Directly from the U.S.-based Defense Tech
organization, this report assesses Russia's current capabilities in cyber
warfare.

- **Non-Government Link**:
  http://www.rferl.org/content/Behind_The_Estonia_Cyberattacks/1505613
  .html. This article in the Radio Free Europe/Radio Liberty organization
  discusses the series of cyber attacks made from Russia on Estonia in 2007.
  This cyber attack swamped multiple websites of Estonian organizations,
  thought to have resulted due to the Russian government's unhappiness
  with the Estonian government's plans to relocate the Bronze Soldier of
  Tallinn.

Booz Allen Hamilton

- **Corporate Link**: http://www.boozallen.com/consulting/view-our-work
  /48383297/defending-against-cyber-espionage. This link goes to the
  official Booz Allen Hamilton website. The website features the challenge,
  the solution, and the role that Booz Allen Hamilton has in defending
  against cyber espionage. Also see Booz Allen's Cyberhub report, cosponsored by the Investigative Unit of *The Economist* at
  http://www.cyberhub.com/
- **Non-Government Link**: http://www.securityweek.com/booz-allen
  -hamilton-confirms-cyber-attack-learning-management-system. This link
  goes to an article off of securityweek.com. The article talks about a cyber
  security attack against Booz Allen Hamilton that occurred in 2011.

Northrop Grumman

- **Corporate Link**: http://www.northropgrumman.com/performance
  /#/cybersecurity/overview. This links one to the Northrop Grumman's
  cyber security page, and as one clicks for more on cyber security, more
  information on how the company deals with cyber threats and protects
  itself from cyber terrorism.
- **Non-Government Link**: http://www.infosecisland.com/blogview/20631
  -Northrop-Report-Examines-Chinese-Information-Warfare-
  Strategies.html. This article, from infosecisland.com, is about a Northrop
  report examining the Chinese government's efforts to centralize cyber
  warfare. It mentions that the Chinese government's hopes to use the
  information warfare to level the playing field, etc.

Microsoft

- **Corporate Link**: http://www.microsoft.com/industry/government /guides/cybersecurity_government/default.aspx. This link goes to the Microsoft page that discusses the company's tactics to defend itself and others against cyber warfare, and its opinion on the importance of protection from cyber threats.
- **Non-Government Link**: http://www.foxnews.com/us/2012/04/30 /microsoft-says-raid-damaged-cybercrime-operation/. This link goes to an article from foxnews.com. It talks about how Microsoft had disrupted a cybercrime operation that had been stealing millions from consumers, what the operation was, ways of dealing with cybercriminals, etc.

South Korea

- **Government Link**: http://www.itu.int/ITU-D/cyb/events/2009/hyderabad /docs/park-korean-cybersecurity-framework-sept-09.pdf. This website outlines the general framework of the Republic of Korea's cyber security. The information is categorized based on the sector (private, public) and it provides background on their National Cybersecurity Strategy Council, how they will respond if information is infringed upon in the future and what steps they will take to prevent a reoccurrence, and the progression of their cybersecurity protection from 1998 until now.
- **Non-Government Link**: http://www.gmanetwork.com/news/story /261615/scitech/technology/alleged-north-korean-cyberattack-foiled-by -sokor-police. This article, from gmanetwork.com, is about North Korea leading a cyber attack against South Korea in the form of a video game. It talks about how this attack was not the first, and how the attack was foiled.

Canada

- **Government Link:** http://www.publicsafety.gc.ca/prg/ns/cbr/index-eng.aspx. This website provides background on cybercrime and security issues generally, then focuses in on how Canada is affected and what counter strategies will be taken. It offers a categorized column on the left of the page with more specific information regarding how Canada reacts nationally, what law enforcement is in place, etc.
- **Non-Government Link**: http://la.trendmicro.com/media/misc/sinkholing -botnets-technical-paper-en.pdf. This website illustrates the process of

sinkholing, a way to locate a botnet and evaluate its abilities. The website describes specifically how to identify from where the botnet originates, what populations the botnet targets, and the original configuration file of the botnet. In doing these things, researchers are able to gather enough information to report the crime to "relevant authorities" and leave it up to them to further investigate the suspect.

Mexico

- **Government Link**: http://www.un.org/disarmament/HomePage /ODAPublications/DisarmamentStudySeries/PDF/DSS_33.pdf. This website offers information about many countries' status, including Mexico's, in the cyber security conflict. It offers resolutions and initiatives, including the amending of their constitution, to combat the problem.
- **Non-Government Link**: http://www.bbc.co.uk/news/technology-16787509. This website illustrates in a condensed picture the weak stance Mexico currently has with respect to cyber warfare and where the country stands among other countries battling cyber crime.

Spain

- **Government Link**: http://www.enisa.europa.eu/activities/stakeholder -relations/files/country-reports/Spain.pdf/view. This is a country report of Spain published by the European Network and Information Security Agency (ENISA). It provides an overview of Spain's strategy and key policies as well as relevant statistics.
- **Non-Government Link**: http://www.realinstitutoelcano.org/wps/portal /rielcano_eng/Content?WCM_GLOBAL_CONTEXT=/elcano/elcano_in /zonas_in/defense+security/ari102-2010#_ftn5. This is a proposal for the management of cyber security made by the Elcano Royal Institute. It introduces cyber security, the risks, and offers an analysis of the current management under the Spanish government.

Vietnam

- **Government Link**: http://mic.gov.vn/Attach%20file/sachtrang /sachtrang2011.pdf. This is the White Book 2011; it was published by the Information and Communication Technology (ICT) sector of Vietnam and it offers analysis on the implementation of a ten-year plan and initiatives to transform Vietnam into an advanced ICT country. It also offers the organizational structure of the committee and its functions as well as relevant statistics on digital infrastructure.

- **Non-Government Link**: http://ethnoblog.newamericamedia.org/2011/07/cyber-war-started-between-china-and-vietnam-over-spratly-islands.php. This is a blog on a dispute in 2011 over the ownership of Spratly Islands, which contributed to the cyber war between Vietnam and China.

United States

- **Government Link**: http://publicintelligence.net/u-s-cyber-command-cybersecurity-legislation-position-letter/. This is a letter from U.S. commander in chief of CYBERCOM Keith Alexander in which he goes into some depth about the outlook for U.S. involvement in cyber warfare and the United States' response to it.

- **Non-Government Link**: http://www.internetnews.com/government/article.php/3827936/US+Official+Cybersecurity+Plans+Not+Just+Talk.htm. The link is an article on how the U.S. cyber security policies are almost always "just talk"; however, recent events and interviews with senior officials have proved otherwise.

  The following link to the Cato Institute, a Washington, D.C.-based think tank, raises doubts about the nature and scope of cyber threats. The February 21, 2012, article, "Cybersecurity Hype," questions whether government contractors are "working to generate an issue." http://www.cato-at-liberty.org/cybersecurity-hype/

Venezuela

- **Government Link**: http://www.cyberwarnews.info/tag/venezuela/. This link includes a detailed history of cyber attacks that Venezuela had faced for the past decade.

- **Non-Government Link**: http://www.bbc.co.uk/news/world-latin-america-12046964. A BBC article on how Venezuelan parliament has enacted new laws on tightening cyber security.

Great Britain

- **Government Link**: http://www.carlisle.army.mil/dime/documents/UK%20Cyber%20Security%20Strategy.pdf. This is a very detailed and current (November 2011) compilation of the U.K.'s cyber security issues, its response, the country's outlook and the possible problems associated with its response, along with its beneficial aspects.

- **Non-Government Link**: http://www.guardian.co.uk/commentisfree/2012 /apr/17/britain-right-take-lead-cybersecurity. The link is from the *Guardian* newspaper and talks about the leading role of Britain in cyber warfare and a critique of techniques Britain is using in the fight.

Luxembourg

- **Government Link**: http://www.investinluxembourg.lu/ict/luxembourg -conference-cybersecurity. This website references a conference hosted by Norway related to cyber security.
- **Non-Government Link**: http://newwww.wort.lu/wort/web/en /luxembourg/articles/2012/01/174398/index.php. This source is a news article appearing in the newspaper *WORT* discussing Luxembourg's Cyber Security Board's recommendation to speed up processes to increase sensitization of the handling of digital information among state employees. "The meeting of the CSB came a week after a security vulnerability in the national Medico Social database was brought to public attention. . . . Especially employees at banks and other institutions handling sensitive information will be called upon to treat data security as an absolute priority. . . . The recent Medico Social scandal was brought about after a doctor left his username and password to the database of registered athletes on a post-it stuck to his computer screen."

Norway

- **Government Link**: http://www.acus.org/natosource/norwegian-military -hit-cyber-attack-after-it-joins-nato-strike-missions-libya. Norwegian military personnel were the targets of what's being described as a "massive" cyber attack this spring 2012, one day after Norway started bombing Libya with other UN- and NATO-backed forces. Newspaper *VG* reported Thursday that the government fended off the attack, which was considered the most serious ever experienced. "It came just a short time after the decision was made to send Norwegian forces to the operation in Libya," confirmed Major Ivar Kjærem of the military's center for protection of critical information. "We haven't seen such an attack so close to conflicts Norway has been involved in earlier, but we can't say there's a connection."

- **Non-Government Link**: http://www.cybercrimelaw.net/documents
  /A_Global_Treaty_on_Cybersecurity_and_Cybercrime,_Second_edition
  _2011.pdf. The source is Judge Stein Schjolberg, chair of the EastWest
  Institute's Working Group on Cybercrime, from his report "A Global
  Treaty on Cybersecurity and Cybercrime, 2011. "Cyberspace. . . is in great
  need for coordination, cooperation and legal measures among all nations. A
  cyberspace treaty or a set of treaties at the UN level, including
  cybersecurity, cybercrime and other cyber threats, should be the framework
  for peace, justice and security in cyberspace. The International Law
  Commission adopted at its 48th session in 1996 the 'Draft Code of Crimes
  against Peace and Security of Mankind,' and submitted it to the United
  Nations General Assembly. Crimes against the peace and security of
  mankind were then established as crimes under international law, whether
  or not they were punishable for binding parties under national law. Crimes
  against peace and security in cyberspace should be established as crimes
  under international law through a Convention or Protocol at the UN
  level."

Egypt

- **Government Link**: http://igf09.eg/brochure.pdf. "The defense systems are
  attacked daily, but it's not often we see such a comprehensive attempt at
  infiltration as this was," [Major General Roar] Sundseth told VG Nett. "The
  trend is increasing, though, and the attackers are more goal-oriented."
- **Non-Government Link**: http://www.bitdefender.com/security/egypt
  -unrest-producing-cyber-attacks.html. "Egypt unrest producing cyber
  attacks." This commercial website is focused on spammers and cyber
  criminals taking advantage of the political unrest in Egypt in January 2011
  to launch cyber attacks on Internet users both inside and outside Egypt.
  With the government blocking the Internet in Egypt, "people are forced to
  use dial-up alternatives to share what is happening through social
  networking, making these alternatives more vulnerable."
- **Non-Government Link**: http://www.sis.gov.eg/En/LastPage.aspx
  ?Category_ID=1213. [This URL references the Feb. 2012 Munich Security
  Conference attended by Egyptian officials and representatives of other
  nations, including the US, at which cybersecurity was discussed.]
- **Non-Government Link**: http://www.egyptindependent.com/news/greek
  -teen-arrested-over-ministry-cyber-attack. This link goes to an article from

the website for the *Egyptian Independent* newspaper. The article talks about a teenager who was arrested for hacking into the Egyptian justice ministry's website, possible accomplices to this crime, charges they may face, etc.

Turkey

- **Government Link**: http://www.washington.emb.mfa.gov.tr /ShowAnnouncement.aspx?ID=153367. This is a statement made by the Turkish Embassy regarding NATO's Deterrence and Defence Posture from May 2012. Throughout the document, Turkey affirms its commitment to NATO's goal of improving cyber security and its agreement that cyber security is a top priority issue.
- **Non-Government Link**: http://www.todayszaman.com/news-285120 -turkey-among-top-10-countries-subjected-to-cyber-attacks.html. This is a news article from July 2012 discussing how Turkey has been affected by breaches in cyber security. It quotes government officials discussing the importance of this issue and suggesting possible solutions for the future.

Switzerland

- **Government Link**: http://www.melani.admin.ch/dokumentation/00123 /00124/01141/index.html?lang=en. The semi-annual report (in pdf format) located at this URL was issued by the Swiss Reporting and Analysis Centre for Information Assurance in 2011. It focuses on information assurance in Switzerland, detailing current problems with cyber infrastructure and examining recent trends in the world of cyber security. There is a helpful glossary of terms on page 33.
- **Non-Government Link**: http://www.swissinfo.ch/eng/swiss_news/Cyber _attack_threats_are_everywhere.html?cid=29205204. This news article from January 2011 features interviews from Kurt Nydegger and Gérald Vernez (both members of the Swiss Defense Ministry). The two experts weigh in on the dangers of cyber crime and protections that are now in place as a result of cyber attacks.

Finland

- **Government Link**: http://www.assembly.coe.int/Mainf.asp?link =/Documents/WorkingDocs/Doc07/ EDOC11325.htm. This page features a report from the Parliamentary Assembly presented by the Finnish delegation to the Council of Europe in 2007. It was drafted in the

Committee on Legal Affairs and Human Rights, and discusses ways that
cybercrime can be prevented.

- **Non-Government Link**: http://www.nextgov.com/cybersecurity/2012
  /01/us-lags-finland-sweden-and-israel-in-cybersecurity/50542/. This
  website features an article from nextgov.com. It gives a bit of information
  on how prepared the Finnish government is for a cyber attack, its plan for
  having a secure information base, information about how a few other
  countries are prepared for a cyber attack, etc.

Israel

- **Government Link**: http://www.gov.il/firstgov/english. This link goes to the
  official Israeli government website. It features information on different
  Israeli government ministries, the history of Israel, current events, etc.
- **Non-Government Link**: http://www.israelnationalnews.com/News
  /News.aspx/152283#.UBAqDe0is20. This link goes to an article from the
  Israeli national news website. It talks about how Israel is among the three
  leading countries ready to fight cyber warfare, the other countries that are
  said to be the most and least prepared for a cyber attack, etc.

Iraq

- **Government Link**: http://www.cabinet.iq/default.aspx. This link that goes
  to the Iraqi executive government website features information such as
  polls, the structure of the cabinet, and cabinet resolutions.
- **Non-Government Link**: http://www.hrw.org/news/2012/07/11/iraq
  -cybercrimes-law-violates-free-speech. This article on the Human Rights
  Watch website talks about how, if a new cybercrime draft law were to be
  passed, it would violate the right of free speech.

Iran

- **Government Link**: https://www.cia.gov/library/publications/the-world
  -factbook/geos/ir.html. This *CIA World Factbook* website gives background
  information about Iran and its infrastructure.
- **Non-Government Link**: http://www.npr.org/2012/04/26/151400805
  /could-iran-wage-a-cyberwar-on-the-u-s. This website includes a
  description of Iran's situation as the U.S. government initiates a wave of
  cyber attacks against Iran. Also describes various implications and
  consequences.

Saudi Arabia

- **Government Link**: https://www.cia.gov/library/publications/the-world -factbook/geos/sa.html. The *CIA World Factbook* gives background information about this country's economy, geography, military, and other basic facts about this country to highlight its essential information.
- **Non-Government Link**: http://www.huffingtonpost.co.uk/faisal-abbas /syrian-electronic-army-de_b_1448517.html. This article examines the cyber war against Syria and Saudi Arabia. While this is one issue that is taking precedence, it's not an isolated incident.

Japan

- **Government Link**: http://www.gbd-e.org/ig/cs/CyberSecurityRecommendation _Nov06.pdf. This is a report on cyber security threats and measures written by Buheita Fujiwara, Chairman, Information-technology Promotion Agency (IPA), Japan.
- **Non-Government Link**: http://jsw.newpacificinstitute.org/?p=5120. An article that explains the future of Japan's cyber warfare policies.

Cuba

- **Government Link**: http://ctp.iccas.miami.edu/FOCUS_Web /Issue139.htm. http://translatingcuba.com/wp-content/uploads /2011/02/Coral-Negro-MININT-video-English-Corrected.pdf. Cuba's Deputy Minister for Information Science and Communication talking about Cuban Internet access and cyber security: a report by Eduardo Fontes Suárez, cybernetic specialist in counterintelligence. From the political Section of the Ministry of the Interior (MININT), Cuba.
- **Non-Government Link**: http://theamericano.com/2012/03/21/cuba-iran -work/. A report that explains the background of Cuba's cyber warfare programs.

North Korea

- **Government Link**: http://www.ists.dartmouth.edu/docs/cyberwarfare.pdf. "A Study on Cyber Warfare—an Analysis of the Means and Motivations of Selected Nation States."
- **Non-Government Link**: http://www.reuters.com/article/2011/06/01/us -korea-north-hackers-idUSTRE7501U420110601. An article explaining North Korea's current position of cyber warfare against South Korea.

SECTION 8—BIBLIOGRAPHY

Aguilar, Michael. *2010 General Assembly First Committee*. n.d. National Model United Nations. Washington D.C.

"Cybersecurity: A Global Issue Demanding a Global Approach." *UN News Center*. UN, December 12, 2011. Accessed September 10, 2012. http://www.un.org/en/development/desa/news/ecosoc/cybersecurity -demands-global-approach.html.

Fosnock, Craig. *Computer Worms: Past, Present, and Future*. n.d. East Carolina University.

"Gauss Virus: Stuxnet-like Cyberweapon Hits Middle East Banks." GE Investigations Blog. n.p., n.d. Accessed September 10, 2012. http://geinvestigations.com/blog/2012/08/gauss-virus-stuxnet-like -cyberweapon-hits-middle-east-banks/.

Geers, Kenneth. *Cyberspace and the Changing Nature of Warfare*. n.d. Estonia, Tallin.

"The History of Cyber Warfare." Lewis University Online. Lewis University, n.d. Accessed September 7, 2012. http://online.lewisu.edu/the-history-of -cyber-warfare.asp.

Bureau of International Information Programs, U.S. Department of State, "Key Cybersecurity Terms That You Should Know." n.d. Accessed September 10, 2012. http://thesop.org/story/technology/2009/09/19/key-cybersecurity -terms-that-you-should-know.php.

Lewis, James A. *Assessing the Risks of Cyber Terrorism, Cyber War and Other Cyber Threats*. Washington, D.C.: Center for Strategic and International Studies, 2002. Print.

Masters, Jonathan. "Foreign Affairs," Council on Foreign Relations, May 23, 2011. Accessed September 10, 2012. http://www.cfr.org/technology-and -foreign-policy/confronting-cyber-threat/p15577.

Maurer, Tim. "Cyber Norm Emergence at the United Nations—An Analysis of the Activities at the UN Regarding Cyber-security." Harvard Kennedy School - Belfer Center for Science and International Affairs, Sept. 2011. Accessed September 10, 2012. http://belfercenter.ksg.harvard.edu/files /maurer-cyber-norm-dp-2011-11-final.pdf.

Patrick Clair. "Stuxnet: the first weapon made out of code," n.d. Accessed September 7, 2012. http://www.patrickclair.com/2011/06/stuxnet-anatomy- of-computer-virus-from.html.

"Q&A of the Week: 'The Current State of the Cyber Warfare Threat' Featuring Jeffrey Carr." *ZDNet*. n.p., n.d. Accessed September 10, 2012. http://www.zdnet.com/blog/security/q-and-ampa-of-the-week-the-current -state-of-the-cyber-warfare-threat-featuring-jeffrey-carr/12066.

Resolution Adopted by the General Assembly; Fifty-seventh Session Agenda Item 84 (c). n.p.: United Nations, January 31, 2003.

Schjølberg, Stein, and Solange Ghernaouti-Hélie. "A Global Treaty on Cybersecurity and Cybercrime." Accessed September 10, 2012. http://www .cybercrimelaw.net/documents/A_Global_Treaty_on_Cybersecurity_and _Cybercrime,_Second_edition_2011.pdf.

"Special Event on Cybersecurity and Development." ECOSOC. United Nations, December 9, 2011. Accessed September 10, 2012. http://www.un.org /en/ecosoc/cybersecurity/summary.pdf.

"TSG IntelBrief: The Evolution of Cyber Governance." The Soufan Group, July 5, 2012. Accessed September 7, 2012. http://www.soufangroup.com/briefs /details/?Article_Id=330.

Ward, Mark. "Hi-tech crime: A glossary." BBC News. May 10, 2006. Accessed September 7, 2012. http://news.bbc.co.uk/2/hi/uk_news/5400052.stm.

SECTION 9—GLOSSARY[18]

APT (Advanced Persistent Threat)—a group, such as a foreign government, with both the capability and intent to persistently and effectively target a specific entity.

Bagle worm (a.k.a. "Beagle")—a mass-mailing computer worm affecting all versions of Microsoft Windows.

Bagle botnet—Discovered in early 2004, it is estimated that this botnet sends roughly 5.7 billion spam messages a day or about 4.3 percent of the global spam volume (estimated as of April 2010).

Botnet—Short for "robot network," this is a large number of hijacked and compromised computers under the remote control of a single person or organization via a net-based command and control system without the knowledge of their owners. Any such infected computer is referred to as a 'bot' or 'zombie.'

Botnet Farm—The colloquial term to describe a number of computers, all compromised by a single third party who uses computer power.

Botnet Herder—One of the names for the controller or operator of a botnet.

"Bot Roast"—The name of an operation by the FBI to track down bot herders, crackers, or virus coders who, without the owners' knowledge, install malicious

---

18 Glossary terms drawn from Wikipedia and ENISA (European Network and Information Security Agency).

software on computers through the Internet which turns the computer into a zombie computer that then sends out spam to other computers from the compromised computer, making a botnet or network of bot-infected computers.

DDoS (Distributed Denial of Service)—An explicit attempt to render a computer or network incapable of providing normal services, performed via coordinated attack from multiple locations. The goal is to make a targeted system unavailable to the intended users.

Flame—Also known as **Flamer, sKyWIper**, and **Skywiper**, this computer malware was discovered in 2012. It attacks computers running the Microsoft Windows operating system. This malware is being used for targeted cyber espionage in Middle Eastern countries. Its discovery was announced on May 28, 2012, by MAHER Center of Iranian National Computer Emergency Response Team (CERT), Kaspersky Lab, and CrySys Lab of the Budapest University of Technology and Economics. The last of these stated in its report that it "is certainly the most sophisticated malware we encountered during our practice; arguably, it is the most complex malware ever found."

Operating System (OS)—A set of software that manages computer hardware.

Patch—A repair to a computer software vulnerability, prepared and distributed by the software creator, such as Microsoft.

Resilience—The ability of a computer system to provide and maintain an acceptable level of service in the face of faults (including both intentional attacks and unintentional or naturally caused interruptions) affecting normal operations.

Spamming—The use of electronic messaging systems to send unsolicited bulk messages, especially advertising, indiscriminately. While the most widely recognized form of spam is e-mail spam, the term is applied to similar abuses in other media. Spamming remains economically viable because advertisers have no operating costs beyond the management of their mailing lists, and it is difficult to hold senders accountable for their mass mailings. Because the barrier to entry is so low, spammers are numerous, and the volume of unsolicited mail has become very high. In 2011, the estimated figure for spam messages is around seven trillion. The costs, such as lost productivity and fraud, are borne by the public and by Internet service providers (ISPs), which have been forced to add extra capacity to cope with the deluge. Spamming has been the subject of legislation in many jurisdictions.

Stuxnet—A computer virus believed to have been developed jointly by U.S. and Israeli government intelligence agencies that targeted Iranian nuclear facilities.

Titan Rain—The designation given by the U.S. federal government to a series of coordinated attacks on American computer systems since 2003; they were known to have been ongoing for at least three years. The attacks were labeled by U.S. officials as Chinese in origin, although their precise nature, e.g., state-sponsored espionage, corporate espionage, or random hacker attacks, and their real identities—masked by proxy, zombie computer, spyware/virus infected—remain unknown. "Titan Rain" is believed to be associated with an Advanced Persistent Threat (APT).

Worm—A self-replicating computer program, similar to a computer virus but unlike a virus which attaches itself to, and becomes part of, another executable program, a worm is self-contained and does not need to be part of another program to propagate itself. In other words a typical computer virus is similar to a parasite and it requires a host. In this case, the host is another executable program. A worm does not need a host; it can spread on its own.

Wormhole—A vulnerability that allows a worm to infect or operate on your computers. Wormholes are there to allow malicious software to infect a victim's computer and in most cases worms will use the same hole to communicate with its author.

Zombie Computers—Another name for a hijacked computer that is a member of a botnet.

Zero-Day Attack—An attack that exploits a previously unknown vulnerability in a computer application, meaning that the attack occurs on "day zero" of awareness of the vulnerability—or the first day that the vulnerability is discovered.

Zero-Day Virus—Any new and previously unknown computer virus.

APPENDIX D:
SAMPLE POSITION PAPER

Syria in DISEC

This position paper was written by a Marshall team in preparing for the National High School Model UN's 2005 conference. As you can see, students should always update their position papers. Just having them available off-the-shelf can quickly leave oneself open to charges of obsolescence.

> **Committee**: Disarmament and International Security (DISEC)
> **Country**: Syria
> **Topic**: Confirming Failure to Disarm
> **Student authors**: Prashanth Parameswaran and Alyssa Katz
> **School**: George C. Marshall High School

Background Information

Syria, officially known as Syrian Arab Republic, is located in the Middle East sector of southwestern Asia and bordered clockwise by Turkey, Iraq, Jordan, Israel, and Lebanon. With a total landmass of 185,180 square kilometers, the terrain entails mainly of semiarid and desert plateaus, with a narrow coastal plain along the Mediterranean Sea and the Euphrates River running across the northeastern region of this country. In 1516, the Ottomans integrated Syria into its empire and were in possession of the region until four centuries later. When World War I broke out, the Allies solicited the aid of Arab nations including Syria to fight against the Turks with promise of postbellum independence, but France took control of the region until it gained independence in 1946. Nevertheless, the vestiges of hostile anti-French sentiments have contributed to Syria's resistance to the West after 1954.

Between 1946 and 1956, Syrian history was marked by a series of political tumults, including its participation in the 1948 Arab-Israeli War, three coups d'état in 1949, and another clash with Israeli forces in the spring of 1951. In 1961, Syria seceded from the United Arab Republic, a short-lived coalition with Egypt initiated three years before. In 1971, The Arab Socialist Renaissance (or the Ba'ath party) became the ruling political system in Syria. General Hafez al-Assad became president and ruled for the next 19 years until his death in June 2000. The unicameral, 250-member People's Assembly currently presides over the legislative branch prescribed by its 1973 constitution, while President Bashar al-Assad (the second son of the former president) and his vice-presidents Abd al-Halim ibn Said Khaddam and Muhammad Zuhayr Mashariqa currently govern the executive branch.

Introduction

On April 17, 2003, Syrian Foreign Minister Farouk Al-Sharaa said, "The Syrian government is ready to sign a treaty under the UN's supervision to make the whole Middle East a zone free from all mass destruction weapons—nuclear, chemical, and biological."[1] The Syrian Arab Republic is dedicated to strengthening the biological and nuclear non-proliferation regime, primarily through the two agreements, Biological Weapons Convention (BWC), and the Nuclear Non-Proliferation Treaty (NPT), while maintaining a defense capability in the field of chemical weapons in the interest of national security and the belligerence of Israel.

History

Israel's belligerent policy toward Syria is the main obstacle to our approach to regional disarmament. War is still a possibility since Israel has not agreed to withdraw peacefully from the Syrian Golan Heights and the zone in southern Lebanon which it has illegally occupied since the Arab-Israeli wars of 1967 and 1978, respectively. In the words of then Syrian ambassador to the United States, Walid al-Moualem, "Syria regards the Israeli occupation of both areas as an affront to Syria's honor, an encroachment on its sovereignty, and a serious threat to its security."[2] Furthermore, Israel is the only nation in the Middle East that has nuclear capabilities, and has launched air strikes and detonated car bombs in Damascus in 2003 and 2004 to escalate tension. Given Israel's systematic infringement of national sovereignty and threats to regional peace and security, the Syrian Arab Republic has decided to develop some defensive capabilities in the field of chemical weapons.

---

1 "Syria proposes Mideast free of WMD," CNN.com, April 17, 2003, http://edition.cnn.com/2003/WORLD /meast/04/16/sprj.irq.un.syria/ (accessed January 2, 2005).

2 Zuhar Diab, "Syria's Chemical and Biological Weapons: Assessing Capabilities and Motivations," *The Nonproliferation Review*, 1997.

Syria's General Position

Therefore, Syria is unwilling to accede to the Chemical Weapons Convention (CWC) until all weapons of mass destruction have been eliminated from the Middle East, and Israel adheres to the BWC and NPT. As Syria's ambassador to Egypt, Issa Darwish, announced in 1999, "All Arab countries have adhered to the nuclear Non-Proliferation Treaty while Israel has refused to do so. . . . By possessing nuclear weapons, the Jewish State threatens the peace and security of the Middle East, the Mediterranean region and Europe. Arabs do not possess weapons of mass destruction."[3] Therefore, Israel needs to adhere to the 2004 General Assembly resolution A/59/462 on "The Risk of Nuclear Proliferation in the Middle East." Operative clause 5 reads as follows: "The Assembly, noting that Israel remained the only State in the Middle East that has yet become party to the NPT, would call upon it to accede to the Treaty without further delay and not to develop, produce, test or otherwise acquire nuclear weapons, and to renounce possession of nuclear weapons and to place all its un-safeguarded nuclear facilities under full-scope International Atomic Energy Agency (IAEA) safeguards."[4] Secondly, Israel must end its illegal occupation of the Golan Heights and the zone in southern Lebanon.

Until the aforementioned conditions are met, the Syrian Arab Republic will continue strengthening its long-range strike and defense capabilities to deter an Israeli invasion. As it has mentioned earlier at the Review Conference and General Assembly sessions, "Syria affirms its adherence to the Charter regarding the right of self-defense when being exposed to any aggression."[5] Should Israel choose to attack, as Mr. Darwish stated, "Damascus will respond by using chemical weapons and Syria is now preparing to face up to any Israeli threat. . . . The response will be severe if Israel goes further in its threats to strike Syria with nuclear weapons . . . Syria is not planning a war or an attack against any party, but it will confront Israeli threats and has a military option."[6] It should be noted that Syria has never responded to this systematic Israeli aggression with weapons of mass destruction, since unlike Israel, Syria is fully committed to seeking a peaceful solution and maintaining regional stability. For instance, when Israel launched air strikes against Syria in 2003, Syria went to the Security Council to seek a diplomatic solution instead of retaliating and causing an outbreak of war.

---

3 The Acronym Institute, "Fierce Israel-Syria Exchange on Chemical Weapons," *The Acronym Institute for Disarmament Diplomacy*, 1999.

4 United Nations General Assembly, Resolution A/59/462, "The Risk of Nuclear Proliferation in the Middle East," 2004.

5 Reaching Critical Will, "Syria: Explanation of Vote on L.50 (HCOC)," First Committee, 2004.

6 "Fierce Israel-Syria Exchange on Chemical Weapons, *The Acronym Institute for Disarmament Diplomacy*, Issue 11, December 1996.

Nevertheless, it should be made clear that Syria is reluctant to reduce its weapons stockpiles in this category unless Israel fulfills the requirements mentioned above. Syria is also dependent on several nations for technological assistance, but their names cannot be disclosed to the public at large. As it is not a signatory to the CWC, Syria does not sign safeguard agreements with the Organization for the Prohibition of Chemical Weapons (OPCW) or subject its capabilities to inspections by the agency.

With regard to nuclear weapons, the Syrian Arab Republic supports the NPT and IAEA in achieving its main goal, a Middle East free of weapons of mass destruction. Syria supports the strengthening of the Non-Proliferation Treaty, and compels the non-signatories, particularly Israel, to sign on to the agreement. Syria signed the 1925 Geneva Protocol banning the use of chemical and bacteriological methods of offensive warfare, and ratified it in 1968, with the reservation that it did not represent recognizing Israel as a nation, only as a geographical location. At the 59th annual session of the General Assembly, Syria voted for resolution A/59/457 on international arrangements to assure nonnuclear–weapon states against the use or threat of use of nuclear weapons, as well as for resolution A/59/459 on moving toward a nuclear free world.

Syria possesses no offensive nuclear capability, and IAEA chief ElBaradei has defended Syria and has said there is no reason to believe Syria was part of Pakistani nuclear expert A. Q. Khan's nuclear proliferation network. As noted by the Nuclear Threat Initiative (NTI), "most of Syria's nuclear program has revolved around research and the production of isotopes for use in medical and agricultural applications, as well as civilian nuclear research."[7] Syria supports treaty provisions that encourage technology-sharing with treaty signatories for the peaceful use of nuclear weapons, and has received assistance from many nations, including Belgium, China, Germany, Russia, Argentina, India, Italy, Hungary, Yugoslavia, and Austria. Further, the Syrian Arab Republic has entered into new cooperative agreements with several countries, including Russia, where the intergovernmental Russian-Syrian Commission on Trade and Scientific and Technical Cooperation signed a memorandum of cooperation. In addition, Syria has established an Atomic Energy Commission (AECS) to manage IAEA assistance programs, which has established analytical laboratories and nuclear reactor construction, and overseas training for Syrian scientists. Syria has also signed a comprehensive safeguards agreement with the IAEA, and has submitted its facilities to annual inspections from 1992, owing to its conviction regarding the need to establish a zone free of weapons of mass destruction in the Middle East.[8]

---

7 The Nuclear Threat Initiative (NTI), "Syria's Nuclear Weapons Capabilities," NTI, 2004

8 Preparatory Committee for the 2005 Review Conference on Parties to the NPT, NPT/CONF.2005/PC.III/19, "Report Presented by the Syrian Arab Republic with a view to the realization of goals and objectives of the 1995 resolution on the Middle East and a strengthened review process for the NPT, " April 28, 2004.

The following report from the NPT Preparatory Session for the 2005 Review Conference summarizes Syria's commitments thus far in working toward a Middle East Nuclear Weapon Free Zone (MENWFZ):

> Syria has long been a front runner, whether in the UN or the League of Arab States, in the appeal to make the Middle East a zone free of weapons of mass destruction, especially nuclear weapons. It has striven tirelessly and effectively for the creation of such a zone. It has worked assiduously, through the annual regular sessions of the IAEA General Conference, for the adoption of a resolution for the application of the Agency's safeguards in the Middle East, requiring that all parties directly concerned to consider in earnest the adoption of suitable, practical measures for the implementation of the proposal to establish a nuclear-weapons–free zone in the Middle East. It has invited the countries concerned to accede to the international non-proliferation regimes, including the NPT, as their means of completing their contribution towards a zone free of all weapons of mass destruction in the Middle East (document GC (46)/16). Israel, however, has not responded to that invitation, but rather insists on continuing to be the sole country in the region to remain outside the international system, refusing to accede to any international call emanating from the UN, whether from the General Assembly or the Security Council.[9]

With regard to biological weapons, Syria signed the Convention on the Prohibition of the Development, Production, and Stockpiling of Bacteriological and Toxin Weapons and on their Destruction (BWTC) in April 1972. Syria thus possesses no offensive biological weapons capability in this area. As correctly noted by the NTI, "on the basis of present knowledge, any conclusions about weaponization or deployment modes with regard to Syria's biological capabilities must be speculative. There are no clear indications that Syria currently possesses an offensive biological weapons capability."[10] Syria does possess a defensive capability against biological weapons, where, as in many countries, scientists engage in limited research on biological agents to identify defensive needs. Research on anthrax, for instance, has been taken in support of efforts to improve the productivity and limit the liability of Syrian agriculture and their vulnerability to bacillus anthracis.

---

9 Preparatory Committee for the 2005 Review Conference on Parties to the NPT, NPT/CONF.2005/PC.III/19, "Report Presented by the Syrian Arab Republic with a view to the realization of goals and objectives of the 1995 resolution on the Middle East and a strengthened review process for the NPT," April 28, 2004.

10 The Nuclear Threat Initiative, "Syria's Biological Weapons Capabilities," 2004.

Data is also analyzed to combat diseases and initiate a program for the vaccination of livestock against anthrax.

All research, development, and production activities and facilities are run by the Center for Scientific Research (CERS). Syria has obtained biological material from twelve national pharmaceutical companies, but does receive substantial foreign technological assistance from nations which cannot be disclosed in the interest of national security. However, the CERS building complex, which also deals in chemical weapons capability, has not been declared to the IAEA for inspection since Syria has not signed the CWC or ratified the BWC. Thus no safeguard agreements are in force, and no inspections by the IAEA have been conducted in this field, although various disarmament institutes have come to an international consensus that Syria possesses no offensive biological weapons and is merely engaging in research and development for agricultural and epidemiological purposes.

Syria's Views on the Current Status of the Issue

Syria believes that the nuclear Non-Proliferation Treaty (NPT) is under severe threat from non-compliance by nuclear weapon states (NWS) and the lack of universality in its scope. The NPT is based on a two-fold agreement by nuclear weapon and non-nuclear weapon states, where the former shares peaceful uses of nuclear technology and reduces its nuclear weapon stockpiles, while the latter group agrees not to pursue nuclear weapons.[11] However, the NWS have fallen behind in their commitments at the 2000 NPT Review Conference under which they agreed to pursue disarmament by entering the Comprehensive Nuclear Test Ban Treaty (CTBT), conduct multilateral negotiations for a treaty banning production of fissile material for nuclear weapons, and promote the principles of transparency and irreversibility in arms reductions and cut in non-strategic weapons.[12]

The United States, in particular, has opposed the CTBT and opposed any verification regime for a Fissile Material Cut-Off Treaty (FMCT) which will ban plutonium production and uranium enrichment. It has undermined negotiations with Russia by withdrawing from the Anti-Ballistic Missile Treaty, and the 2002 Moscow Treaty signed by the two nations lacks any provisions on verification, transparency, irreversible dismantlement of destruction.[13] The United States also supports Israel's refusal to enter the NPT, and has long opposed the establishment of a Middle East Nuclear Weapon Free Zone. Syria views this as a threat to international peace and security,

11 Kennedy School of Government at Harvard University, "Project of Managing the Bomb: Initiatives on Arms Control and What Needs to be Done," 2004.

12 Jim Wurst, "U.N. Disarmament Committee Addresses Proliferation," Global Security Newswire, 2004.

13 Kennedy School of Government, "Project of Managing the Bomb," 2004.

since every other nation in the Middle East is party to the NPT. Moreover, due to Israel's nuclear arsenal, other Arab nations have begun to develop their own defensive capabilities in the event of an Israeli invasion. The United States also rejected Syria's draft proposal to the United Nations Security Council in the latter half of April 2003 for the elimination of all weapons of mass destruction——chemical, biological, and nuclear—from the Middle East for all nations including Syria herself.[14] The establishment of a nuclear weapon–free zone is in the interest of all Middle Eastern nations, but the United States and Israel continue to threaten the stability of the region.

The United States also continues its attempts to destabilize the IAEA by eavesdropping on the atomic agency with activities such as, but not limited to, listening in on phone calls, and even reported meetings. ElBaradei was furious with these alleged espionage activities, arguing that it would be "a major violation of our right to independence, and tampering with their (the IAEA's) intelligence would be tampering with the whole fabric of multilateralism and the United Nations system as we know it."[15] From Syria's perspective, the United States still bears a grudge against ElBaradei since he stood up against U.S.-alleged reports of Iraq's WMD possession and found evidence to the contrary, and on a number of key occasions found Iraq to be complying with the IAEA. Regardless of motive, however, Syria feels that this destabilizes the nonproliferation regime and is not the proper moral conduct for the world's superpower.

Although Syria has yet to ratify the Biological Weapons Convention (BWC), it notes with deep regret that the BWC still lacks a verification protocol. Once again, the unilateralism of the United States is to blame, since it systematically criticized the Ad Hoc Group formed by the parties of the Convention. The Ad Hoc Group spent six years developing a protocol for states to submit to an international body of declarations, which included the possibility of challenge inspections and routine on-site visits. The United States rejected the protocol offered by the Group and was the only nation in favor of terminating its mandate. Since the negotiations are based on consensus, they failed. Further, Syria feels that more coordination needs to be fostered between the BWC and the World Health Organization (WHO) so that the organizations can organize a joint aid team in the event of a major biological hazard or disease outbreak.

Syria has not signed the Chemical Weapons Convention (CWC) as part of its protest campaign with Egypt and other Arab countries to seek the dismantlement

---

14 Preparatory Committee for the 2005 Review Conference on Parties to the NPT, NPT/CONF.2005/PC.III/19, "Report Presented by the Syrian Arab Republic with a view to the realization of goals and objectives of the 1995 resolution on the Middle East and a strengthened review process for the NPT," April 28, 2004

15 "UN nuclear chief warns US against eavesdropping on IAEA," Agence France Presse, January 5, 2004.

of Israel's nuclear program before other states adhere to arms agreements. However, Syria believes there is a strong foundation with regard to the CWC. Despite this fact, Syria contends that this part of the nonproliferation regime is also under the greatest degree of threat from advances in science and technology, as well as globalization. Millions of chemicals are being proliferated and synthesized in more efficient and surreptitious ways and means as we look to the future. Furthermore, there still remains a significant amount of chemical weapons stockpiles in various nations that need to be secured and destroyed, and kept out of the hands of terrorist organizations. Moreover, national implementation of the CWC also lacks the participation and coordination with other international agencies as part of a global outbreak alert system.

Possible Solutions

The following are possible measures or solutions that Syria advocates the international community should undertake to overcome the aforementioned problems with regard to the nonproliferation regime:

Nuclear Weapons and the NPT

1. Syria believes the first step to a comprehensive solution is that the international community needs to secure Israel's entrance into the NPT and take significant steps to establish a NWFZ in the Middle East. The former PrepCom session suggested that the MENWFZ would come together with the road map to peace, but Syria disagrees with this notion and contends that "the importance of the nuclear weapon free zone should not be underestimated or tied to specific kinds of political or regional developments."[16]

2. Secondly, arms export controls need to be strengthened and linked to the implementation of Additional Protocols with the IAEA to ensure verification.

3. Syria believes in IAEA Director General Mohamed ElBaradei's initiative to multilateralize the sensitive parts of the fuel cycle, such as enrichment and reprocessing activities, thereby limiting highly enriched uranium and plutonium from the fuel cycle. As agreed at the PrepCom session, the IAEA Director General should appoint an expert panel for examining possible solutions to this risk and provide an interim report by the 2005 Review Conference.[17]

---

16 Jean du Perez, "2003 NPT Preparatory Committee: Progress Towards 2005 or Business as Usual?," 2004.

17 "Curbing Nuclear Proliferation: An Interview With Mohammed ElBaradei," *Arms Control Today*, 2004.

4. The IAEA, NPT, and the UN Security Council also need to coordinate their efforts to energize the collective security system for member states to delegitimize nuclear weapons.[18]

5. There should be a verified, transparent, and irreversible reduction of arsenals of NWS leading to their elimination along the lines of the 2000 Review Conference.

6. The CTBT needs to be put into force and ratified by all NWS as agreed at the 2000 Review Conference.

7. Negotiate a Fissile Material Cut-Off Treaty (FMCT) covering all materials in weapons-separated plutonium and highly enriched uranium.

8. Work toward a universal or multilateral negotiated legally binding establishment of a Convention for the Prohibition and Elimination of Nuclear Weapons comparable to the one for chemical weapons.

9. Strengthen the review process through regular reporting, and emphasize and strengthen IAEA safeguards. The Additional Protocol needs to be universalized, and the IAEA safeguards system should be adequately funded to carry out its function.[19]

10. Disarmament and nonproliferation education need to be instituted at the global and national level.

11. A system of either the institution of sanctions or massive pressure by the Security Council needs to be developed in order to prevent member States from obtaining fissile material and then withdrawing, such as North Korea, since this severely paralyzes the nonproliferation regime.[20]

Biological Weapons and the Biological Weapons Convention (BWC)

1. Syria believes that the Protocol to the BWC established by the Ad Hoc Group has potential for success, and should be reconsidered, and the Ad Hoc Group should be reconvened and their proposals reconsidered, since the United States is the only nation opposing their mandate.[21]

2. Regional initiatives should also be taken to strengthen the BWC, such as implementing national legislation, holding regional conferences, and establishing networks to monitor the outbreak of disease.[22]

---

18 Ibid.

19 NPT/CONF.2005/PC.III/WP.27, Chairman's Summary of the Committee Sessions, May 10, 2004.

20 Du Perez, "2003 NPT Preparatory Committee," 2004.

21 Arms Control Association, "Briefing Paper on the Status of Biological Weapons Nonproliferation," May 2003.

22 Iris Hunger, "Bulletin 19: BWC Conference Fails: What Needs to Be Done Next?" International Network of Engineers and Scientists Against Proliferation, 2002.

3. Work with the World Health Organization (WHO) to be part of a global outbreak response team which will react quickly to an outbreak of disease or release of harmful biological agents by rapid deployment.
4. Begin discussions on the Conference topic for 2005, namely establishing standards for how scientists work with dangerous biological agents.
5. Consider the U.S. proposals presented at previous conferences, provided that they are all conducted within the framework of the re-established Ad Hoc Group.[23]

Chemical Weapons and the CWC

1. Syria believes that member states should focus on speeding up the destruction of chemical weapons stockpiles.[24]
2. State parties should improve national implementation of the CWC within the frameworks of domestic legislation.
3. The response capacity of the OPCW needs to be strengthened in coordination with other international agencies such as the WHO, and it needs to join the BWC to play a role in the international task force or team to respond to biological or chemical attacks.

Relevant Bloc Positions and Current Issues

As a member of the Arab League, Syria will continue to work with Arab nations for a Middle East free of nuclear weapons, and urge Israel to live up to its disarmament commitments.

Syria is also a falsely suspected weaponized or weaponizing state and accusations have been hurled regarding its possible acquiring of weapons of mass destruction and using its arsenal for offensive capabilities. As mentioned earlier, Syria only possesses a defensive capacity, and it hopes that the international community will not be duped into falling for false American intelligence once again, which was used to invade Iraqi national sovereignty based on the same threat of WMD.

The United States has recently stepped up its efforts to undermine Syria's security and position in the world, by suggesting that the Syrian leader Mr. Assad is going on a "shopping spree for missiles" to the Russian Federation in January 2005. Once again, Syria denies all such false intelligence as the Russian Federation has,

---

23 Jenni Rissanen, "BWC Report: Left in A Limbo: Review Conference Suspended on Edge of Collapse," *Disarmament Diplomacy* 62, January–February 2002.

24 Director General of the OPCW Rogelio Pfirter, "The Global Ban on Chemical Weapons Commitment and Confidence in the OPCW," Disarmament Watch, 2003.

and would like to call on the United States to start acting like a superpower rather than undermining the very spirit of the nonproliferation regime which Syria strives to achieve.

(Student Authors' Note: This paper was written in mid-January 2005, to make the NHSMUN deadline of February 1. The last paragraph may need to be amended, pending the results of President Assad's visit to Russia.)

Bibliography

Agence France Presse. "UN nuclear chief warns US against eavesdropping on IAEA." January 5, 2004.

Arms Control Association. "Briefing Paper on the Status of Biological Weapons Nonproliferation." May 2003.

"Curbing Nuclear Proliferation: An Interview With Mohammed ElBaradei." *Arms Control Today*. 2004.

Diab, Zuhair. "Syria's Chemical and Biological Weapons: Assessing Capabilities and Motivations." *The Nonproliferation Review*. 1997.

Director General of the OPCW Rogelio Pfirter. "The Global Ban on Chemical Weapons Commitment and Confidence in the OPCW." *Disarmament Watch*. 2003.

"Fierce Israel-Syria Exchange on Chemical Weapons. *Disarmament Diplomacy* (The Acronym Institute): 11, December 1996, http://www.acronym.org.uk /dd/dd11/11issyr.htm.

Hunger, Iris. "Bulletin 19: BWC Conference Fails: What Needs to Be Done Next?" International Network of Engineers and Scientists Against Proliferation. 2002.

Jean du Perez. "2003 NPT Preparatory Committee: Progress towards 2005 or Business as Usual?" 2004.

Kennedy School of Government at Harvard University. "Project on Managing the Bomb: Initiatives on Arms Control and What Needs to be Done." 2004.

Microsoft Encarta Online Encyclopedia 2004. "Syria." http://encarta.msn.com /encyclopedia_761569233_3/Syria.html#s19. Accessed January 14, 2005.

The Nuclear Threat Initiative (NTI). "Syria's Biological Weapons Capabilities." 2004.

The Nuclear Threat Initiative (NTI). "Syria's Nuclear Weapons Capabilities." 2004.

Preparatory Committee for the 2005 Review Conference of the Parties to the Treaty on the Non-Proliferation of Nuclear Weapons (NPT).

NPT/CONF.2005/PC.III/19: "Report presented by the Syrian Arab
  Republic . . . with a view to the realization of goals and objectives of the
  1995 resolution on the Middle East within the framework of and a
  strengthened review process for the NPT." April 28, 2004. http://www.un.org
  /ga/search/view_doc.asp?symbol=NPT/CONF.2005/PC.III/19.
Reaching Critical Will. "Syria: Explanation of Vote on L.50 (HCOC)." First
  Committee. 2004.
Rissanen, Jenni. "BWC Report: Left in A Limbo: Review Conference Suspended
  on Edge of Collapse," *Disarmament Diplomacy* (The Acronym Institute): 62,
  January–February 2002, http://www.acronym.org.uk/dd/dd62/62bwc.htm.
"Syria." *CIA World Factbook.* https://www.cia.gov/library/publications/the-world
  -factbook/geos/sy.html.
"Syria proposes Mideast free of WMD. CNN.com, April 17, 2003. http://edition
  .cnn.com/2003/WORLD/meast/04/16/sprj.irq.un.syria/. Accessed January 2,
  2005.
"Syrian Arab Republic History and Government." *Syrian Arab Republic.* October
  3, 2004. AME Info: Middle East Business and Financial News Source.
  January 13, 2005.
United Nations General Assembly. Resolution A/59/462: "The Risk of Nuclear
  Proliferation in the Middle East." 2004.
Wurst, Jim. "U.N. Disarmament Committee Addresses Proliferation." Global
  Security Newswire. 2004.

APPENDIX E: LESSON PLANS

Lesson Plan: Speaking Opportunities

Name of Course: Model UN

Exercise Title: Speaking Opportunities

Methods: Lecture

Training Aids Needed: Projector to show where you are in the rules of procedure. If you want to outline this lecture, show the main chronological flow of the MUN session so that the students can follow along. An example follows this lesson plan.

Student Handouts Needed: Copies of rules of procedure, cheat sheet

Special Instructions: Bring water. You'll be talking a lot in this session.

Your Actions: Straight lecture. No special actions needed.

Your Commentary:

Model UN offers you numerous opportunities to score points by speaking. The key thing to remember: Always take the opportunity to speak, no matter how minor. Many Chairs simply keep a tally of how many times delegates speak, with no differentiation between a long, brilliantly argued tour d'horizon of the substantive issues before the committee and a very short "I think we should close debate" observation. So speak often, get yields, ask questions.

Here's the general line of march of a typical MUN committee session. There will be some differences in some of the historical simulations, but we'll discuss those special situations when we are attending a conference that offers them.

There are two types of speeches: substantive and procedural. Substantive speeches talk about the issues that the UN is considering— terrorism, narcotics trafficking, child soldiers, budgetary issues, etc. Procedural speeches look at how the committee is going about its business—creating speaker lists, voting on resolutions, and the like.

When a committee session starts, the Chair will give various welcoming remarks, then hand out the placards for each delegation. After that, the Chair will call **roll**, to determine how many delegations are necessary for a quorum. Although there are 193 countries with formal voting rights in the UN General Assembly, and a few other countries and organizations that have observer status, it is very unlikely that all of these entities will be represented at most of the conferences that you will be attending. So the Chair will call the roll, tally how many countries are in that committee, and determine what the quorums are for discussion and for voting. (Some rules make this distinction. Usually quorums for discussion are smaller than quorums for voting.) Be sure to speak up, and just say "present." Do not say "present and voting," which in strict parliamentary terms means that you may not abstain from a vote. There is no upside to doing this.

After that, the opportunities for you to speak begin, starting with **substantive speeches**.

The first opportunity is called **General Debate**. You might have seen this in news media coverage of the UN General Assembly's autumn opening ceremonies, when heads of state from around the world flock to New York City to give their views on global issues. This is your opportunity to give what will probably be the longest speech at the conference—three minutes, if you are lucky. You can cover any of the topics that are on the agenda for your committee, so use your research well, and try to at least touch on all of the topics, focusing on those that are critical to your country.

General Debate begins with the Chair opening the Speakers' List. The Chair asks the delegates who wants to speak. Those who do raise their placards, and the Chair begins a long list (this can run into sixty to seventy names, if not more, at the larger conferences) of what countries will speak, in the order in which he/she calls them. This list is usually shown on a white/blackboard or projected on a screen. Delegates may add their names to the end of the Speakers' List by sending a note to the dais. Even if you have already spoken, you can usually get added to the end of the Speakers' List.

At some point, those who are at the end of the Speakers' List, or those who are not on the list at all, will give up hope of getting a chance to speak, and will move to **set the agenda**. This means that the delegate proposes a specific sequence in which the main topics—usually two or three for each committee—will be discussed. You want to make sure that the topics come in an order that is most beneficial to you as a delegate, as well as to your country. Although there may be an issue that is especially unwelcome to your country, you might want it to be addressed first, so that you can demonstrate your skills at playing defense. You will get more chances to speak if everyone is inveighing against your policies. But you do *not* want to say "bring it on" by moving to bring that specific issue to the fore.

A motion to set the agenda is usually debatable, although often limited to two speakers in favor and two opposed. Make sure you are one of those four speakers.

After the agenda has been set, the committee moves into a discussion of the first **topic**. The Chair retires the General Debate Speakers' List, and opens a new one on that topic. Get on this new Speakers' List. Things move along in the same fashion as in the General Debate, with the Chair going seriatim through the Speakers' List.

There are a few new wrinkles in the system once you get to the topics debate. You can move to switch to a **moderated caucus**. This means that the Speakers' List —and much of the rest of the rules of procedure—is suspended, usually for five to ten minutes, and the Chair calls upon delegates at random, independent of the Speakers' List. This allows for more back-and-forth between delegates, and usually for livelier debate. Again, get your placard up early and often, and get called upon.

You can also move to an **unmoderated caucus**, in which the committee goes into a recess—usually ten or so minutes—allowing delegates to get a snack, go to the restroom, and more importantly, to discuss privately the possibilities of writing resolutions with like-minded delegates. Usually, the motions for moderated and unmoderated caucuses are subject to limited debate. If your delegates are making a motion for an unmoderated caucus, they should be prepared to give a reason—for example, to allow delegates to confer on a working paper.

Resolutions will be introduced at some point during the topic's debate. The initial draft of a resolution is called a **working paper**. There are two phases of the resolution discussion that permit several speaking options. During the **Introduction of the Resolution**, sponsors read aloud the resolution—at least the operative paragraphs, and sometimes the preambular clauses. Make sure that you get to read at least one paragraph; do not let the principal drafter read everything. Once the resolution has had its reading, the Chair will open the floor to questions. There are two question periods. One is for checking typos, infelicitous language, spelling errors, and other nonsubstantive issues. If you're in the audience and spot something, raise it. The second period allows for substantive questions. This gives both the audience and the resolution's sponsors great opportunities to get in speeches. As a member of the audience, no matter what the topic, you should try to get in some question. These questions often are counted in the tally as much as speeches. In turn, if you're not the primary sponsor, you should nonetheless attempt to answer virtually every question, even if it has been adequately covered by another sponsor. We'll have a separate practice session devoted to **Q&As**.

Once the introductory phase has finished, the resolution then comes up for its own debate. A separate Speakers' List for **speeches regarding the resolution's merits** is opened, and things move along much the same way as you have already seen with general and topic debate.

Amendments might be introduced during the debate on the resolution. If they show up, the Speakers' List for the resolution temporarily closes, and a new Speakers' List is formed. There are two types of amendments: **friendly** and **unfriendly**. An amendment is deemed friendly if all of the sponsors say that it's fine by them to include the amendment in the text of the resolution. In that case, it's adopted without debate, and debate continues on the resolution. However, if even one sponsor balks, the amendment is considered unfriendly, and thus becomes open to debate and voting.

Procedural speeches are the second main class of speeches. They are much shorter than the substantive speeches, and are focused on how the committee is conducting its business. If you sneak in a substantive point without the Chair calling you to order, fine, but in general, you want to speak to the topic at hand—the conduct of the meeting.

Procedural speeches can include speaking for or against certain parliamentary **motions**, such as opening and closing the Speakers' List, changing the time limits on speeches, and changing the number of questions that can be asked of a speaker.

One can also get short amounts of time through **yields** from other delegates. While a speaker can yield time back to the Chair, you should never do this—it's just a waste of the time you were given. More effective is getting and giving yields to **like-minded speakers**. Again, the time will be short, but at least you're getting credit for speeches. If a delegate yields to **questions**, make sure to get your placard up quickly. In some conferences, the Chair permits **comments** regarding the previous speech. Again, this is worth your time. The rules usually say that the comments have to be directly relevant to the previous speech, but Chairs usually give you wide latitude to speak about the overall topic.

Finally there are some opportunities for speaking during **voting** procedures. Most votes will be by simple placard count, but there are occasions in which a roll-call vote will be taken on substantive resolutions, and perhaps even amendments. Delegates are permitted to request an explanation of vote following the announcement of the vote tally. You get on this Speakers' List by saying "Yes, with right of explanation," or "No, with right of explanation," when your country's name is called during the roll call. The rules usually state that these explanations are to be used to explain the reason why you voted "out of character" (sometimes known as "out of policy") on a vote, e.g., voting "yes" on something that you would normally oppose.

However, Chairs again usually look the other way and give you wide latitude during these speeches.

In our next session, we'll practice writing and delivering some of these specialized speeches.

OUTLINE OF OPPORTUNITIES TO SPEAK: PARLIAMENTARY PROCEDURE

Substantive Speeches
- Following Opening Remarks, Hand out of Placards, and Roll Call
- General Debate
- Set Agenda
- Topics
- Speakers' List
- Moderated Caucus
- Unmoderated Caucus
- Resolutions
- Introduction of the Resolution, Q&As
- Speeches
- Amendments
- Friendly
- Unfriendly

Procedural Speeches
- Motions
- Open Speaker' List
- Close Speakers' List
- Change Time of Speeches, Number of questions
- Questions
- Yields
- Chair
- Another Speaker
- Comments
- Voting
- Placard
- Roll Call
- Explanation of Vote

Lesson/Exercise Plan: Speechwriting

Name of Course: Model UN

Exercise Title: Speechwriting

Methods: Short lecture, student writing assignments, student delivery of short speeches

Training Aids Needed:

Student Handouts Needed: Writing tablet, note cards

Special Instructions: None

Your Actions: Hand out the writing materials to the students.

Your Commentary:

Today we're going to look at the process of creating speeches. Some call this speech *writing*, but there will often be times when you won't have time to actually write down anything, but will have to speak off the top of your head. But whether you have had weeks to create an eloquent presentation, minutes to draft notes for an extemporaneous observation, or seconds to put down your placard, stand up, and speak, the principles we'll examine all apply.

In any MUN speech, you have to put foremost the diplomatic character you are creating. You are no longer a high school student, you are the ambassador from your member nation. You thus have to create a persona appropriate for that role. This is done via the uniform our team wears—either Western business attire or country-specific native costume—and by the style of speech we employ.

We will always be polite to the Chair. This attitude is established in the very first words that we will use in *every* speech you give: "Thank you, Mr./Madam Chair, fellow delegates." It is crucial that you show proper respect to the Chair and your audience up front. We're often nervous getting into our speech, but setting this tone will help in how the audience and Secretariat receive your message.

We will also use language and style appropriate to that of a senior representative of a government. This includes:

- Avoiding "youthspeak" in its various forms, including
  - a lilt at the end of a declarative sentence that makes the sentence sound like a question. Linguistically, the implied question mark is being used to say "you agree with me on this, right?" but sounds to the audience like you are unsure of yourself.

    – slang, in any form

    – references to pop culture that would not be used in a Foreign Ministry's public pronouncements

- Using *le mot juste* (the right word), rather than an informal term. Informality in general is not prized in this form of speech.
- Being attentive to the cultural sensitivities of the nations represented, as well of as the individuals in the room.
- Avoiding "I" language. You are representing the government, not yourself. Use "the government of _____ believes X" rather than "I think X."
- Dropping unneeded fillers, including "ums," "ers," "ehs," and more sophisticated fillers, such as "if you will."
- Using pauses effectively. Although our interior monologue—that little voice in your head—is saying "come on. You've got to say something right now!" ignore it. Pauses let the audience catch up to you, and makes you look thoughtful. And a pattern of naturally pausing means that the audience won't notice it if/when you pause because you have forgotten what your next point is and you have to stop to think.

The structure of a Model UN speech is fairly simple:

- **Greeting**: "Mr./Mme. Chair," etc.
- **General observation**: "Our country supports X."
- **Reasons** for supporting X: Usually you will have time for no more than three reasons. The audience also won't be able to remember anything much more complex, so keep it simple for them.
- **Conclusion**: "We look forward to working with like-minded delegations on getting X enshrined in a resolution." Or "Please join us in voting against the motion to close debate."

The way you dress up your speech goes a long way in establishing the issues that *you* want discussed on the topic. Remember, you are trying to make *your* speech the one that everyone else will be talking about. You're there to set the table; everyone else picks from it.

Among the techniques you'll find helpful:

- **Facts**: You're trying to establish credibility on the topic, letting the Chair know that you have done the research and are the go-to person in the room on the issue. A simple way of doing this is what pundits do on the Sunday morning public affairs television shows. Offering three facts—no matter what they are—on an issue gives the impression of knowledge about that issue. You can even echo those three facts in follow-up speeches. These three facts could be as simple as citing a paragraph from the UN Charter, quoting from a treaty, and quoting from some notable in the field of inquiry.

- **Statistics**: A subset of the Facts technique is to use statistics. Citing from UN studies, public opinion surveys, learned journals, government reports, and the like all give the impression that there is empirical backing for your position.

- **Narrative**: Facts, however, are often difficult to remember. Some facts are difficult to "wrap one's head around," i.e., to understand the magnitude. Saying "300,000 child soldiers are adversely affected" is difficult for the mind's eye to see. Instead, try personalizing the point you're making by creating a story about one child who was so affected. Give him a name, a backstory, friends, hobbies, and then tell how his life changed dramatically for the worse when the issue came to his village. Then multiply that story by 300,000. "*This* is why we must act."

- **Parallel construction**: Sometimes simply echoing the same point, stated slightly differently, can drive the point home. In parallel construction, the speaker starts a series of sentences with the same words, but then ends each sentence with a slightly different twist. So, for example, "The nation of X calls itself a land of opportunity. But we all see a land of opportunity in which child mortality is the worst in the world. A land of opportunity in which literacy is the lowest in the world. A land of opportunity rife with rioting. A land of opportunity in which freedom of expression is unknown."

[**Instructor Action**]: Now have the students draft short—no more than one minute—speeches in which they use one of these techniques. (Just keep it to one for the moment.) Work with them on the flow and tone of it, but let them keep it in the style that best fits them. If you run out of time, you can have them deliver these speeches at the next practice session.

Lesson/Exercise Plan: Basic MUN Public Speaking, with emphasis on Projecting/Audibility

Name of Course: Model UN

Exercise Title: Basic MUN Public Speaking, with emphasis on Projecting/ Audibility

Methods: Short lecture, student speech practice

Training Aids Needed: Microphone

Student Handouts Needed: Any speech, or even text, will do. If the students would like to give a speech they have written, great.

Special Instructions: It is helpful if you have rooms roughly the same size as the meeting halls the students will experience at each conference. Many committee rooms are the size of thirty-student classrooms, but at large conferences, students will find themselves facing two hundred to four hundred delegates in committees. At large conferences, plenary sessions can hold well over two thousand students. Try to book the school's cafeteria and/or the auditorium for these practice sessions.

Your Actions: Model appropriate microphone use. Do *not* tap it, do *not* blow into it. Mikes are not going to make up for a soft voice—you'll still need to project, but not yell, into it.

Your Commentary:

All the knowledge in the world regarding the UN, your country, and the issues in your committee does not matter if you don't put that knowledge to work. You have to communicate that knowledge, in your position papers, your resolutions, and perhaps most importantly of all, in your public speaking, both substantively and procedurally.

Persuasive Speaking also has a triangle, and each point has a sub-triangle. The key points of the triangle are **style**, **research**, and **persuasion**.

For **style**, consider **character**—accurately representing the government of your country; costume (either native costume or business attire); and eye contact. Don't bother reading your speech; speak from your notes. Keep in mind that you are no longer a student—you are the ambassador of a country. Most Chairs prefer that you *not* use first-person pronouns. Rather than say "we believe" or "I think," try "the delegation of Republic of Fiji wishes to underscore that . . . " or "the people and government of Republic of Fiji believe . . ."

Get comfortable with having your microphone an inch from your mouth at all times. Gesture often, but only with one hand, not both, if you're holding a microphone. Despite what you have seen other speakers do, do not tap the microphone. Do not blow into it. Microphones are very delicate instruments. If you want to test whether the microphone is working, just say something into it.

When people are initially learning public speaking, they will want to write out every word of their speech to make sure that they "get it right," and then want to keep their head down and read every word aloud. Try to get away from using this crutch as soon as you can. A successful speaker is not one who drones on from prepared text. Effective speakers look the audience members in the eye. It's okay to bring up a short list of key talking points that you want to make, and to refer to them—quickly—as needed. If you get stuck for the correct word and lose your train of thought, do *not* look up, down, or to the side. Rather, look a delegate in the back of the room in the eye to search for that word. These pauses look to the audience like you are pausing for effect. While this pause seems like minutes are passing by, this is not the impression that the audience gets. The pause gives the audience a chance to catch up to the thoughts you are offering, and makes you look thoughtful.

MUN speaking times are very short. A comparatively long general debate speech might be limited by the rules or the committee to only three minutes; parliamentary procedure supporting speeches are usually thirty to sixty seconds. This is not academic debate, an entirely separate sport, in which speakers try to race through all of their arguments in an attempt to answer every issue that's been raised. Their goal is to win every argument. That's not what you're trying for here. You should attempt to slow down and be memorable, focusing on no more than three facts and three key points that you want to make. Trial attorneys will tell you that if they have ten great points they could offer to the jury, the jury will remember none of these points. So boil it down, make it simple, and make it memorable. What you are trying to do is get the other delegations to cite a point you made in their speech, "as the delegate from X so eloquently said," rather than hoping that the Chair will remember that you covered fourteen points in thirty seconds.

You can develop **stage presence**, giving the impression that you are in charge of what's going on. "Taking over the room" requires you to know in your heart of hearts that you are a great speaker, and to let that self-confidence flow into your speech. Although most speeches will be run-of-the-mill, your speech will be the one that makes the audience cut short their private chats, sit up, and listen. While some speakers have a certain native ability, stage presence can be developed, even among the most initially timid speakers.

You're going to feel nervous the first time you give a public speech. This is quite normal. Even the most polished speakers, including famous standup comedians, who earn their livelihood from looking like they are comfortable, are exceptionally nervous before they go on stage. Nervousness is your body's way of acknowledging that something that needs extra energy is coming up in a few seconds or minutes. It gives you that shot of adrenaline that you need to perform at a higher energy state than normal. It's up to you to recognize that, and channel that extra energy into presence, rather than nervous tics. Think of this as using the Star Wars "force." You can direct that force to make you a confident, energetic speaker.

One simple trick to establish credibility and authority with your audience is to **project** your voice. In these following exercises, you can mimic some of the techniques that drama coaches and singing coaches employ in teaching how to use your diaphragm in projecting your voices. One can easily be heard by an audience of two hundred, even without a microphone, with the proper projection techniques. The diaphragm allows volume; yelling from the throat merely tires out one's throat, and quickly causes hoarseness—as well as irritation on the part of the audience.

Exercise One: Finding the Diaphragm front to back. [Instructor Action]: To give the students a feeling for how the diaphragm works, have them place one hand on their stomachs, and the other hand on the small of their back, then talk. They'll feel the vibrations of the diaphragm.

Exercise Two: Finding the Diaphragm with a punch. [Instructor Action]: Another technique for finding the diaphragm is to have them pretend that they've just been punched in the gut. That forceful expulsion of air comes from the diaphragm, and has a different feel than expelling air from the voicebox. They'll quickly get the idea.

Gestures—which should be given individualized attention for every student— can also help with projection. Keeping one's hands to the side, or worse, behind one's back, constricts the diaphragm. Arm movement helps, not only with the diaphragm, but also with channeling the speaker's nervous energy. Students should not gesture for the sake of gesturing; gestures should be natural to the speaking style of the student. If it doesn't look natural, it's not going to work.

To get students used to projecting once they've found their diaphragms, try the following exercises:

Exercise Three: Murmuring. [Instructor Action]: Have half of the audience (the other students getting ready to give their speech) murmur to each other. In most MUN committees, easily half of the delegates are chatting with their friends, texting, talking about resolutions, etc., and not listening to the speaker. The rookie speaker should get used to being initially greeted with this din, and should develop projection techniques accordingly. Have them give their speech, projecting gradually louder until they can be heard.

Exercise Four: Auditorium Projection. [Instructor Action]: Take the students to a cafeteria, an auditorium, or a hallway, with a 50- to 100-foot gap between the two halves of the team. Speakers in turn give their speeches to the faraway team, with the distant teammates giving immediate feedback as to whether they can be heard. You'll need to do this often in practice, particularly with the quiet-spoken students, as well as with the otherwise outgoing students who will mistake projection for yelling.

Exercise Five: Stand up Speaking. [Instructor Action]: Require the students to speak while standing. Students should not speak while seated—it is difficult to get the full projection effect of one's diaphragm in such a position. Standing also commands more authority in your efforts to take over the room.

Exercise Six: Losing the Lectern. [Instructor Action]: Encourage students to get away from the lectern. Grabbing on to the sides of the lectern dissipates their energy into the furniture, and thereby erodes their projection. Standing to one side, or on occasion pacing, focuses their energy into their speech. It also makes it easier to gesture, which in turn adds to the energy and interest of the presentation.

Start slowly on this one. Let them get comfortable giving a speech at all—they'll initially need that crutch of their notes. But wean them away from this habit as soon as you can. If they need their notes, they can keep them on the lectern—that's why it was invented—but look at the crowd, not the notes.

Exercise Seven: Microphones. [Instructor Action]: If you have a microphone, have each student use it, getting them comfortable with gesturing with one hand. Always keep the microphone an inch away from your mouth. They might also want to keep the microphone slightly off center from their mouths, so that words beginning with explosive *p*'s do not get distorted.

Lesson/Exercise Plan: Rules "Cheat Sheets" and Finding Loopholes

Name of Course: Model UN

Exercise Title: Rules "Cheat Sheets" and Finding Loopholes

Methods: Short lecture, followed by student workups in classroom discussion format of the rules of procedure

Training Aids Needed: Projector, computer with copy of the rules of procedure and blank cheat sheet running in separate windows

Student Handouts Needed: Note paper, copy of the rules of procedure for upcoming conference (a copy of the University of Minnesota's Model UN Rules of Procedure Long Form used by George Mason University's conference is appended). You can use either the Minnesota Long Form or the UVA Long Form to create the "cheat sheet" for practice. You can use paper separated with the following columns

RULE #	NAME OF MOTION	MAJORITY TYPE	DEBATABLE	INTERRUPT	COMMENT

along the top. A template with grid lines is available at the end of this Lesson Plan for you to photocopy.

Special Instructions: This activity, which converts the Long Form or Short Form version of a set of conference rules into an easy-to-use and understandable cheat sheet, can get tedious if you run this longer than an hour. Once you've hit an hour, pulse the audience, and if they've hit the wall, assign the rest as homework. But be sure to check their homework to make sure that they have understood the nuances of the specific conference's rules—they *all* are different.

You might also look over the cheat sheet constructed for the University of Virginia Rules of Procedure that appeared in the Parliamentary Procedure chapter of this book.

Your Actions: Run the two screens on the wall.

Your Commentary:

Today we're going to look at the rules of procedure for the next conference we'll be attending. Most teams don't bother doing this, and it's to our benefit. We'll go into the conference knowing how to use the rules, where the loopholes are, how to help the Chair in tricky situations—Chairs will remember you for this assistance—and how to use these rules for the triangle offenses and defenses.

Some teams believe that all they need to know are Robert's Rules of Order, a commonly used set of parliamentary rules used in many civic associations. This could not be further from the truth. They are *not* used in the UN or MUNs. They have absolutely no bearing on what you will be doing. All that matters is what the rules for that particular conference say. Each conference will have a different set of rules; everyone believes they can write rules better than the UN did. Rules can be as little as only one page, or up to multiple pages. Today we're going to take a look at the University of Minnesota's Long Form Rules of Procedure used by George Mason University in Fairfax, Virginia. **[Instructor Action]:** Or use a set you've obtained from an upcoming conference.

Let's first read the Rules, then create a spreadsheet/chart that we'll use as a cheat sheet. Sometimes we will get this from the conference organizers. Most often, we won't. This doesn't matter to us. We'll write our own for every conference we attend, because we're looking for different things than the conference organizers.

On a separate piece of paper, let's figure out the order of precedence of the motions (things like motion to recess; motion to call the question—let's vote on this resolution; motion to amend; etc.) and points of procedure (these will be separate, and are things like Point of Order—your new best friend; Point of Personal Preference; and the like). That means that some things, when moved, have to be considered before what the group had been considering. For example, a motion to amend a resolution has to be voted upon before you vote on the resolution as a whole. Don't worry if it takes awhile for us to get it just right; the folks who wrote the rules often haven't worked all the bugs out of the system, and we will find conflicts.

[Instructor Action]: Now facilitate the discussion. You might find that it takes most of the session to tease out this ranking. If so, fine. The second part of this lesson plan—drafting the cheat sheet—can be run in a follow-up session.

Now that we've figured out that precedence, along the top of the spreadsheet, you'll see:

RULE #	NAME OF MOTION	MAJORITY TYPE	DEBATABLE	INTERRUPT	COMMENT

Majority Type notes that some motions require a simple majority of those present, some require an absolute majority (every member of the group, no matter whether they are present or not), two-thirds majority, majority of quorum, etc.

Debatable refers to whether there are limits to debate on the motion. Some are not debated at all—the Chair simply rules on the matter, then moves on to the next issue on the agenda. Some are debatable only by a set number of speakers—usually two in favor, two against. Yet other motions—usually resolutions and amendments—do not have preset limits on how many speakers are eligible, or whether they have to take a side in favor or opposed to the motion.

Interrupt speaker—in this column you'll simply write in yes/no. These are generally high-precedence parliamentary questions—I can't hear, what are we doing, and the like.

Comment allows us to capture the oddities/special circumstances about the rule as to how it works in this conference. We will find that sometimes the rule writer has unintentionally—or intentionally—thrown strange things into the rules. Be alert to what appear to be typos—they might be intentional. Also note whether the rules supersede the UN Charter in specific instances, or rewrite parts of the

Charter. But remember, the Charter does not always trump conference Rules, and if you find a conflict between the Charter and the conference rules in advance of the conference, bring it to the attention of the conference Secretariat and ask for a ruling. If the conflict arises in committee, bring it to the attention of the Chair and ask for a ruling.

So let's start. What's the topmost item? Point of Order? Good. Let's continue with the order of precedence. Write it on the side of your sheets. Let's now go on to complete each section of the grid for each rule.

Commentary on the Rules of Procedure for George Mason University MUN Conference Using University of Minnesota MUN Rules

1. **Functions of the Chair**: The Chair is responsible for facilitating debate and for enforcing these rules of procedure (Rules section 1.5). The Chair will rule on points of order, put question to votes, announce decisions, and recognize speakers. The Chair may use discretion to alter the rules of procedure in whatever manner he or she deems necessary to enhance the debate. The Chair will maintain order in the committee. Note in Rule 7.5 that rulings by the Chair on certain rules and motions are not appealable, but others are.

2. **Quorum**: At least one-quarter of any committee must be present in order to open debate. A majority is required before a substantive question can be put to a vote. Quorum will be assumed to be present unless challenged by a member of the committee.

3. **Setting of the Agenda**: A motion to set a topic (this is the consideration at the start of a conference whereby the delegations vote on the order in which topics or agenda items [Section 1.7] are taken up) requires two speakers for and two speakers against. A simple majority of present delegations is necessary for passage. Once the vote on the agenda has been taken, typically a motion is made to open the Speakers' List for speeches by delegates, with speaking times set in advance (typically for 60–90 seconds) (Rule 2.3). Note, however, that the Minnesota rules (2.4) bans Speakers' Lists, preferring to have the Chair call upon delegations (Rule 2.3). At a point in the proceedings when delegate speeches have sufficiently defined the various perspectives on the topic, the Chair may begin to accept draft resolutions (i.e., working papers) for review and approval (Rules 4.1 and 4.2). If accepted, the committee will immediately enter formal voting procedure on all resolutions and amendments that have been introduced.

4. **Closure of Debate**: A motion to close debate (Rule 7.4) may allow two speakers for and two speakers against. A simple majority of present delegations is necessary for passage. If accepted, the committee will immediately enter formal voting procedure on all resolutions and amendments that have been introduced.

5. **Tabling of Debate**: A motion to table debate (Rule 7.3) requires two speakers for and two speakers against. A simple majority of present delegations for passage. If debate on a topic is tabled, the agenda will be considered undetermined and resolutions and amendments will not be voted on. Discussion of table topics may be resumed at a later time.

6. **Speeches**: No delegate may speak in formal debate until recognized by the Chair (Rule 2.3). Conference rules often grant the Chair the authority to maintain a Speakers' List for those wishing to speak after it is motioned open by the committee. And typically each topic will have a separate Speakers' List. However, in the Minnesota rules, note that the Chair is not obligated to open or maintain Speakers' List for each topic (Rule 2.3).

7. **Time Limits**: Time and question limits may be set by the committee. They require a simple majority.

8. **Yields**: While the Minnesota rules do not address yields (when one delegation gives up part of its speaking time to another delegation), there is often opportunity to give or receive yields. Should a speaker choose, he or she may yield time in one of three ways. If time is yielded to the Chair, the delegate will give up the floor. If time is yielded to questions, the Chair will entertain questions from the body for the speaker until the question limit is exhausted. Time yielded to another delegation may be used only to speak. No questions are allowed after a yield to another delegation.

9. **Rights of Reply**: Should a delegate feel that the honor of his or her country has been insulted by a speaker, he may submit a motion for a right of reply to the Chair in writing (Rule 2.5). If the Chair agrees, the Chair shall grant time for the insulted delegate to address the speaker's comments. This motion is rarely granted as delegates are almost always courteous.

10. **Point of Information**: A delegate may rise with this point if confused or unsure of the rules of procedure (Rule 6.2). Such a point of parliamentary procedure may not interrupt a speaker.

11. **Point of Order**: A delegate may rise to this point to bring a rule infraction to the attention of the Chair. It may only be used to interrupt a speaker if the speech violates parliamentary procedure. Also under Rule 6.1, if physically

uncomfortable or unable to hear the speaker, a delegate may rise to this point. Such a point may interrupt a speaker.

12. **Caucusing**: A motion for a caucus (or a consultative session as referred to in Rule 8.3) is in order whenever the floor is open and formal debate is in effect. It must specify a time limit and may be followed by a brief explanation of its purpose. A simple majority vote is required for its passage.

13. **Moderated Caucusing**: A moderated caucus is proposed similarly to a regular caucus. It must specify a total time and may include a time limit for individual speakers. During a moderated caucus the Chair will recognize those wishing to speak at random. Although they are a common feature of most MUN rules, the Minnesota Rules make no specific mention of moderated caucuses. Rule 2.3, however, grants the Chair broad discretion in calling on delegates to speak and to answer previously posed questions when speaking.

14. **Resolutions**: Any document meeting the requirements of a formal resolution, which includes the signatures of at least 20 percent of the assembled committee, may be submitted as a resolution (Rule 4.2). Signature does not imply support. Each document submitted as a resolution must be sponsored by one or more delegations. Sponsors are assumed to have contributed the bulk of a resolution and to be in support of it. After submission the Chair will review the document. If it meets the necessary requirements any sponsor may formally introduce it as a resolution when the delegate has the floor in formal debate. The time required to read the resolution and to answer points of clarification only will not be counted against the speaker's time limit.

15. **Amendments**: Amendments under Rules 4.3 and 4.4 may be introduced to any formal resolution. Each must have the signature of 20 percent of the body in order to be considered. If all sponsors to the resolution being amended state that the amendment is friendly, it will be automatically added to the resolution. If any sponsor considers the amendment unfriendly, it can be added to the resolution by a majority vote of the committee.

16. **Voting Procedure**: Formal voting procedure may only be entered into by closing debate. Under some conference rules, during voting procedure, the doors will be shut and no moving about or speaking by the delegates will be permissible. The Minnesota Rules on voting procedures (Section 5) are silent on this procedure. All formally introduced resolutions will

be voted on typically in the order of introduction unless otherwise motioned for and voted for by a majority vote of the committee. Note that the Minnesota Rules are silent on order of voting. Incorporation of unfriendly amendments will be voted on immediately before the resolution to which they apply. A simple placard vote will be taken on each item unless a roll call is requested. The passage of a resolution on specialized committees (like the Security Council, which has five veto nations) may be subject to different requirements. Rule 4.4 instructs that friendly amendments cannot be accepted after a vote has been taken on a contested amendment.

17. **Roll-Call Voting**: Should any delegate motion for a roll-call vote on a resolution, such a vote will automatically be taken, according to Rule 5.4, but typically such a motion will be subject to the Chair's discretion. During a roll-call vote, the Chair will ask for the vote of each delegation in alphabetical order. Delegates may reply either yes, no, abstain, or abstain from the order of voting, as noted in Rule 5.4. In other conference rules, allowing delegations to "pass" is fairly common. The Chair will call again on all nations who pass after proceeding through the committee. Each nation that has passed will then vote either yes or no, with no abstentions allowed. It is also fairly common in conference rules to find an allowance for delegations to vote "yes with rights" or "no with rights." Voters with rights of explanation will be granted thirty seconds following the vote to explain why their nation voted in apparent contradiction with its policy.

18. **Division of the Question**: This motion under Rule 7.8 is in order after debate on a topic has been closed but before the resolution to which it applies is voted on. It must specify those parts of the resolution to be voted on apart from the resolution body. The Chair may call for two delegations to speak for and two delegations against, and a simple majority vote will divide the resolution into two parts to be voted on separately.

19. **Adjournment of the Meeting**: This motion, under Rule 7.2, is not debatable, requires an immediate vote, and requires a simple majority vote to pass. When passed, the committee will be suspended until the next annual session, if there is one.

20. **Motion to Vote on Competence**: Should a delegate feel that the topic under discussion is outside the jurisdiction of the Committee or is more appropriate for another committee, he or she may bring the topic to a vote of competency (Rule 7.6). The Chair may call for two speakers for and

two speakers against. The motion requires a second, and the vote requires a simple majority to end all further debate on the topic.

Cheat Sheet Template

RULE #	NAME OF MOTION	MAJORITY TYPE	DEBATABLE	INTERRUPT	COMMENT

UMMUN RULES OF PROCEDURE: GENERAL ASSEMBLY AND ECONOMIC AND SOCIAL COUNCIL

1. Administrative

1.1 The Secretariat. The Secretariat consists of the volunteer staff members of the University of Minnesota Model United Nations.

1.2 Credentials. All questions concerning the validity of representative credentials shall be submitted in writing to the Secretariat
- The Secretariat has sole authority to decide all questions concerning credentials,
- Representatives must wear approved credentials at all times while at the Conference.

1.3 Quorum/Majority. A quorum will be one-fourth of the member delegations in attendance at the conference,
- A quorum must be present at all times during Committee/Council sessions,
- A majority is required for a substantive question to be put to a vote,
- Questions concerning quorum or majority should be directed to the Chair,
- It is the responsibility of the Chair to ensure that a quorum is present at all times.

1.4 Committee/Council Officers. The Secretariat shall appoint the President/Chairperson and Vice President/Vice Chairperson for each

Committee/Council and Shall Select any other positions necessary to help conduct the sessions of UMMUN.

1.5   **General Authority of the Chairperson.** In addition to exercising such authority conferred upon the Chair elsewhere in these rules, the Chair shall have the authority to:

- Declare the opening and closing of each session,
- Ensure the observance of the rules,
- Direct the discussions of the Committee/Council, and accord the right to speak,
- Advise the Committee/Council on methods of procedure that will enable the body to accomplish its goals,
- Rule on points and motions, and subject to these rules, shall have complete control of the proceedings of the Committee/Council and the maintenance of the order at its meetings

During the course of the session the Chair may propose:

- Limits on Debate, Closure of Debate, Enter Consultative Session and Suspension and Adjournment of the Meeting.

The Chairperson is under the direct authority of the Secretariat, and may be directed to inform the body on matters of procedure and/or the body's topical competence if such action is deemed necessary.

1.6   **Absence of Chairperson.** If the Chairperson should find it necessary to be absent during any part of a Committee/Council session, he/she will designate an individual, normally the Vice Chair, to perform the duties with the same authority. At no time will the Chair be accorded the right to vote.

1.7   **Selection of Agenda Items.** Agenda items shall be selected by the Secretariat prior to the start of the conference. Once selected, these items are fixed for the duration of the conference.

1.8   **Observer Statues.** Those delegations recognized as having Observer Status by UMMUN shall be accorded all rights in the Committee/Council except following:

- They may not vote on any item,
- They may not make or second the following motions:
  - Adjournment of the Meeting (rule 7.2),
  - Adjournment of Debate (rule 7.3),
  - Closure of debate (rule 7.4),
  - Decision of Competence (rule 7.7).

2. General Rules

2.1   **Statements by the Secretariat**. The Secretary-General, or any member of the Secretariat, may make verbal or written statements to the Committee/Council at any time.

2.2   **Diplomatic Courtesy.** Representatives must accord diplomatic courtesy to all other Representatives and Secretariat members at all times,
  - Any Representative or visitor who, after being advised by the Chair, persists in an obvious attempt to divert the meeting from its intended purpose, or who otherwise attempts to disrupt the proceeding, shall be subject to disciplinary action and expulsion form the Committee/Council by the Chair,
  - The Secretariat reserves the right to expel any Representative/ delegation from the Conference,
  - Decisions of the Chair on diplomatic courtesy are not appealable.

2.3   **Speeches.** No delegation may address the Committee/Council without previously obtaining the permission of the Chair,
  - The Chair shall call upon delegations in the order in which they signify their desire to speak,
  - Speakers must keep their remarks germane to the subject under discussion,
  - A time limit may be established for speeches (see rule 7.9),
  - Representatives, at the conclusion of a substantive speech, will be allowed, if they are willing, to answer questions concerning their speech,
    - A delegation that desires to ask a question should signify by raising a Point of Inquiry (see rule 6.3),
    - All questions and replies are made through the Chair,
  - A speaker who desires to make a motion may do so after their speech and questioning, but prior to yielding the floor,
    - By making a motion the speaker yields the floor,
    - Motions may not be made from: Points of Order (rule 6.1), Information (rule 6.2), or Inquiry (rule 6.3), or from any procedural speeches.

2.4   **Recognition of Speakers.** Delegations wishing to speak on an item before the body will signify by raising their placards
  - The exception to this rule occurs on any Point of Order (rule 6.1), Information (rule 6.2), or Inquiry (rule 6.3), at which time a Representative should raise their placard and call out "Point of_____" to the Chair,
    - Points will be recognized in the order of their priority,
  - Speakers will be recognized in a fair and orderly manner,
  - Speakers lists will not be used.

2.5   **Right of Reply.** The Chair may accord a right of reply to any Representative if a speech by another Representative contains unusual or extraordinary language clearly insulting to personal or national dignity.
Requests for a Right of Reply shall be made in writing to the Chair,

- Requests shall contain specific language which was found to be insulting to personal or national dignity,
- The Chair's decision is not subject to appeal,
- There shall be no reply to a reply,
- The Chair may limit the time for reply.

2.6   Withdrawal of Motions. A motion may be withdrawn by its proposer at any time before voting on it has begun, provided the motion has not been amended,

- Seconds to a motion may also be withdrawn; if a withdrawn sponsorship or second brings the proposal below the required number the motion is withdrawn,
- A withdrawn motion, sponsorship or second may be reintroduced or sponsored, either verbally or in writing, by any other delegation.

2.7   Dilatory Motions. The Chair may rule out of order any motion repeating or closely approximating a recent previous motion on which the Committee/Council has already rendered an opinion, this ruling is not subject to appeal.

3. Rules that Relate to the Rules

3.1   Rule Priority and Procedure. The rules contained in this document are the official rules of procedure of the University of Minnesota Model United Nations and will be used for all Committee/Council sessions. These rules take precedence over any other set of rules.

3.2   Precedence of Rules. Proceedings of the UMMUN Security Council shall be conducted under the following precedence of rules;

1. UMMUN Rules of Procedure,
2. UMMUN GA/ECOSOC Precedence Short Form,
3. The Charter of the UN.

3.3   The Order of Precedence of Motions. The order of precedence of motions is listed in order of priority in both the GA/ECOSOC Precedence Short from and in these rules under Section 7, Motions in Order of Priority. These motions, in the order given, have precedence over all other proposals or motion before a Committee/Council or the General Assembly.

3.4   Rule Changes. The Secretariat reserves the right to make changes to these rules at any time. Should a change occur, it will be communicated to the representatives in a timely manner.

4. Draft Resolutions, Amendments & Statements.

4.1   Definition of Draft resolutions. A draft resolution is a proposal consisting of at least one preambular and one operative clause.

4.2   Draft Resolutions. Draft resolutions may be submitted to the Chair for approval at any time during the conference,

- These draft resolutions will be approved if they are legible, organized in content and flow, and in proper format,
- Draft Resolutions must have 20% minimum signatures of delegations in attendance, the final number of signatories will be determined by the Secretariat at conference registration and announced at the opening of each committee session,
- Once approved, draft resolutions will be distributed in a timely fashion to all Committee/Council delegations,
- Once a draft resolution is on the floor for discussion, additional sponsors may only be added to that draft resolution with the consent of the original sponsors,
- See also rule 7.13.

4.3   Definition of Amendments. An amendment to a draft resolution is a written motion that adds to, deletes from, or revises any part of the draft resolution.

4.4   Amendments. All amendments to draft resolutions must be signed by 20% of the delegations in attendance,

- The final number of signatories will be determined by the Secretariat at conference registration and announced at the opening of each committee session,

An amendment is submitted to the Committee/Council Vice Chair for approval.

- Amendments will be approved if they are legible, organized in content and flow, and in the proper format,
- Approved amendments will be assigned an identification letter by the Vice Chair,
- Typographical errors will be corrected by the Chair and announced to the body,

One or more amendments on any draft resolution, which is on the floor, may be considered at the same time.

- See also rule 7.14 for bringing amendment to the floor.
- See also rule 7.4 for bringing amendments to a vote.

An amendment will be considered "friendly" if all sponsors of the draft resolution are also sponsors to the amendment,

- A friendly amendment becomes part of a draft resolution upon receipt by the Chair,
- The Chair shall announce the acceptance of a friendly amendment on the first opportunity at which no speaker has the floor,
- Friendly amendments can not be accepted after a vote has been taken on a contested amendment,
- No vote is required to add a friendly amendment to a draft resolution.

5. Voting

5.1   Voting Rights. Each member delegation shall have one vote in each Committee/Council on which it is represented,

- No Representative/delegation may cast a vote on behalf of another country.

5.2   Simple Majority. Unless otherwise specified in these rules, decisions in the Committee/Council shall be made by a majority vote of those nations present. If there is an equal division between yes and no votes, the motion fails.

5.3   Adoption by Consensus. The adoption of amendments and draft resolutions by consensus is desirable when it contributes to the effective and lasting settlement of differences, thus strengthening the authority of the UN,

- Any Representative may request the adoption of an amendment or draft resolution by consensus at any time after Closure of Debate has passed,
- The Chair shall ask whether there is any objection to a consensus, and shall ask if any nations wish to abstain from consensus,
  - If there is no objection, the proposal is approved by consensus,
  - If any Representative objects to consensus, voting shall occur as otherwise stated in these rules.

5.4   Method of Voting. The Committee/Council shall normally vote on motions by a show of raised placards,

- The votes of Council members on all substantive matters shall be officially recorded,
- Any nation may request a roll call vote on substantive matters, unless adopted by consensus; this request shall then automatically be granted by the Chair,
- When applicable, roll shall be called in English alphabetical order beginning with a nation selected at random by the Vice Chair,
- Representatives shall reply "yes," "no," "abstain," or "abstain from the order of voting,"
  - A nation may abstain form the order of voting once during a roll call: a second abstention from the order of voting will be recorded as an abstention.

5.5   Conduct During Voting. Immediately prior to a vote the Chair shall describe to the Committee/Council the item to be voted on, and shall explain the consequences of a "yes" or a "no" vote. Voting shall begin upon the Chair's declaration "we are in voting procedure," and end when the results of the vote are announced,

- Once in voting procedure, no Representative shall interrupt the voting except on a Point of Order or Information concerning the actual conduct of the vote,

- Following Closure of Debate, and prior to entering voting procedure, the Chair shall pause briefly to allow delegations the opportunity to make any relevant motions,
    - Relevant motions prior to a vote include: Suspension of the Meeting (7.1), Adjournment of the Meeting (7.2), Decision of No Action (7.5), Decision of Competence, Division of the Question (7.10), Important Question (7.12), or Adoption by Consensus (5.3).

5.6   **Changes of Votes.** At the end of roll call, but before rights of explanation and subsequent announcement of the vote, the Vice Chair will ask for any vote changes. Any delegation that desires to change its recorded vote may do so at that time.

5.7   **Rights of Explanation.** Rights of Explanation are permitted on all substantive votes after voting. Rights of explanation may be limited in time by the Chair.

6. Points of Procedure in Order of Priority

6.1   **Point of Order.** During the discussion of any matter, a Representative may raise a Point of Order if he/she believes that the Committee/Council is proceeding in a manner contrary to these rules,
- The Representative will be immediately recognized by the Chair and the point ruled on,
- A Representative rising to a Point of Order may not speak substantively on any matter,
- If a Representative's ability to participate in the Committee/Council's deliberations is impaired for any reason related to the Council's physical environment the Representative may rise a Point of Order,
- A Point of Order may interrupt a speaker.

6.2   **Point of Information.** A Point of Information is raised to the Chair if a Representative wishes to obtain a clarification of procedure or a statement of the matters before the Council,
- Representatives may not interrupt a speaker on a Point of Information.

6.3   **Point of Inquiry.** During substantive debate, a Representative may question a speaker by rising to a Point of Inquiry,
- Questions must be directed through the Chair and may be made only after the speaker has concluded his/her remarks, but before he/she has yielded the floor,
- Representatives may not interrupt a speaker on a Point of Inquiry,
- See also rule 2.3.

7. Motions in order of Priority

7.1   Suspension of the Meeting. During the discussion of any matter, a Representative may move to suspend the meeting, except when such a motion would interrupt a speaker. Suspending a meeting recesses it for the time specified in the motion,
- The motion is not debatable,
- The Chair may request that the delegation making the motion modify the time of suspension,
- If the motion passes, the Committee/Council, when it reconvenes, will continue its business form the point at which suspension was moved.

7.2   Adjournment of the Meeting. The motion of adjournment means that all business of the Committee/Council has been completed, and that the Committee/Council will not reconvene until the next annual session,
- A motion to adjourn is not debatable and may not interrupt a speaker,
- A motion to adjourn will be put to an immediate vote,
- This motion requires a second and a majority vote for passage,
- The Chair may refuse to recognize a motion to adjourn the meeting if the Committee/Council still has business before it,
- This decision is not appealable.

7.3   Adjournment of Debate. During the discussion of any resolution or amendment, a Representative may move the Adjournment of Debate on that matter,
- Adjournment of Debate on a draft resolution or amendment has the effect of tabling that item and allows the Committee/Council to move onto another draft resolution/amendment,
- This motion requires a second and a majority vote for passage,
- Two delegations may speak in favor of the motion and two opposed; the motion shall then be put to a vote,
- An item upon which debate has been adjourned must pass a vote of Reconsideration before it may be brought back to the floor for consideration (rule 7.11).

7.4   Closure of Debate. A Representative may move to close debate on an issue before the Committee/Council at any time, except when such a motion would interrupt a speaker,
- This motion requires a second and a majority vote for passage,
- Two delegations may speak for and two against closure, the motion will then be put to a vote,
- Representatives should specify whether the motion for closure applies to an amendment or a draft resolution,
- If closure passes on draft resolutions, all amendments on the floor will be voted on in the reverse order from which they were moved to the floor,

– After voting on all amendments is completed, the draft resolution shall be voted upon in accordance with these rules.

At conclusion of voting procedure, the draft resolution or amendment being voted on is removed from consideration for future discussions, regardless of whether it passes or fails. Debate then continues in the current topic under discussion.

7.5 **Appealing a Decision of the Chair.** Rulings of the Chair are appealable unless otherwise specified in these rules,

- This motion requires a second and a majority vote for passage,
- Two delegations may speak in favor and two opposed to the motion,
- An appeal must be made immediately following the ruling in question,
- The Chair shall put the question as follows: "Shall the decision of the Chair be sustained?" A "yes" vote supports the Chair's decision; a "no" vote signifies objection,
- The decision of the Chair shall be sustained by a tie,
- Rulings by the Chair on the following rules or motions are not appealable: Diplomatic Courtesy (2.2), Right of Reply (2.5), Dilatory Motions (2.7), granting of a roll call vote (5.4), Adjournment of the Meeting (7.2), and any time a ruling by the Chair is a direct quotation from these rules of procedure.

7.6 **Decision of Competence.** A motion calling for a decision on the Competence of the Committee/Council to discuss or adopt a proposal is in order at any time prior to the proposal being put to a vote,

- This motion requires a second and a majority vote for passage,
- Two delegations may speak in favor of the motion and two opposed,
- If a Committee/Council decides it is not competent to discuss or vote on an amendment or draft resolution, the effect is the same as adjourning debate. (See also 7.11 on Reconsideration.)

7.7 **Limits on Debate.** A motion to limit or extend the time allotted to each delegation, or limit the number of times each delegation can speak on a proposal, is in order at any time. This motion may be proposed by the Chair or a delegation,

- This motion requires a second and a majority vote for passage,
- Two delegations may speak in favor and two opposed to the motion,
- The time allotted for substantive speakers shall be no less than three minutes,
- This motion may limit the number of points of inquiry a speaker may accept to a minimum of one,

A motion to limit the time of debate on an agenda topic, draft resolution, or an amendment is also in order.

7.8 **Division of the Question.** A motion to divide the question, proposing that clauses of an amendment or draft resolution be voted on separately, is in order at any time prior to entering into voting procedure on the amendment or draft resolution,

- This motion requires a second and a majority vote for passage,
- Two delegations may speak in favor and two opposed to the motion,
- The first motion for division to pass shall determine the order in which the amendment/draft resolution is voted on. Those clauses of the amendment/draft resolution which are approved shall then be put to a vote as a whole,
- If division causes a draft resolution to no longer be improper format (rule 4.1), the proposal as a whole is rejected.

7.9   Reconsideration of Proposals. A motion to reconsider is in order on an amendment or draft resolution which has passed or failed when put to a final vote. The motion is also in order for proposals on which debate has been adjourned (rule 7.3), on proposals on which no action was decided (rule 7.5), and on proposals upon which the Committee/Council has decided it was not competent to discuss or adopt (rule 7.7),

- This motion requires a second and a majority vote for passage,
- Two delegations may speak in favor and two opposed to the motion,
- If the motion passes it brings the issue back before the body for debate, and to be voted on again.

7.10   Consideration of Draft Resolutions. Any draft resolution with at least 20% sponsoring delegations may be considered, one at a time, from the floor. A draft resolution may be moved to the floor by a motion for Consideration of Draft Resolutions

- This motion requires a second and a majority vote for passage,
- This motion is not debatable,
- If the motion passes, the delegation moving consideration will be allowed to speak first on the draft resolution, if desired,
- Draft resolutions with fewer than the required number of sponsoring delegations may not be moved to the floor,
- If no draft resolution has the required number of sponsoring delegations, discussion may focus on the topic under consideration, or the Chair may suggest a Suspension of the Meeting for delegations to consider the draft resolutions available.

7.11   Consideration of Amendments. An amendment, once approved and assigned an identifying letter, may be moved to the floor by any delegation that receives recognition by the Chair,

- No verbal second is required,
- The delegation moving consideration will be allowed to speak first on the amendment, if desired.

8. Rules Relating Only to the Economic & Social Council

8.1   Interchangeability of Rules. All Committee/Council rules apply to the conduct of business in the Economic & Social Council. The priority of rules for motions specific to the council shall be in the order in which they are listed under Section 8, and they shall follow all other GA/ECOSOC rules in overall precedence.

8.2   Participation of Non-Member States. The Council may invite a non-represented state or intergovernmental organization to participate in its discussions on any item before the body. This includes all United Nations member states, recognized non-member states, and any other organization or individual recognized by the United Nations whose participation would enhance the proceedings of the Council,

- Non-Members may be invited into the Council by request made to the Chair from any member state,
- Non-member states of the Council have all the rights as observers (rule 1.10) in the General Assembly,
- Organizations or individuals may speak, but have no rights to make any motion or vote.

8.3   Consultative Session. The council may choose to suspend its rules and enter an informal, consultative session if the members determine that this process will enhance members understanding on a particular issue,

- The motion to move into consultative session must include the amount of time that such session is to be in effect,
- The council will move immediately into a formal session at the conclusion of discussions on the consultative topic.

8.4   Formation of Committees. A delegation may propose the formation of a Committee to deal with any issue(s), including topics not already on the agenda of the Economic and Social Council. The motion must be submitted in writing to the Chair prior to being made from the floor, and must contain the following:

1. Membership of Committee;
2. Issues(s) to be investigated;
3. Objectives of the Committee;
4. Duration of the Committee's existence.

- A Committee, once established, shall elect its own officers and determine its rules of procedure, within the bounds of the Council rules,
- The motion to from a Committee requires a second and is debatable,
- Upon the conclusion of the Committee's work, it will report its findings to the Council.

8.5   Formation of Commissions. The Council has the authority to establish commissions on topics that require long-term consideration,

> - A commission may be established to develop a convention, treaty, or deal with an issue that requires more in-depth deliberation than the Council can provide,
> - The motion to establish a commission should be in the form of draft resolution, it should detail the commission's membership, and establish the mandate for its formation,
> - Once the establishment of commission has been recommended by the Council, the Secretariat will review the proposal for potential implementation at the next year's conference,
> - Upon the conclusion of the commission's work, it will report to the Council as a whole for approval on its findings.
>
> **8.6　Creation of Conventions and Treaties.** The Council may decide to draft a convention or treaty on any given topic. The format of such a document shall be determined by the Council.
>
> http://www.tc.umn.edu/~unsa/resources.html

Lesson/Exercise Plan for Researching Public and Private Position Papers

Name of Course: Model UN

Exercise Title: Researching Public and Private Position Papers

Methods: Lecture, student research, student writing (homework outside of the practice session)

Training Aids Needed: UN articles and books, hardcopy or CD of *CIA World Factbook*, Internet connectivity

Student Handouts Needed: Copies of exemplary position papers (you can photocopy any that appear in the body of this book)

Special Instructions: It would be nice if you had Internet access for all attendees. Failing that, access to the school's library; hosting the session in the library would also be helpful. If you have a dedicated set of books regarding the UN, bring them.

Your Actions: Your call on whether you want to have a simple slide showing the main sections of a position paper.

Your Commentary:

Some conferences require a **position paper**; some do not. Some give awards for research and writing, as evidenced in part by your position paper; some do not. In all instances, we *will* write position papers. They are useful ways of providing some structure to our research, ensuring that we include everything we want to in our conference preparation. View them as a checklist. They should have at least five paragraphs—although each section can be longer than a paragraph—with at least one section each devoted to

- straightforward **assessments** by your country **of the issues** before your committee
- your **country's views** on those issues
- what you would like to **accomplish**—or prevent from happening—on those issues
- who your **friends and opponents** could be
- what **tactics** you will use in getting the best deal for your country

In some cases, you will write an **external** and an **internal** position paper. The external paper is one you can share with other delegations, letting them know where your country stands on the issues. The internal paper is close-hold, to be read only by members of your delegation, as it gives no-holds-barred tactical and strategic plans on how you will play offense and defense.

Conference organizers often hope that the starting point for delegation position papers will be the background guides they send out before the conference. (See appendix D of this book for an example.) It's a nice sentiment, but we've found that too often Secretariats send out these backgrounders much too late for them to be useful. We will not wait for the Secretariat's backgrounders to arrive, and instead get our country/committee assignments from the conference host as soon as we learn what committee topics will be discussed.

We can use absolutely anything to research these five topics. Among the resources you might want to consider:

- interviews—in person, via e-mail, via phone, etc. of the real UN delegation we are mimicking
- interviews, in the forms listed above, of the embassy, consulates, and interest sections of the country we are representing
- correspondence with private research firms, serving and former diplomats (U.S. and foreign), academic specialists, journalists, pundits, scholarly authors, and others recognized as authorities on these subjects
- Internet sites, including those made available by our assigned country, the

State Department, other federal agencies, interest groups, nongovernmental organizations, lobbyist groups, and others
- Books
- Newsletters
- Scholarly journals
- Background guides from other MUN conferences
- Background guides from the upcoming MUN conference

For the rest of this session, I'd like you to start researching your country's position on the topic(s) you'll be discussing in your committee. I'll be here to help you at any point.

Lesson/Exercise Plan: Resolution Writing

Name of Course: Model UN

Exercise Title: Resolution Writing

Methods: Lecture, student writing exercise

Training Aids Needed: Projector with UN resolution loaded up

Student Handouts Needed: A copy of any UN resolution, from any committee or plenary organization; the UN Charter; sample resolution format (you may want to photocopy the one that follows this lesson plan); lists of **Frequently Used Preambular Phrases** and **Frequently Used Operative Paragraph Phrases** (photocopy the ones that follow this lesson plan)

Special Instructions: You might want to have the students write resolutions tailored for the conference they are about to attend. Some conferences require resolutions to be submitted before the conference begins. Others prohibit prewritten resolutions believing that wisdom comes from the debate at the conference. It cannot hurt to have some plug-and-play language available for when the resolution-writing phase of the conference begins, so that your delegates are credited with being the principal drafters.

Your Actions: Walk the students through the structure of the UN resolution.

Your Commentary:
The lifeblood of UN sessions is **consideration of the resolutions**, which have three parts:

- Sponsors/cosponsors
- Preambular paragraphs (which you'll often see written as preambulatory paragraphs. "Preambulatory" means "crawling." Do *not* make this mistake vocally, but do not complain if other delegates—or the Chair—makes the error.)
- Operative paragraphs

Sponsors write the resolutions. You'll find that, particularly for this early MUN experience, it's much easier to let someone else write the resolution, then offer to cosponsor it. (Some delegates will crassly "hijack" as many resolutions as they can, putting their names on everything considered by the committee in an attempt to "brand" themselves as the movers and shakers of the room.) What you'll want to do is get a copy of the resolutions, before the conference if you can, figure out which one(s) you can support, and contact the sponsor to offer to cosponsor it. It's important for you to be the first cosponsor because this will increase the likelihood that you will get on the Speakers' List early.

Once you're comfortable with MUNing, it's time for you to consider playing offense and writing resolutions, rather than just sponsoring or trying to defeat them.

Each resolution is written as **one** long, involved **sentence**. Good news: we will not bring in the grammarians to try to diagram these sentences!

Resolutions start as working papers with the name of the committee, a resolution number (usually the first digit refers to the number of the topic on the formal agenda; the second digit refers to the sequence of that resolution for that topic), the name of the topic, the names of the sponsors, the names of the signatories, and follows with the name of the organization engaged in the activity (e.g., ultimately the General Assembly, not its subsidy committees, takes the action).

Preambular paragraphs set up the facts of the situation, and why action is needed by the organization.

Operative paragraphs explain the action(s) to be taken by the organization. They can be as simple or as complex as you wish.

[Instructor Action]: Walk the students through the sample resolution. Have them ask any questions they have. Then assign them to write a simple resolution on any topic they want. Have them share it with the rest of the group.

Sample Resolution Format

Special Political Committee Resolution 2.1

Topic: Resolution Format

Sponsors: United States, Senegal, Fiji, Cameroon, Mexico

Signatories: Zimbabwe, Australia, Russia, France, Japan

The General Assembly
Recalling that five spaces should be indented before preambular clauses,
Gravely concerned that delegates may forget to use a comma at the end of preambular clauses,
Desiring to see some reference to the UN Charter authorizing such action,
Further recalling the preambular phrases cannot be amended,
Aware that the format of a working paper or resolution may be changed by the Secretariat,

1. Notes with confidence that this format is used at most conferences;
2. Welcomes clean and simple wording, and splitting complex ideas into operative sub-paragraphs:
   a. With a colon introducing the first sub-paragraph,
   b. With no underlining within the sub-paragraph,
   c. With a comma at the end of each sub-paragraph and a semicolon at the end of the entire operative clause;
3. Observes that a resolution, being only one sentence, always ends with a period.

Frequently Used Preambular Phrases

Affirming	Convinced	Noting
Alarmed by	Declaring	Observing
Approving	Desiring	Reaffirming
Aware of	Emphasizing	Realizing
Bearing in Mind	Expecting	Recalling
Believing	Guided by	Recognizing
Cognizant	Having adopted	Referring
Concerned	Having considered	Regretting
Confident	Having studied	Seeking
Conscious	Keeping in mind (or	Taking Note of
Contemplating	Mindful that)	Welcoming

These words can also be modified by "fully," "deeply," "further," etc.

Frequently Used Operative Paragraph Phrases

Accepts	Deplores	Recommends
Affirms	Designates	Regrets
Approves	Emphasizes	Reminds
Authorizes	Encourages	Requests
Calls upon	Endorses	Resolves
Condemns	Expresses its hope	Supports
Confirms	Invites	Takes note of
Congratulates	Notes	Trusts
Considers	Proclaims	Urges
Declares accordingly	Reaffirms	

Again, modifiers are acceptable for these terms. Note that some operative words are the sole function of the Security Council, such as authorizing certain actions, establishing sanctions, etc. Consult the UN Charter for a listing of these specific responsibilities.

Lesson/Exercise Plan: Playing Offense

Name of Course: Model UN

Exercise Title: Playing Offense

Methods: Lecture, facilitated discussion

Training Aids Needed: A notional resolution for the students to use in practicing these plays

Student Handouts Needed: Copies of rules of procedure, cheat sheet (preferably, the students have already attended your session on the rules of procedure and cheat sheets, so that they understand the terminology of parliamentary procedure)

Special Instructions: Write a notional resolution ahead of time so that the students do not waste time writing their own. The key here is how to pass a resolution, not how to write one.

Your Actions: For this Lesson Plan, the Instructor Actions appear within the text of the commentary.

Your Commentary:

WIIFM (What's in it for me, the student): There are two different situations you will be in during a committee meeting or plenary assembly. One is when you want to get some resolution passed that our country likes. You use all of the techniques we will cover in the Offensive section to do so. Sometimes you'll be in a Defensive position, in which you're trying to kill off a resolution, or at least prevent its passage. We'll have separate exercises for those situations. For now, although you might be trying to get a resolution stopped, it's helpful to know what techniques that other side will use against you.

Overview of the Triangle System

We use an adaptation of the Triangle Offense that Phil Jackson used with the NBA Chicago Bulls when Michael Jordan was playing on the team. We call it the Triangle Offense and Triangle Defense. There are three overall parts of the Triangle system that we'll explore:

- parliamentary procedure plays
- public speaking styles and coalition formation in the Model UN context
- research

We'll cover the rest of those issues in other exercises. In today's session, let's look at how to get a resolution gets passed.

On Offense, you're trying to **move things along and get your resolution(s) passed.**

[Instructor Action]: Hand the students the Playbook: Here's a simple **Par - liamentary Procedure Playbook.**

Remember that your country delegation's **goal** is *not* to solve a crisis, resolve issues, etc., but to **represent your country's position accurately** and get the best deal for your country that you can. You want to get your country's position heard by all, and your country mentioned favorably (and never negatively) as early and often as you can.

Plays mentioned early in the following discussion can be used at any time later, e.g., General Debate defensive plays can also be used when discussing the topic, discussing the resolution, etc. Your use of them and their timing, however, depends on whether you're on Offense or Defense. Items that are centered in this table mean that either Offense or Defense can use the tactic at that time.

[Instructor Action]: Walk the students through the Playbook below. Have them explain what they believe the terms mean.

Table 3. Parliamentary Procedure Playbook

OFFENSE	DEFENSE
Goal: Move things along. Get yes votes.	Goal: Stall, avoid voting, get no/abstentions.
Initial roll-call to establish quorum[1]	
General debate	
Get your speech in, and make sure that students from your school representing other countries also get heard; i.e., do not vote to end debate before they have spoken! You're also trying for a Best School award.	Get your speech in, keep debate going. You don't want any hostile resolutions introduced, much less voted upon.
Move to shorten speaking time; speak for it	Speak against shortening speaking time
Speak against lengthening speeches	Move to extend speaking time; speak for it
Move to close Speakers' List	Speak against it
Move to close debate	Speak against it
Right of reply	
Set agenda	
Move to set agenda topic	Fine, but not the offending topic; speak for it
Speak on your topic's importance	Argue that other topics are more important
	Comment on speech (if rules allow it)
	Get yields
	Ask questions
	Move for moderated caucus (informal debate)
	Move for unmoderated caucus (short recess)
Discuss topic	
	Stay on Speakers' List, give speech
	Get back on Speakers' List
	Get yields from other speakers
	Yield to questions; never to the Chair
Ask friendly question ("do you agree?")	Ask questions (cost, relevance, committee authority/competence)
Discuss resolution	
Get your resolution first on the agenda	Get anything else discussed first
	Point out typos

1 Do *not* say "present and voting"; just say "Present." "Present and voting" means that you cannot abstain. There is never a reason for you to throw away your option to abstain.

Table 3. Parliamentary Procedure Playbook (continued)

OFFENSE	DEFENSE
	Point of order (question whether sponsors/signatories agree with each friendly amendment by having Chair ask them individually)
	Try to get some sponsors/signatories to withdraw
	Move to recess early (e.g., lunch, etc.)
	Offer seemingly friendly amendments (poisoned apple)
	Move to amend (several times)
	Move to open Speakers' List on amendment
	Move to amend amendment (if it isn't yours, and if allowed by the rules)
	Move to substitute resolution
	Appeal Chair (on amending preambulars)
	Point of order (is there a quorum to vote?)
Voting	
Quick show of placards	Request roll-call vote
	Try to get others to pass, thereby killing time Use right of explanation
	Move to divide the question
	Move for Important Question
	Move to reconsider

When trying to combat what the Defense is doing, your key weapon is the word "dilatory." You want to suggest to the Chair that a particular motion (in our parlance, "play") by the Defense is "dilatory"—that is, time-wasting, and should be declared by the Chair to be out of order. Such a decision helps you, because while most Defensive plays require a simple majority, in most sets of Rules it requires the Defense to get a two-thirds majority to overrule the Chair.

Exercise: The Instructor will serve as the Chair.

[Instructor Action]: Assign the students their countries, and make some of them sponsors, some signatories, and some against the resolution. Forgo general and topical debate. Just announce that the resolution has been introduced. In turn, have them try each of the above plays, both playing Offense to try to pass the resolution, and playing Defense to try to kill the resolution.

Lesson/Exercise Plan: Asking and Answering Questions: Hostile and 2nd Speaker

Name of Course: Model UN

Exercise Title: Answering Questions

Methods: Brief introductory lecture, followed by student exercise

Training Aids Needed: Gavel

Student Handouts Needed: Notional resolution for all students. Topic does not matter, but it would be helpful if it was one that the students have written in earlier practices on resolution writing, and/or that they will use in an upcoming conference.

Special Instructions: This will have four exercises that give the students practice in answering hostile questions, and being second answerer.

Your Initial Actions: Split the students into two groups. One will have a notional resolution that has been sponsored by the countries that this group is representing. The students in the "questioners" section will include delegations that support, oppose, or are on the fence regarding the legislation.

Your Commentary:

Today we are going to look at another way for you to get points as speakers when you are having difficulties getting on the Speakers' List. You can ask questions of a speaker, if they have agreed to yield to questions. If you have been a speaker, you can also yield to questions. While we would prefer that you take up all of your speaking time with your speech, yielding to questions is fine, in that it gives you yet more opportunities to speak.

Another way to get a chance to answer a question or two comes immediately after delegates initially present their proposals. After they read the resolution out loud, they can then yield to questions from the floor. This gives you, a nonsponsor, the opportunity to pose questions, and you as the sponsor an opportunity to answer questions. While you will initially have a fear of the unknown—What if I'm not ready for what they ask me?—you will soon discover that the question period is very helpful.

There are usually two types of question periods. The first is devoted to making sure that the resolution is grammatically correct, that there are no typos, no missing words, and it means what the sponsors meant for it to say. This period is usually deemed by the Chair to last for only five minutes, but if things are going well, they will frequently ignore that limitation until all delegates who have this type of query are called upon.

In both instances—either after a speech or after the introduction of a resolution—the tactics that you can use on offense and defense (in this case, questioning and answering) are much the same. For purposes of today's practice, we will concentrate on the questions phase of a resolution's introduction.

So let's try our **first exercise**, in which speakers can yield to questions. This gives you terrific opportunities, as the questioner as well as the speaker. Take out your copy of the resolution. If you're a member of the audience, look for any typos first. If there are any, ask about them.

[Instructor Action]: At this point, call upon anyone who notices any. If you wish, you can "salt" your resolution with a few typos, infelicitous phrases, etc.

Now that we're done with that phase of questioning, we move on to the substantive types of questions. You can strategically ask questions of speakers:

- How's this proposal going to help the people of my region?
- What is this going to cost?
- How much money—give me a precise dollar/Euro figure—have you given/will you give to fund this project? If you're not willing to fund it, why should we take this seriously?
- There are inconsistencies in the argument you've just presented. Here they are: _____. Which is correct?
- These paragraphs are vague. What precisely do you mean?

So let's try a few questions as part of our second exercise. Those of you in the audience, see how many questions you can generate.

[Instructor Action]: Call upon as many students as raise their placards. It's fine if they use variations on the questions above. You're just trying to get them comfortable with this style of speaking.

Now we come to the delegates who are proposing the resolution or who are speaking. If you find you have extra time on your hands, you should always offer to yield to questions. You can use shills in the audience who will ask friendly questions. (Although in many conferences, Chairs, rather than the delegates, determine who asks the questions. Check your local rules for what will be the custom at your specific conference.)

Yielding to questions gives you yet another way to get your point across. Delegates should keep in mind that they are trying to stay on point. A hostile question doesn't need to be answered directly. If there is no legitimate answer to a question, or it raises issues that you wish to brush aside, it is perfectly acceptable to rephrase the question, or answer the question that you wanted to answer. (Consider candidates in presidential debates. They always reframe the hostile question fired by the debate's moderator into something far more palatable.) The rules generally prohibit follow-up questions or to-and-fros between interlocutors. You're there to frame the debate, not to respond to the agenda of others.

So let's try that as our **third exercise**. Each of you sponsoring the resolution gets to take a hostile question from the audience.

[Instructor Action]: Call upon as many audience members as you can, and parcel out the questions to each resolution sponsor. Look for how they deflect the question, while sounding like they are intent on giving a legitimate answer to the questioner.

In some cases, there will be a mix of friendly and hostile questions. Of particular importance when you are before the committee as a resolution sponsor is to attempt to answer nearly *every* question asked, even if another sponsor has already adequately answered the question. This gives the impression that you are the power-behind-the-throne, and actually in charge of the resolution. You should also be standing very near to the microphone so that you can throw in your two cents before the Chair turns to the next questioner. It's perfectly fine to paraphrase what the initial answerer said—don't parrot, paraphrase. It's ok to underscore a particular point that your colleague made. Remember, most of the delegates in the audience were not paying attention the first time, but may catch the idea if you reiterate it.

So let's give it a try as part of our **fourth exercise**. I'd like members of the audience to ask softball questions of the resolution writers. I'd like one of the resolution writers to answer the question. I'd then like the delegate standing next to the initial sponsor to gently grab the microphone and also answer the question. We'll do this for several rounds so that everyone gets to be the primary and secondary question answerers.

You've all done very well today. Give yourselves a hand. The key takeaway from these exercises: Questions and answers are important arrows in your quiver. You get points for asking and answering questions, and should always step up whenever the opportunity to ask or answer presents itself.

Lesson/Exercise Plan: Playing Defense

Name of Course: Model UN

Exercise Title: Playing Defense

Methods: Lecture, facilitated discussion

Training Aids Needed: A notional resolution for the students to use in practicing these plays

Student Handouts Needed: Copies of UN Charter, rules of procedure, cheat sheet

Special Instructions: Write a notional resolution ahead of time so that the students do not waste time writing their own. The key here is how to kill a resolution, not how to write one.

Your Actions: For this Lesson Plan, the Instructor Actions appear within the text of the commentary.

Your Commentary:

WIIFM (What's in it for me, the student): There are two different situations you will be in during a committee meeting or plenary assembly. One is when you want to get some resolution passed that our country likes. You use all of the techniques we've covered in the Offensive section to do so. You're also trying to combat those who do not like the resolution, and are trying to stop its passage via Defensive techniques. Although you might be trying to get a resolution passed, it's helpful to know what techniques that other side will use against you. And in some cases, you might have a resolution that's not in our interests, so you'll want to stop the resolution.

Defensive techniques aim to **stop passage**. It does *not* necessarily mean that you want other delegations to directly kill the resolution. There are far more subtle ways to ensure that something doesn't pass than a direct frontal assault. You may well need the support of a sponsor of a hostile resolution a few votes from now, so let's not make them aware that we're in opposition directly. Try this:

- **Stall Ball** tries to use up the remaining time before the other side can pass the resolution (this is similar in football or basketball when the team in the lead holds the ball to prevent the other team from scoring). The conferences have a very limited amount of time. If you're pretty sure that you have very few votes on your side on a substantive issue, period, then all you're trying to do is to kill the clock. You can do that by calling for:

- **Quorums.** Every committee has a limitation on how few countries are
  needed to get business done. For example, it wouldn't make sense for
  just a handful of countries to speak for the entire 193-member General
  Assembly. So check the Rules, usually within the first ten paragraphs, for
  how many delegations are required to discuss a topic. Sometimes there
  are separate regulations on how many delegations are needed to vote on
  a topic. Usually this request is not debatable and the Chair goes ahead
  with the head-count. This is usually good for killing about five
  minutes—the Secretariat has to read off the names of every delegation
  that could be there, even the ones that didn't establish that they were
  present at the opening session of the committee. With this play, you
  don't actually vote; nothing gets done, but the clock runs down.
- **Caucus time** is less annoying to the Chair, but always welcome by the
  delegates. Everyone likes to take a break from the formal sessions and
  talk with their friends, hit the restroom, get a sandwich, etc. If you're not
  too obvious about it, even the Secretariat will appreciate you doing this,
  because they're under stress and could use the break. Call for a ten-
  minute caucus—moderated or unmoderated. In either case, no voting
  may occur. Things never get started on time, and you'll have taken
  another twenty minutes off the clock.
- **A roll-call vote** requires the Chair to ask each delegate in turn for their
  vote. In some cases, delegates can "pass," meaning they won't vote
  immediately, because they want to see how others are voting. There are
  good strategic reasons for doing this; if you're a permanent member of
  the Security Council, you can see if there are enough "no" votes and/or
  abstentions to kill a resolution without you having to commit to a veto
  by voting "no." Do this only if you have a chance of winning a vote. If
  it's going to be 192–1 against you, just accept the defeat gracefully.
- **Misdirection** takes the other side's attention away from what they're trying
  to do—get a specific resolution passed. This is the equivalent of saying
  "Hey, how 'bout them Yankees," or "look, a shiny object," in getting out of
  an awkward social situation. Resolutions will be considered in the order in
  which the Secretariat sets them. Let's suppose that you don't like Resolution
  1, are neutral on Resolution 2, but would support Resolutions 3 and 4.
  Rather than try to kill off Resolution 1, move to alter the agenda to consider
  Resolution 3 first. (If you can, try to get the sponsor of Resolution 3 to make
  this move. You thereby don't alienate the sponsor of Resolution 1, have

gotten the sponsor the Resolution 3 to think you're with him/her, and have gotten what you want on the agenda. It's ok to second this motion. People will think you're just doing something minor in parliamentary procedure, but the sponsor of Resolution will get the flak if this doesn't work.

- **Substitution** of an entire resolution can confuse the other side, and chew up time. If misdirection doesn't work, try this. Move to substitute the entire text of Resolution 1 with the entire text of a resolution you like. (You might not want to substitute 3—you already know that you don't have the votes to do this, because your misdirection vote lost. Try it with Resolution 4. Again, if you can, try to get the sponsor of Resolution 4 to do this, with you seconding the motion. The reasoning behind this is the same as with Misdirection.

- **Salami Amending** entails you trying to amend, paragraph by paragraph, the offending resolution. If the previously mentioned plays don't work, try killing off individual offending paragraphs of the resolution with amendments that delete the paragraph entirely, water it down, substitute a better paragraph, or otherwise help your position. You can do this as many times as you want (assuming you haven't alienated the Chair and a majority of delegates by now) and pick apart the resolution. In some instances, you can actually get the original sponsor to try to withdraw the resolution in disgust. Check your rules to make sure they can do this. If the rules are written correctly, the resolution is the property of the committee, not the sponsor. There's no greater victory for the Defense than hacking up an offending resolution so badly that the sponsor is forced to vote against his/her own resolution!

- **Deleting sponsors and signatories** is something that you can do behind the scenes. If the Chair notices you orchestrating this, you'll get extra points come awards time for excellent subtle use of the rules, parliamentary maneuvering, and interpersonal skills. Sometimes rules of procedure require a set number of sponsors and signatories. If you can get a few of those delegations to drop their sponsorship/signatory status before a vote takes place, the resolution dies without a formal vote. This is a fairly rare gadget play, but has a wonderful element of surprise and can confuse the Offense.

- Get the resolution declared an **Important Question**. The UN Charter is very clear about what constitutes an Important Question—requiring a two-thirds majority, rather than a simple majority—in the UN General Assembly: budgetary questions, admission of new members, use of force, and the like. However, MUN rules of procedure often are not as clear. You can argue "This is clearly an Important Question. What's not important about this issue?" Many delegates who have not done their research on the UN Charter can be swayed by such a specious argument. After all, they've put some work into writing their position papers and looking up the positions of their allies, so it's now emotionally important to them. If you obtain the simple majority needed to declare a resolution an Important Question, you've made it that much more difficult for the sponsors to get the resolution passed. Of course, if you're playing Offense, make sure that you argue vigorously that Important Question is irrelevant in this instance. You might also ask the Chair to rule that this is not an Important Question (and to rule that s/he cannot be appealed on this decision).

Exercise: The Instructor will serve as the Chair.
[Instructor Action]: Hand the students the Playbook.
Tell the students: Here's a simple **Parliamentary Procedure Playbook**
[Instructor Action]: Assign the students their countries. Make some of them sponsors, some signatories, and some against the resolution. Forgo general and topical debate. Just announce that the resolution has been introduced. In turn, have them try each of these plays, both playing defense to try to kill the resolution, and playing offense to try to parry the plays.

Lesson Plan: Practice Sessions

Name of Course: Model UN

Exercise Title: Practice

Methods: Simulation of a simulation

Training Aids Needed: Room large enough to facilitate discussion by all of your delegates. Tables and chairs are welcome, but you can get by with just chairs if it's an auditorium.

Student Handouts Needed: Copies of rules of procedure, UN Charter, cheat sheet, country placards, one or two resolutions that the students have written in earlier practice sessions—on the topic of the day.

Special Instructions: Your choice on whether you want to chair the meeting, or give one (or more) of your students the practice time. You might try it once yourself to give your budding Chairs a role model, then turn the gavel over to them during an unmoderated caucus. To make this simple, limit the session to just one topic. It's fine for the debate to consider setting the agenda, but ultimately, you do not want to burden the students into having to prepare in-depth for several topics.

Your Actions: Assign the same UN topic to all of the students, and give them individual country assignments. Make sure you have a mix of delegations that will play offense and defense. Feel free to use any of the background guides elsewhere in this book as the material they should read ahead of time. It's your choice on whether you want them to write position papers; while it's excellent practice, it is time-consuming, and you are competing for the time they will spend on homework assignments for the other courses they are taking and other extracurriculars in which they are involved.

Your commentary:

Today we put it all together—your research, caucusing, speechwriting/delivering, interpersonal jockeying for position, and everything else we have talked about. We'll try out aspects of offense and defense.

The meeting will come to order. We will begin by calling the roll.

[Instructor Action]: From here, run the session the way it would be held in any committee, going through the following line of march:

Roll call
General debate
Motion to set the agenda
Debate on specific topic
Introduction of a resolution
    Nonsubstantive question period
    Substantive question period
    Debate on the merits of the resolution
Introduction of an amendment to the resolution
    Ask sponsors if it is friendly or unfriendly (privately ask one sponsor to balk)
    Debate on the merits of the amendment
    Vote on the amendment
Vote on the resolution
    (privately ask a delegate to request a roll-call vote)
    Explanations of votes

Throughout this practice, encourage each delegate to make at least one parliamentary motion on offense or defense. Also encourage all of the delegates to try all of the tactics that have been covered in the previous practice sessions. The more they see all of this come together, the easier it will be for them to understand, and employ at conferences.

APPENDIX F: FURTHER READING

There are numerous websites that offer suggestions for quality delegate perform-ance, and a few books written are for delegates. We have seen precious few books that are designed for MUN coaches per se. Among the few books/articles that might be helpful to you are the following:

American Model United Nations. *Model UN "In a Box,"* http://www.amun.org /model-un-in-a-box-simulation-guides/. Many rules and procedures described in this guide are specific to the American Model United Nations (AMUN) conference.

Liu, Eric. *Guiding Lights: The People Who Lead Us Toward Our Purpose in Life.* New York: Random House, 2004. Liu includes a profile of an inspirational debate coach.

Mickolus, Edward. "Models of the United Nations: Contemporary Developments in Research and Teaching." *The Social Studies* 67, no. 4 (July–August 1976): 171–74.

Rocca, Christopher M., Robert F. Simmons, Julie Christiano, and Edward Mickolus. *Preparing a Delegation for a High School Model United Nations: A Bibliography.* New York: National Collegiate Conference Association, 1974.

Woodall, Marian K. *Thinking on Your Feet: Answering Questions Well, Whether You Know the Answer—Or Not.* Lake Oswego, OR: Professional Business Communications, 1987. A straightforward guide on how to ask questions, how to answer them, and how to answer the question you wanted to answer.

INDEX

ABOUT THE AUTHORS

J. Thomas Brannan is the faculty advisor to the George C. Marshall High School Model United Nations team in Falls Church, Virginia. He has been teaching International Baccalaureate classes in history and theory of knowledge at the high-school level for over ten years. In 2005 he was Teacher of the Year and in 2012 was named a Teaching Fellow by the Choices Program at Brown University. The "My First MUN" training conference he created at Marshall High School with coauthor Ed Mickolus has trained more than two thousand high school and middle school students in the essential skills of Model UN since 2004. Before becoming a teacher, he served in the U.S. Navy, as a newspaper reporter, and as the assistant city manager in the City of Alexandria, Virginia—careers in which he developed the writing and diplomacy skills needed in Model United Nations conferences. He holds a bachelor's degree in political science from Catholic University and a master's degree in public administration from George Mason University. He was introduced to Model United Nations by his children, who learned diplomacy from Albert VanThornout, the beloved MUN club advisor at Yorktown High School in Arlington, Virginia.

Dr. Edward Mickolus is president of Vinyard Software, Inc., a northern Virginia software company that specializes in computer databases of political events. He has written twenty books on international terrorist events and biographies of terrorists, and is head of the International Terrorism: Attributes of Terrorist Events (ITERATE) project, which provides a computer-readable chronology of 13,000+ international terrorist events coded for 150+ variables from 1968 to today. He also runs Vinyard's Data on Terrorist Suspects (DOTS) project, a compendium of some 15,000+ biographical entries on terrorists. As an undergraduate at Georgetown University, he led teams to regional and national MUN championships; was president of the National Collegiate Conference Association, which hosts the college national MUN championship; chaired at the North American Invitational Model

United Nations and National College Security Council; and ran Georgetown's summer MUN institute, which coached high school teams. While completing his doctorate in political science, he founded and coached the Yale University MUN team and started the Yale MUN conferences. His daughter, Ciana, was on Marshall's MUN team, on which he served as team parent and coach. He and coauthor Tom Brannan founded the "My First MUN" Training Conference, now in its tenth year. They were awarded the Sister Anne Award as the best coaches at the North American Invitational Model United Nations, hosted by Georgetown University's International Relations Association.

In the 2003–2004 season, Marshall's MUN team attended fourteen weekend conferences, winning multiple speakers' awards at every conference and winning Best School awards at several high school and college conferences, including the University of Virginia conference and the national Model Arab League championship. Of the forty-seven students who attended a conference, forty-one won a speaking award. The team won a total of eighty-nine awards. Since 2004, the Marshall MUN Club has won Best School awards at college conferences hosted by international relations organizations at Princeton University, the College of William and Mary, the University of North Carolina at Chapel Hill, and the Model Arab League at Georgetown University. George C. Marshall High School's Model UN Club, in partnership with the University of Virginia's International Relations Organization, since 2004 has hosted "My First MUN," an annual noncompetitive teaching conference for novice MUNers and their advisors and teachers.